Modern Japanese Literary Studies

MICHIGAN MONOGRAPH SERIES IN JAPANESE STUDIES

NUMBER 106

CENTER FOR JAPANESE STUDIES
UNIVERSITY OF MICHIGAN

Modern Japanese Literary Studies

Seth Jacobowitz and Jonathan E. Abel, Editors

University of Michigan Press
Ann Arbor

Published in the United States of America by the
University of Michigan Press
First published February 2026

A CIP catalog record for this book is available from the British Library.

Library of Congress Cataloging-in-Publication data has been applied for.

ISBN 978-0-472-07795-3 (hardcover : alk. paper)
ISBN 978-0-472-05795-5 (paper : alk. paper)
ISBN 978-0-472-90572-0 (open access ebook)

DOI: https://doi.org/10.3998/mpub.12899731

The University of Michigan Press's open access publishing program is made possible thanks to additional funding from the University of Michigan Office of the Provost and the generous support of contributing libraries.

Cover image: *Takekurabe* (*Comparing Heights*), *Gojūnotō* (*The Five-Storied Pagoda*), *Asakusa kurenaidan* (*The Scarlet Gang of Asakusa*), *Taiyō no nai machi* (*The Streets Without Sunlight*), *Midaregami* (*Tangled Hair*), *Kokoro* (*The Heart*).

The authorized representative in the EU for product safety and compliance is Easy Access System Europe, Mustamäe tee 50, 10621 Tallinn, Estonia, gpsr.requests@easproject.com

Contents

Digital materials related to this title can be found on the Fulcrum platform via the following citable URL: https://doi.org/10.3998/mpub.12899731

Acknowledgments

This project began as a series of conversations sparked by John Treat's article "Japan is Interesting: Modern Japanese Literary Studies Today" in *Japan Forum* (2018). Energized by his polemical essay and the passionate responses it garnered, Seth Jacobowitz organized a state-of-the-field workshop later that year, sponsored by the Council on East Asian Studies at Yale, which featured many of the contributors to the present volume. Colleagues who took part in those early conversations also include Nina Cornyetz, Yukiko Hanawa, and Joseph North (English literature). Our efforts were also bolstered by generous intellectual support from Markus Nornes, Charles Exley, Christopher Lupke, and Christopher Lowy, among others.

The editors further wish to thank our predecessors, who have written about the state of the field in recent years, such as Michael Bourdaghs, Harry Harootunian, Norma Field, Naoki Sakai, Alan Tansman, and Tomiko Yoda. We would also like to thank some of the many friends, colleagues, and *senpai* who served as interlocutors along the way: Andre Haag, Christopher L. Hill, Sari Kawana, Karatani Kojin, Shion Kono, Komori Yoichi, Tom Lamarre, Aaron Moore, Satoko Shimazaki, Doug Slaymaker, and Yoshikuni Hiroki. Lastly, we would like to express our gratitude to Brett de Bary and Christine Marran, who have long served as mentors.

Introduction

Stating the Field

Seth Jacobowitz and Jonathan E. Abel

Modern Japanese Literary Studies assembles a spectrum of interdisciplinary and institutional perspectives on the state, or rather, multiple states of the field into a single volume. Drawing upon the work of sixteen scholars based in North America, Asia, and Europe, the book strives to make a timely intervention that renews critical dialogue and registers major changes that have arisen since the late 1990s. In contrast to previous efforts that sought to singlehandedly assess the state of the field, we have adopted a collaborative approach because modern Japanese literary study has long since transcended the point at which the lone, intrepid scholar could attempt to adequately address its complexity, whether in terms of chronology, thematic organization, methodologies, or theoretical frameworks. This volume is addressed to specialists and non-specialists alike as we set forth a broader vision for a globalizing Japanese culture in the early 21st century. *Modern Japanese Literary Studies* presses for overdue recognition by our colleagues in other disciplines that ours is not only a national or regional (i.e., East Asian) literature, but also deserves equitable representation in the humanities. Modern Japanese literature today is not studied as an end in itself, but consists of, and is, in fact, read in unison with colonial and postcolonial literature, women's literature, LGBTQ literature, diasporic literatures, indigenous literatures, visual cultures, disability studies, and more. It is a field, moreover, that has made innovative contributions to critical theory and comparative literature; film and media studies; gender and sexuality studies; and more recently, transnational, medical, and environmental humanities. Our main objective here, as we take stock of how the field has been studied and taught, or researched and catalogued, is to address the challenges and opportunities for growth that lie ahead for the study of modern Japanese literature amid the crises of relevance that continue to reshape the contemporary academic landscape.

There have been several individual essays published since the late 1990s that assess Japanese literary studies from a primarily Anglophone and US-based viewpoint. Although Japanese culture had been the object of intellectual inquiry in the West since at least the late nineteenth century, the first wave of what is now recognizable as Japan Studies emerged in the postwar era. Led by those scholars who Norma Field in her own state-of-the-field essay, "'The Way of the World': Japanese Literary Studies in the Postwar United States" (Brill, 1998) called "tastemakers," the field was as concerned with producing anthologies in translation and introductory studies of classical, early modern, and modern Japanese literature to a Cold War-era American audience as they were to addressing fellow literary critics and scholars.[1] Luminaries at the time included Donald Keene, Edward Seidensticker, Ivan Morris, and Helen Craig McCullough, whose careers were facilitated by the education they received from the US Navy Japanese Language School and their firsthand experiences during WWII.[2] Despite playing a formative role in establishing the field, their generation would be criticized by Field for endorsing essentialist approaches to Japanese literature and culture that relegated the Japanese to an inferior and posterior role in relation to the industrially advanced and democratic West. The modern writers most frequently upheld as exemplars of high literature (or "pure literature" *junbungaku*) in the postwar American literary scene—Kawabata Yasunari, Akutagawa Ryūnosuke, Tanizaki Jun'ichirō, and Mishima Yukio—had been represented to American and international readers as purveyors of traditional Japanese aesthetics and mores, while "mass literature" (*taishū bungaku*) in the nomenclature of the time and literature that employed avant-gardist experimental techniques were largely ignored or dismissed as derivative.[3]

Prominent national literature (*kokubungaku*) scholars in Japan during the same era such as Nakamura Mitsuo and Etō Jun made valuable contributions that prompted reconsiderations of key philosophic concepts, authors, and texts in the modern Japanese literary canon, which these scholars then sought to bring into dialogue with postwar political and ideological frameworks. As Ann Sherif has observed of the latter, beginning in 1956, "Etō succeeded brilliantly in challenging established notions of [Natsume] Sōseki's conception of individualism and in relating the novelist's works to the historical conditions of the Meiji era (1868–1912). [. . .] Etō also produced a provocative assessment of the literary criticism of Kobayashi Hideo in 1961."[4] Elevated to the status of public intellectuals, these postwar establishment figures engaged in spirited debates with leftist students and Marxist colleagues, facilitated translation of some of their scholarship into English, and served as de facto cultural ambassadors to the West.

A second wave of modern Japanese literary studies came in the 1970s and 1980s in the wake of protest rallies against the US-Japan Anpo Security Treaty and the Vietnam War, as well as internal critiques within the field prompted by the publication of Edward Said's *Orientalism* (1978). In consequence of the changed atmosphere on American university campuses, self-reflective re-evaluations of East Asian Studies and new comparative frameworks emerged from institutions like the University of Chicago and the *Journal of Critical Asian Studies*. Katō Shūichi's *A History of Japanese Literature: From the Manyoshu to Modern Times* (1979), a three volume history of Japanese literature appeared in English translation, while Harry Harootunian, Masao Miyoshi, and William Sibley welcomed Maeda Ai to the University of Chicago in the spring quarter of 1981, where he taught a seminar based on materials that would form the basis for his groundbreaking *Literature of Urban Space* (*Toshi kūkan no naka no bungaku*, 1982).[5] Katō and Maeda contributed to training a new generation of literary scholars, who became intellectual conduits for the latest approaches from Japan. In 1984, Donald Keene published his two-volume compendium *Dawn to the West: Japanese Literature in the Modern Era*, which surveyed a broad range of prose fiction, poetry, drama, and literary criticism. Taken together, these second wave efforts helped transform Anglophone Japanese literary studies into a more robust and accessible field of inquiry.

In his critical introduction to *The Linguistic Turn in Contemporary Japanese Literary Studies* (University of Michigan Press, 2010), Michael Bourdaghs recounts a series of debates in 1985 initiated by literary scholars Komori Yōichi and Ishihara Chiaki over iconoclastic interpretations of Sōseki's novel *Kokoro* (1914). The debate itself brought forth standing tensions between the academic study of literature in Japan in relation to linguistics (*gengogaku*) and national language studies (*kokugogaku*).[6] It also signaled an ideological spinoff from the collapse of the New Left. By insisting on the reader's autonomous relationship with the text (*tekisuto-ron*), Komori and Ishihara established a kind of poststructuralist reading that moved beyond the orthodoxy of author-based (*sakkaron*) and works-based (*sakuhinron*) approaches that had heretofore defined the modern literary canon.

The 1990s and early 2000s experienced a third wave of innovative collaborations and translations that bridged Japanese and American scholarship, and brought lasting impacts to the study of modern Japanese literature. Standing fast as the polestar in this firmament, Karatani Kōjin brought key insights from poststructuralism to the still-conservative world of Japanese national literary studies in Japan after a stint as a visiting scholar at Yale in 1975 during the heyday there of Paul de Man and Derridean deconstruction. Karatani primarily made his mark in Anglophone Japanology through *Origins of Modern Japanese Literature* (*Nihon kindai bungaku no kigen*, 1977–1980), translated by Brett de Bary and her then-graduate students at Cornell beginning in the late 1980s, including Ayako Kano and Joseph Murphy, and subsequently published by Duke University Press in May 1993. Karatani's mentoring of American doctoral students at Hōsei University in Tokyo, and his participation as a frequent visiting professor at Columbia further solidified his centrality for this next generation of American scholars. Although his early work, *Man in Awe* (*Ifu suru ningen*, 1972), lay the foundation for Komori and Ishihara's rereading of Sōseki, Karatani's signature achievement in *Origins* was a series of epistemic ruptures that he dubbed "discoveries" (*hakken*) in categories he defined as landscape, interiority, confession, disease, childhood, and the power to construct. His Foucauldian-inflected analysis of modern subjectivity led to an overhaul of the conceptual apparatuses away from the individual in society *pace* Etō, or even Maeda's topographic and topological methods of close reading. No matter how vociferously critics at home or abroad found fault with his philosophical methods or lapses in historical specificity, in his aftermath it was no longer sufficient for Japanese or American scholars to claim mastery of the Japanese language and literary canon alone. Henceforth, one also had to demonstrate a working knowledge of continental European philosophy, critical methodologies, and an expansive East-West dialogue of counterparties and interlocutors. It is a testament to Karatani's stature at the time that field leaders in comparative literature, notably Frederic Jameson and, later, Franco Moretti, enthusiastically endorsed his paradigms and sought to reconcile them within their understandings of Western and global modernities.[7]

Karatani was hardly alone in shaping the field in the United States and beyond during this period. Kamei Hideo at Hokkaido University, the aforementioned Komori Yōichi at the University of Tokyo-Komaba, Kōno Kensuke at Nihon University, and Hideto Tsuboi at Nagoya University (now at Waseda University and a contributor to this volume), boldly shaped the direction of the field on both sides of the Pacific in terms of narratology, modernist poetics, colonial/postcolonial literature, and the history and sociology of Japanese print culture.

In the late 1980s and early 1990s, polemical critiques emerged that were leveled at Japan Studies and Area Studies, castigating them not only for an underlying Orientalism and modernization theory, but also for an inability to free themselves from Western hegemonic thinking due to an inadequate command of, or engagement with, "theory." The *South Atlantic Quarterly* 87, no. 3 (Summer 1988), edited by Masao Miyoshi and Harry Harootunian, which was subsequently published in expanded form as *Postmodernism and Japan* (Duke University Press, 1989), marked a watershed intervention in Japan Studies. Featuring essays by Miyoshi, Harootunian, Tetsuo Najita, Marilyn Ivy, Isozaki Arata, Karatani Kōjin, Brett de Bary, Alan Wolfe, Norma Field, Naoki Sakai, Asada Akira, and Stephen Melville, as well as Japanese novelist and soon-to-be Nobel laureate Ōe Kenzaburō (1994), it helped shift the discipline of modern Japanese literature away from its patriarchal, depoliticized, and aestheticized approaches to the canon.[8] In his essay, Masao Miyoshi argued that modern Japan needed to recognize that the Japanese *shōsetsu* was qualitatively different from the Western novel in order to press his case that Japanese literary studies ought to make common cause with Third World Literature.[9] Naoki Sakai's "Modernity and Its Critique: The Problem of Universalism and Particularism," which diagnosed the solipsisms inherent in the field's constructions of Japan relative to the regulative idea of the West and the non-West, subsequently became the rare essay originating in Japan Studies that has been widely adopted in graduate seminars and re-circulated throughout the humanities.[10] In toto, this collection of essays amounted to a clarion call to overturn how the discipline of studying Japanese literature had previously been practiced. The volume and its contributors had a decisive impact in bringing about the theoretical turn in Japan Studies whose results are in evidence throughout this volume.

Published a decade later, Field's state-of-the-field essay, while generally opposed to American exceptionalism and the politics of literary canonization, and thus accepting of their broad critique, mostly sidesteps Miyoshi, Harootunian, and Sakai's anti-essentialist critiques of Japan Studies. Another outlier to these critiques was UC Berkeley's Alan Tansman, whose essay, "Japanese Studies: The Intangible Act of Translation" (2003), implicitly endorses Miyoshi, Harootunian, et al., but identifies the field's locus classicus in the act of translation as "a gesture of goodwill."[11] Tansman professes that the desire to understand and communicate ideas from another culture and language supersede the effort to dominate or exploit them. To be sure, the anti-essentialist critique of Orientalism in the 1990s was a powerful corrective to prevailing stereotypes in the writings of previous generations. It deftly critiqued any inherent comparison between modern Japanese literature and Asian American literature based solely on notions of an immutable ethnic or racial identity. But by now, it is also clear that recent studies of diasporic communities, such as those under the banner of a "global Japan" or "global Asias" offer more nuanced and ecumenical approaches to the many cultural continuities and connections which transcend language, epoch, and geographical region.

By the early 2000s it became de rigueur for East Asian Studies and Comparative Literature departments to recruit and train scholars well versed in critical theory. Since then, the field has increasingly defined itself through the disavowal of Orientalism, imperialism and nationalism, as well as by challenging what is seen as exploitative regimes of late capitalism, sexism, homophobia, and racism embedded in Japanese and American (or Western) literary, social, and cultural discourses.

A handful of other trends have helped to further mold the field. The advent of cultural studies has generally supported the growth of visual studies, film studies, and studies of popular culture. An upsurge of interest in Japanese colonial and imperial literature in Taiwan, Korea, Manchuria, and China came about as East Asian Studies belatedly responded to the widespread adoption of postcolonial theory advanced by English and comparative literature programs. Renewed emphases on gender and sexuality studies for much the same reasons brought women's literature, LGBTQ literature, and queer theory to the forefront of modern Japanese literary studies. Work on genre fiction has accordingly become more accepted as an extension of the literary canon, while studies on immigrant literature, transnational diaspora, and Japanophone or exophone literature are now in ascent on both sides of the Pacific.

It should come as no surprise that these critical discourses have also coincided with an explosion of interest in Japanese popular culture around the world. By the onset of the 21st century, Japanese cuisine, music, architecture, fashion, and television shows (including "reality TV") became ubiquitous signifiers of a borderless cosmopolitanism. In spite of the puncturing of Japan's economic bubble in 1991, the eclipse of Japan's preeminent technology companies by Silicon Valley in the early 2000s, and against many of the prescient objections registered in *Postmodernism and Japan*, Japan has enjoyed more than three decades as a globalized soft power superpower. "Cool Japan," an unironic moniker coined around 2002 that panders to depoliticized consumerism and nationalistic pride, has largely, if inadequately, filled the void left by 1990s *Rising Sun*-style accounts of Japan Inc. taking over the world.[12] Early responses to this shift already underway within the field of Japanese Studies can be found in John Whittier Treat's edited volume *Contemporary Japan and Popular Culture* (1996).[13]

The fact remains that scholars today often find themselves caught between the irresistible force of popular culture and the immovable object of high theory. Although approaches to modern Japanese literature have expanded to a remarkable degree, it is also true that the field has occasionally suffered losses of disciplinary specificity and critical acumen as a tradeoff for these new commitments. For better or worse, the infusion of film, anime, and popular culture, combined with heavy doses of theory has fundamentally altered modern Japanese literature's original remit. If there is no question of a "return to tradition" (itself a loaded term from the prewar era), modern Japanese literature nevertheless needs to come to terms with how our ongoing additions and subtractions have irrevocably transformed the discipline.

This volume offers no readymade solutions to narrow the gap between an idealized sense of pure literary studies on the one hand, and the complexities of the lingua franca of critical theory or the broad allure of popular culture on the other. But this volume demonstrates how even now, as we more easily make our claims legible to scholars outside of our field, we do so at the risk of erasing cultural specificity to render Japan as yet another iteration of a homogeneous global modernity. Conversely, when scholars play up the fetishism of small differences, they risk sliding down that regressive slope to exoticism and Orientalism, pandering to the knee-jerk, hobbyist's stereotypes of a "weird" or "quirky" Japan. Another issue often seen in small, insular fields is the cultivation of obscurantist concerns only intelligible to insiders. The recourse to rigorous archival work to circumvent these dangers is a necessary first step, even if it invites accusations of further reifying the positivism already found in Area Studies. We believe the present moment is an ideal time to reflect on the state of the field, recognizing the persistence of a tension between anti-essentialism (Miyoshi) and translating difference (Tansman). These ethical stakes, however, are bracketed by vastly larger existential threats such as the defunding of language study and cutbacks to the humanities, which render the study of modern Japanese literature more precarious than ever.

While the contributors to this volume assess a wide range of field-specific developments that are reinvigorating Japanese literary studies, they also pose questions about the structural and seismic shifts in the humanities writ large. It goes without saying that the study of modern Japanese literature in Japan and around the world is not alone in finding itself in the crosshairs of a neoliberal administrative model that sees foreign languages and literatures only through the lens of language enrollments, insists upon popular culture to "give the students what they want," and prioritizes American identity politics at the expense of teaching about similar (but also sometimes very different) struggles elsewhere in the world.

On these and many other points, we signal a debt to John Whittier Treat's article "Japan is Interesting: Modern Japanese Literary Studies Today," first published in *Japan Forum* in 2018,[14] and his related scholarly monograph, *The Rise and Fall of Modern Japanese Literature* (University of Chicago Press, 2018), for fundamentally reopening the discussion about the landscape of modern Japanese literary studies. This argument is reprised and updated in his essay for this volume. In 2017, Seth Jacobowitz organized a state-of-the-field workshop sponsored by the Center for East Asian Studies at Yale University, which provided a springboard for thinking about what form new models of the field might take. This volume emerged from such ongoing dialogues and debates that recognize Japanese Studies must surmount the zero-sum notion that an economically ascendant China (or Korea, whose cultural contributions have been even more woefully ignored by many of the leading research universities) translates into a diminished Japan. Whereas an earlier generation of scholars struggled to define the changing definition of modern Japanese literature within the context of a national canon in Japan, and within Area Studies (and to a lesser degree, comparative and world literature) in North America and Europe, the essays in this volume call attention to issues of visuality and language, as well as matters of ethnicity, race, gender, and sexuality. *Modern Japanese Literary Studies* pays special heed to emerging trends such as the advent of eco-criticism, transnational migration studies, and the concept of a Japanophone literature pioneered by comparatist Nishi Masahiko, which see it as a distinct outgrowth from mainstream Japanese literature.[15]

One of the conspicuous developments in the field since the 1990s has been the emergence and maturation of queer theory and LGBTQ studies. Although several preeminent scholars working at the intersection between gender and sexuality studies and modern Japanese literature are included here (Angles, Copeland, Tsuboi, and Treat), their essays in the volume focus on other topics. Translation has long been integral to the representation of Japanese literature in the West, and some of its earliest practitioners were gay and lesbian intellectuals who found alternative gender constructions and sexualities of premodern Japanese culture of particular interest and importance.[16] But it was not until the 1990s when the intersection of queer identity and literature became a major topic of study. The arc of Anglophone scholarship on homosexuality in modern Japanese literature likewise aptly fits between two literary bookends, the translation anthologies edited by Stephen Miller: *Partings at Dawn: An Anthology of Japanese Gay Literature* (Gay Sunshine Press, 1996) and *Queer Subjects in Modern Japanese Literature: Male Love, Intimacy, and Erotics, 1886–2014* (University of Michigan Press,

2022). The first volume made teaching Japanese gay literature possible in the English language world, while the second appeared at a moment when such stories had already long been included in syllabi, integrated into curricula, and read within the broader canon. It was not only in this realm of translation however where queer studies and the study of modern Japanese literature crossed. There was also pathbreaking scholarship by Steven Dodd, Paul Schalow, James Reichert, Jeffrey Angles, Sarah Frederick, J. Keith Vincent, Reggie Jackson, Christopher Lowy, Julia Bullock, Clare Maree, and many others.[17] But much of this scholarly work was preceded by an essay, "AIDS Panic in Japan, or How to Have a Sabbatical in an Epidemic" (*positions* 1994), and then a monograph, *Great Mirrors Shattered: Homosexuality, Orientalism, and Japan* (Oxford University Press, 1999) by John Whittier Treat. Regarding the latter, "*Great Mirrors Shattered* is not a work of conventional scholarship. Written in 1999, it is a postmodernist work of literature in its own right, equal parts confessional memoir, a documentary of the AIDS crisis that decimated gay communities around the world, and as per its title, a reflection on Orientalism and Japan."[18] More recently there have also been significant contributions to queer studies by Japanese scholars such as the work of Takeuchi Kayo and Iwakawa Arisa.[19]

The emphasis on a variety of methodological and experiential perspectives in the present volume should yet again drive home the point that no one speaks as the sole authority at the level of the field. *Modern Japanese Literary Studies* is a collection of essays in which our contributors each provide insights into the expansion of disciplinary, linguistic, and institutional approaches to the field. Although several of the essays engage with premodern and early modern Japanese literature (i.e., Sinographic writing and manga studies), the volume primarily attends to modern through contemporary literary matters. If this appears to reproduce a problem in the field today by prioritizing modernity, we can assure the reader that many of the essays in this volume also account for the temporal construction of the premodern and early modern.[20] Similarly, though we as the co-editors of this volume locate our own scholarly work at the intersection of literary and media studies, we have not included essays covering those disciplinary approaches, having published on the subject elsewhere.[21] Absent here are also the voices of scholars from prominent sites of Japan Studies including Australia, Brazil, France, Germany, New Zealand, and the United Kingdom. Such limitations notwithstanding, it is nevertheless our hope that the present book will generate productive dialogue with scholars within and beyond our immediate subject area(s). Apropos of Deleuze and Guattari's *A Thousand Plateaus*, we have not sought to claim the field in its entirety, but instead conceive of this collaboration as a series of multi-faceted openings onto a body of scholarship that solicits further rhizomorphic assemblages and interfaces from its readers,[22] the occasion for a growing awareness of the scope of the field rather than a claim of presenting the entire field as such.

Despite the fact that Japanese language, literature, and related fields are thriving in many sectors of today's academia, there is an entrenched, if unwarranted, perception by university administrators that interest in Japanese culture is waning in tandem with the country's supposedly diminished economic standing in the world. To this end, John Whittier Treat's contributing essay focalizes key points from the well-attended (standing room only) roundtable panel, "The Death of Japan Studies," that he organized for the Association of Asian Studies in 2019. To a certain degree, this comes down to accepting painful truths that are by now inescapable: Japan Studies has suffered from the broader defunding of non-Western humanities and declining student interest in the humanities since the Great Recession. Japan is erroneously held to no longer serve as a national geostrategic or economic concern by the US government; and in the eyes of many neoliberal administrators, a rising China or South Korea means corresponding cutbacks to Japan Studies in East Asian departments. And yet, judging by the unshakable commitment of our students to studying Japanese literature and culture, not to mention the robust diversity of scholarship and viewpoints on display in this volume, modern Japanese literature remains a vital discipline in the humanities.

The fact remains that modern Japanese literature has always exceeded its status in the Western imagination as a rarified cultural product or esoteric academic discipline. Since the mid-nineteenth century, Japanese literature and culture were consumed in the West under the sign of a perpetually evolving discourse of "Japonisme," and exerted an extraordinary historical impact on the project of invigorating Western mainstream culture and avant-gardist aesthetics.[23] At the level of popular culture, it is fair to say that younger generations around the world today are already conversant, and yearn to become fluent, in Japanese anime, manga, music, fashion, and cuisine. It is not surprising when they reach college age that many gravitate toward the study of Japanese language and literature, eager to deepen their understanding of a culture with which they feel a special bond.[24] As Japan becomes increasingly open to foreigners living and working there, with a record 3.4 million foreign residents in 2023, according to the Immigration Services Agency, the possibilities to realize professional goals in, and related to, Japan are also more available to our students than ever before.[25]

And yet the boundaries of "things Japanese" have undergone a remarkable metamorphosis in the last several decades. In 2017, the Nobel Prize for Literature was awarded to British author of Japanese descent, Kazuo Ishiguro, "who, in novels of great emotional force, has uncovered the abyss beneath our illusory sense of connection with the world."[26] In perhaps anticipation of one future direction of modern Japanese literature, author Kudan Rie admitted in 2024 that her Akutagawa Prize-winning novel *Tōkyo-to dōjōtō* (*Tokyo Metro Sympathy Tower*, 2023) included 5% of prose which came directly from ChatGPT, primarily through a scene in which a character interacts with generative AI.[27]

In response to the ways the field has evolved in recent decades, Rebecca Copeland's essay in this volume makes evident that while the nearly exclusive masculinist lineage of Japanese literature once taught in the United States ignored the significance of women writers, now women writers appear prominently on modern Japanese literature syllabi. This is to say nothing of the upsurge in women writers on the contemporary Japanese literary scene at home and overseas. Although Yoshimoto Banana broke the glass ceiling in the 1980s for the recognition of contemporary Japanese women writers outside of Japan, they have long been successful bestsellers in Japan from Kōno Taeko to historical fiction writer Setouchi Jakuchō. Since Yoshimoto, women writers have become increasingly popular in translation whether in popular genre fiction (Kirino Natsuo, Miyabe Miyuki, and Taguchi Randy) or belles lettres (Tawada Yōko, Kawakami Mieko, and Kanehara Hitomi). It is noteworthy that in 2020, Yū Miri's *Tokyo Ueno Station* (2014) was awarded a National Book Award in the United States for translated literature. Contemporary Japanese women writers are increasingly capturing new and appreciative audiences around the world through works translated into a myriad of languages. Recent developments such as these have unquestionably contributed to dynamic growth, renewal, and promise for students and scholars alike.

Nevertheless, even as modern Japanese literature experiences healthy reinvigoration, the rigor of a field demands that certain forms of autonomy must be respected and preserved. To the extent that modern Japanese literature has been a launching pad for studies of Japanese film, anime, and other forms of media, we should acknowledge the foundational and centering place of literature in these operations.[28] There has been a persistent blind spot in cultural and media studies of Japanese cinema, anime, television, and social media, which all too frequently fail to signal, much less repay, their disciplinary, conceptual, and institutional debts to literary studies.

Amid the efflorescence of Japanese visual studies since the 1990s, Norma Field's contention that we would all need to become better visual art readers has only partially come to pass. If Field's call "to sharpen our understanding of verbal art by comparison with visual art" by now seems like a quaint whisper from a time when verbal arts still seemed in ascendancy, we now know that the presumed demise of literature in favor of new media was never really the problem. Rather, the reprioritization of STEM-friendly and social scientific discourses over those of humanistic inquiry poses an existential threat to existing theories and best practices in literary studies. Field astutely anticipated some of the challenges ahead and elaborated her notion of media literacy as follows: "It only makes good intellectual and pedagogical sense for us to become film literate. We will need to do this thinking with our eyes resolutely open to institutional context, to budget cuts, to demands for ever-accelerated professionalization, to the claims of 'globalization' that may paradoxically produce a new parochialism as English's lingua franca status is reinforced."[29]

Having largely followed Field's advice, a new generation of scholars raised on television, video games, and film came to Japanese literature already predisposed toward the visual. The successful incorporation of Japanese film is an integral component of the discipline; in fact, it preserves the narrative economy we were trained to analyze in prose fiction. Prior to the vast video archives enabled by the World Wide Web, television was largely deemed too ephemeral, vast, and unwieldy for most scholars to embrace as an object of inquiry. By a perversely contrarian logic, it would be too easy to argue that the Internet has or will lead to the demise of literary study in general or Japanese literature in particular. If anything, the existence of the Internet has been the impetus for an even broader dissemination and a diversification into new forms of poetry and prose, whether by allowing the latest Japanese language novels to be bought in digital form anywhere in the world—almost simultaneously with their official domestic release—or through the superterranean piracy asserted through crowd-sourced "fanlations" (fan-based translations) of the latest manga series and trendy dramas. Needless to say, smartphones, tablets, e-readers, and computers have dramatically, if not yet entirely, supplanted traditional print media, while AI seems to render complex prose into accessible, statistically likely translations that frequently distort or even "hallucinate" Japanese literature. This threatens to mirror what was already prevalent in the data collated for the large language models upon which they draw.

Accordingly, we may accept that certain factors have perhaps irrevocably changed in early 21st century forms of literacy such as the speed and space of publication and circulation; the closing of the discursive loop between reader and writer, or producer and consumer; the vibrancy with which new identities and communities coalesce and dissipate; increased propensities to borrow ideas and intellectual labor without proper attribution, and the shortening of our collective attention span, which has us chasing more headlines, summaries, and social media posts, but fewer lengthy stretches of thoughtfully composed prose. It is fair to say that the range and intensity of the present circumstances are fundamentally shifting in accordance with emerging forms of networked, mobile, and wearable digital media.

The same technological systems that facilitated economic, cultural, and geopolitical upheavals are driving a slow bleed of the humanities. Despite the defunding of language study, the rise of a managerial class of non-academic administrators, and the pushing of STEM for pre-professional training in lieu of a traditional liberal arts education, enrollments in Japanese studies on the whole remain strong. According to the most recent pre-pandemic MLA data (2020), Japanese continues to be among the top five languages studied in North American institutions, though because the numbers of majors may be down, those committing to four years of language may have dropped slightly.[30] And the state of Japanese language study in North America to the degree we can measure it in numbers (i.e., before the pandemic) has been reassuringly stable since it reached a peak in the late 1990s and early 2000s. Language study, however, is but one external factor to the study of literature and culture. How these other external factors will continue to affect this discipline and its institutions of learning are a source of considerable consternation, yet offer some glimmers of optimism.

It is axiomatic in today's university culture that constant self-assessment is essential to the future planning of a discipline or academic program. Given the magnitude of contemporary challenges, now is the time for modern Japanese literary studies to undergo a much-needed review of its best methods and practices. Our central task for this book was to gather statements from a diverse cross-section of experts in order to consider where Japanese literary studies is today, how far it has come since previous rounds of fieldwide assessment, and to suggest pathways going forward. It is a testament to a shared sense of purpose that overlapping thematic clusters and through lines arise with regularity. As noted earlier, expansion of what the field of Japanese literature means in terms of belonging to a national language and/or canon has been well underway for thirty years or more. These essays in the aggregate are concerned with several interlocking issues: what new forms of research are emerging? Who is supporting them institutionally? What should be taught in the classroom, and what should be off-limits? When literary scholarship is ever more concentrated upon ideological and material conditions of production and consumption, can aesthetics still be considered dispositive? In pragmatic terms, are we training graduate students for what they will encounter on the job market, and are we properly addressing the intellectual concerns for a rising generation of undergraduate students? Rather than continue to go it alone or surrender to university administrations that want to dissolve us into omnibus departments of world languages and literatures, we offer the present volume to resume badly needed forms of critical engagement and dialogue. We trust that the issues raised in this volume will resonate with colleagues in other literary and humanistic fields as well.

Despite continual rhetoric about "worlding" comparative literature, decolonizing the curriculum, or overcoming a Eurocentric bias in higher education, modern Japanese literature has not been widely embraced outside its traditional postwar Area Studies configurations. While this volume includes scholars with expertise in Sinophone literature—Matthew Fraleigh and Christopher Lupke, in particular—our focus is on Japan, which has the longest modern literary history in East Asia. Chinese and Korean literary modernity were to varying, but significant degrees, shaped by explicit and implicit tutelary efforts during the era of the Japanese empire, and revolutionary literary activity against the Japanese empire must also be calculated in this regard.

Another rationale for this project is the need for a counterbalance to the widespread misrepresentations of modern Japanese literature that continues to dominate much of what is represented to mainstream and commercial global audiences. Notwithstanding the visibility of the short-lived, but much-beloved Vertical, Inc. (2004–2019) that championed the publication of contemporary Japanese literature, publishing houses in the United States routinely double down on the persistent idea of quirky or weird Japan, skewing cultural perceptions and consigning contemporary Japanese literature to a niche readership. This is oftentimes nothing more than an updating of Japoniste and Orientalist tropes, a sad reality made more pernicious by the enthusiastic endorsement of social media influencers and the like. In taking stock of critical work on modern Japanese literature, the editors and contributors to this volume seek to intervene in reshaping popular perceptions of the material that actually forms the basis for our studies, especially when its field of view is occluded by these latter-day "tastemakers."

The emergence of new geopolitical crises in the last twenty years has prompted reconsideration within Japan of the nation's place in the world. The return of Japanese abductees from North Korea in 2004, a series of North Korean nuclear and ballistic missile tests between 2006 and 2024, the Fukushima triple disaster of March 11, 2011, and most recently, the Covid-19 pandemic have profoundly unsettled tidy notions of the Liberal Democratic Party-led managerial state. The geopolitical tensions posed by a militarily assertive China and Russia, and potentially unreliable postwar allies, have put further pressure on Japan to upgrade its military responsiveness. Toward the end of 2021, Japan surprisingly even signaled its willingness to defend Taiwan, a democratic ally that for half a century (1895–1945) had been its colonial possession. Meanwhile, the closure of Japan's borders in response to the pandemic had measurable impacts on the cultural sphere and pummeled Japan's international standing. After the delayed and deeply unpopular 2020 Olympics brought down the short-lived Suga administration, former Prime Minister Kishida Fumio appeared determined to enact an isolationist policy as a buffer not only against the omicron variant of Covid-19, but also any political threats to the LDP's grip on power. Nevertheless, given Japan's aging and shrinking population, it is to be expected that the country was once again turning more insular well before the onset of the pandemic. In the face of broader cultural shifts and the demographic risks to Japan's global competitiveness, the "Ministry of Education, Culture, Sports, Science and Technology began full-scale efforts to internationalize higher education in 2009 with Global 30, a project to establish a network for internationalization. Significant progress has been made over the last 12 years, with the Go Global Japan Project, which launched in 2012 to support universities foster [sic] people capable of aggressively challenging global issues and playing active roles on the global stage, and the Top Global University Project (TGU), launched in 2014."[31] The TGU project, which ran until 2023, set the ambitious goal of attracting 300,000 foreign students by 2020 and having ten Japanese universities rank among the top 100 universities in the world by 2030.[32] How these plans will be affected by Japan's post-pandemic footing, and response to its own demographic pressures of a shrinking and aging population, remains to be seen.

Needless to say, these are anxious times for contemporary Japanese, whose authors have applied unremitting scrutiny to issues of modern alienation, loneliness, and the hollowing out of family and domestic life. Not all is gloom and doom: the charms of one's neighborhood and small mysteries of daily life, continue to captivate readers at home and abroad. Bestselling works such as Yū Miri's *Tokyo Ueno Station* (2014) and Murata Sayaka's *Convenience Store Woman* (2016) have reflected upon diminished horizons and wasted lives for an audience that is understandably worried about its own potentially foreshortened prospects. An overriding question the present volume explores is how best to respond to emerging changes in present-day Japan, even as scholars in the field continue to assert the need to teach the literature *qua* literature, critical methodologies, and hold the center for a discipline with an uncertain future.

Part I, on "Negotiating Disciplinary Formation," features six essays that examine the dramatic turns in terms of canon formation and reformation, as well as the emergence of new theoretical and disciplinary frameworks that have redrawn the boundaries of literary inquiry. Rebecca Copeland's "Modern Japanese Women Writers and Evolving Trends in North American Japanese Literature Scholarship" opens the section with an account of the struggles she and other women scholars faced over the span of several decades to overcome prejudices against Japanese women's literature and place it front and center in research and the classroom. Davinder Bhowmik's "The Inclusion of Okinawa in Japanese Literary Studies" narrates a parallel effort to bring modern Okinawan literature out of the shadows. She highlights the tensions even at institutions such as University of the Ryukyus and Okinawa University to juggle teaching of Okinawan literature together with the mainstream national canon, a phenomenon which echoes the curricular struggles by ethnic studies for representation in the North American university system. William H. Bridges IV's "Do Black Lives Still Matter to Japanese Literary Studies?" insists on the importance of the African American experience for the study of modern Japanese literature and its canonicity. Bringing attention not only to the institutional frameworks that necessitate the continued and continual argument for Black lives, but also for the history of modern Japanese literature itself, Bridges pushes us beyond the trope of the black body that formed a focal point for so many postwar narratives. He leaves us with the aspirational and optimistic idealism of Esperantism in Japan and its deep imbrication with the foundational role of the Japanese Black Studies Association in the 1950s (when it was The Japanese Association for Negro Studies). Jon Pitt's "Ecocritical Precedent, Present, and Possibility in Japanese Literary Studies" explores how quickly and strategically ecocriticism has been positioned as a new center for the field in response to the still-unfolding global catastrophes of the Anthropocene, and insists the value of such work will only increase in the near future. Two very different essays on manga in the curriculum complete this section. Adam Kern's "Comixing Frameworks: Rethinking the Euroamerican Critical Paradigm from the Perspective of Manga Studies" advocates for a revitalized commitment to the teaching of comic books, graphic novels, and the like, insisting that they "may be able to provide a constructive critique of the ethnocentrism, chronocentrism, and ocularcentrism engendered by this modern Western critical framework dominating literary studies and other fields, including Comics Studies."[33] Deborah Shamoon's "Approaches to Researching and Teaching Manga as Literature" demonstrates how the "marginal status" of manga has been remedied in recent years with the continual development of translations, curricula, and manga studies as a field.

Part II, "The Question of Language" investigates literary production in the Japanese-language literate community beyond the ethno-linguistic unity of the modern nation-state. These next five essays mark a transition toward the emerging discourse of "Japanophone literature" (*Nihongo bungaku*) that has become a prominent feature of modern Japanese literary studies in the last two decades. Together with exophony, the concept of a Japanophone literature has gathered around a disparate collection of non-native Japanese writers and those former Japanese subjects taking up positions outside the boundaries of what Oguma Eiji famously called "the myth of a homogeneous Japan."[34]

The ranks of prominent non-native Japanese writers includes the recent Akutagawa Prize winning novelists Li Kotomi (2021; pen name of Li Qifeng, born in Taiwan in 1989) and Yang Yi (2008; pen name of Liu Qiao born in the People's Republic of China in 1964), and an immigrant writer such as Matsui Tarō (1917–2017), who was born in Japan but spent most of his life in rural Brazil. Remarkably, Matsui was in his 90s when his long-form novels *Utsurobune* (The empty vessel, Shōraisha, 2010) and *Tōi Koe* (A distant voice, Shōraisha, 2012) were championed by literary scholars Nishi Masahiko and Hosokawa Shūhei. They described Matsui as a masterful storyteller and contemporary voice of the Japanese Brazilian diaspora still writing in Japanese, albeit from unfamiliar grounds. We would do well to remember, too, that one of our contributors, Jeffrey Angles, is at the forefront of the Japanophone wave in poetry and one of only a handful of American scholars to gain recognition for their literary activities in Japan.[35] In 2016, his poetry collection *Watashi no hizukehenkōsen* (My International Date Line) won the Yomiuri Prize for Literature, making him the first American to receive this prestigious prize in Japan.

Hideto Tsuboi's "World Literature and Japanese-Language Literature," assesses how the concepts of global, international, and world literature relate to the ways the field of modern literary studies have historically been constituted in Japan. He critiques the tendency of world literature to understand global culture as Eurocentric homogeneity: such trends divide the planet in terms of what Stuart Hall (1991) and Niall Ferguson (2011) called "the West and the Rest" and are consonant with elevation of a particular mode of Japanophone literature (exemplified by the work of Murakami Haruki), one linguistically simple and translation-friendly. Yoshitaka Hibi's "The History and Present of Japanophone Literature: Migration, Border Crossing, and Materiality," meanwhile, considers the implications for the primarily prewar Japanese-language community that achieved its zenith with Japanese imperial expansion in East Asia coupled with mass migration to the Americas, particularly the United States and Brazil. In "Modern Japanese Literature and Sinitic Literary Traditions," Matthew Fraleigh characterizes the protracted afterlife of Chinese poetry, a mainstay of premodern Japanese literary and cultural production, which, since the Meiji era, was largely eclipsed by Japanese-language and Western-derived modern poetic forms. Nevertheless, he calls attention to how competing forms of classification and cataloguing have sought to define modern Japanese Sinitic texts. These categorical confusions revolve around what is essentially the composition of Chinese poetry by Japanese poets. Fraleigh makes the case for Sinitic poetry and prose (*kanshibun*) to be understood as exophonic literature, or "literary activity that is undertaken in a language other than the writer's native language."[36] Youngran Kō's "Literature and the Cultural Politics of Immigration: Between Lee Hoesung and Yang Yi in the 'Era of the Immigrant,'" evaluates the life and times of Lee Hoesung, the first resident (*Zainichi*) Korean to win the award in 1972, against the backdrop of Japan's restrictive immigration policies and the modishness of the Japanophone boom, which elevates the exotic spectacle of foreign authors while conveniently forgetting the presence of Japan's minority communities. Jeffrey Angles's "Translation and the Crisis of Relevancy in Japanese Studies" explores the dynamics of translation studies and the rise of world literature, noting that despite the status of translation as "secondary, derivative activity," it remains indispensable for making Japanese cultural life accessible to non-specialists. He mobilizes an impressive array of data showing how institutional support for translation has not only sustained the field at the academic level, but also expanded the readership and appreciation of modern to contemporary Japanese literature through prestigious literary awards such as the National Book Award in Translation and the Man Booker International Prize.

Part III, "Institutional Responses to the Field," presents three essays that assess modern Japanese literature's positionality within the humanities and liberal arts in the United States and Europe. Writing about the state of the field of modern Japanese literature in Europe, Italian scholar Gala Maria Follaco describes some of the innovative research that has emerged in recent years on modern urbanization and the literature of urban space, as well as the critical dialogues our European colleagues have enjoined with their counterparts in Japan and North America. While elaborating on the topographical genres that help to structure our understanding of the ever-changing facets of city life, she offers a timely reminder that we should strive "to continue with work capable of valorizing non-canonical texts, authors, and contexts, clarifying the centrality of literary discourse in the colonial space and urban experience in the context of migrations."

In its wide-ranging analysis, John Whittier Treat's "The Problem of Scale in Japanese Literary Studies," takes stock of the much-touted "end of literature" and the crisis in the (especially non-Western) humanities that continues to buffet the field. Treat further makes the case that modern Japanese literature has become the victim of its own diversification at the expense of its core identity. In its attempts to transcend the structural problems of the humanities, he avers, advocates of digital humanities and other supposedly more "objective" methodologies have unwittingly repeated all the subjective claims present in the worst of humanist inquiry, minus self-awareness or critical distancing.

Lastly, Christopher Lupke's "Signposts for the Non-Specialist: Thoughts on a Renewed View of the State of Modern Japanese Literary Studies" concludes the volume by offering the perspective of a seasoned Sinologist based in Canada on the fourteen essays in the volume and their impact on the progress of modern Japanese literary studies into the early twenty-first century.

Notes

1. Norma Field, "'The Way of the World': Japanese Literary Studies in the Postwar United States," in *The Postwar Developments of Japanese Studies in the United States*, ed. Helen Hardacre (Brill, 1998), 227–93.

2. It is essential to recall that the location and composition of the Japanese Language School faculty were affected by Franklin Delano Roosevelt's Executive Order 9066, which mandated the evacuation and internment of Japanese Americans following the attack on Pearl Harbor. As Brian Niiya observes, "Originating at Harvard and the University of California Berkeley in the fall of 1941, the school moved to the University of Colorado at Boulder in June 1942 due the exclusion of Japanese Americans from the West Coast. Around 150 Japanese Americans made up the vast majority of the faculty, many of them recruited from detention camps holding the removed Japanese Americans." *Densho Encyclopedia*, accessed January 1, 2025, https://encyclopedia.densho.org/Navy_Japanese_Language_School/. Other leading scholars of that generation, such as Howard Hibbett and Earl Miner, also received language instruction from the military.

3. See Edward Seidensticker, "The 'Pure' and the 'in-Between' in Modern Japanese Theories of the Novel," *Harvard Journal of Asiatic Studies* 26 (1966): 174–86. Muta, Orie, "Popular Literature," *Japanese Studies*, September 1, 1992. Suzuki Sadami, "Three Themes and a Few Points of View—for Rewriting of Japanese Modern and Contemporary Cultural and Literary History," *Japan Review*, no. 5 (1994): 125–44. Matthew C. Strecher, "Purely Mass or Massively Pure? The Division Between 'Pure' and 'Mass' Literature," *Monumenta Nipponica* 51, no. 3 (1996): 357–74.

4. Ann Sherif, "The Politics of Loss: On Etō Jun," *positions* 10, no. 1 (Spring 2002): 113–14. Sherif's article further assesses the controversies in Etō's later writings, which followed his two years of study at Princeton funded by the Rockefeller Foundation, and which contributed to his defense of a deeply conservative "ahistorical

symbolic order" predicated on "the nation as family" (118).

5. Katō Shūichi's *History of Japanese Literature* was published by Kodansha International as *The First Thousand Years* (1979), *The Years of Isolation* (1983), and *The Modern Years* (1983). Major sections of Maeda's study appear in James Fujii, ed. *Text and the City: Essays on Japanese Modernity* (Duke University Press, 2004), as do Harry Harootunian and William Sibley's reminiscences of Maeda's visit to Chicago in Foreword, vii–xiv, and Afterword, 351–73, respectively.

6. See linguist John Whitman's excellent essay in the same volume, "*Kokugogaku* versus *Gengogaku*: Language Process Theory and Tokieda's Construction of Saussure Sixty Years Later," 227–54.

7. Karatani's later work would take a more philosophical and explicitly Marxian turn. Karatani, Kojin, *Architecture as Metaphor: Language, Number, Money* (MIT Press, 1995); *Transcritique: On Kant and Marx* (MIT Press, 2005); *History and Repetition* (Columbia University Press, 2012); *The Structure of World History: From Modes of Production to Modes of Exchange* (Duke University Press, 2014); *Isonomia and the Origins of Philosophy* (Duke University Press, 2017); *Nation and Aesthetics: On Kant and Freud* (Oxford University Press, 2017); *Marx: Towards the Centre of Possibility* (Verso Books, 2020). These efforts would go on to have impacts that far exceeded the field of Japanese literature such as when Slavoj Žižek drew on Karatani's *Transcritique* as the impetus for *The Parallax View*. See Slavoj Žižek, *The Parallax View* (MIT Press, 2009).

8. Its successors, Masao Miyoshi and Harry Harootunian, eds., *Japan in the World* (Duke University Press, 1993) and Harry Harootunian and Tomiko Yoda, eds., *Japan After Japan* (Duke University Press, 2006) were similarly pitched as interdisciplinary commentaries on "recessionary era" Japan's struggles with globalization.

9. See also Masao Miyoshi, *Off Center: Power and Culture Relations between Japan and the United States* (Harvard University Press, 1991); Miyoshi, *Learning Places: The Afterlives of Area Studies* (Duke University Press, 2002).

10. The essay was later reproduced in Sakai's *Translation and Subjectivity: On "Japan" and Cultural Nationalism* (University of Minnesota Press, 1997).

11. Alan Tansman, "Japanese Studies: The Intangible Act of Translation Location: Global, Area, and International Archive," in David L. Szanton, ed., *The Politics of Knowledge: Area Studies and the Disciplines* v.3 (University of California Press, 2004), 184–216. Previously published as "Japanese Studies: The Intangible Act of Translation. Location: Global, Area, and International Archive," UniversiAlifornia, Berkeley, GAIA Books, Global, Area, and International Archive, 2003, 1–23. Notable here is his more recent attempt to present Japanese literature in a summative way: Alan Tansman, *Japanese Literature: A Very Short Introduction* (Oxford University Press, 2023).

12. See the discussion of odorless Japanese cultural products designed for the global market in Koichi Iwabuchi, "From Western Gaze to Global Gaze: Japanese Cultural Presence in Asia," in *Global Culture* (Routledge, 2002) and Koichi Iwabuchi, *Recentering Globalization: Popular Culture and Japanese Transnationalism* (Duke University Press, 2002), 24–29. Douglas McGray, "Japan's Gross National Cool," *Foreign Policy* (2002) 130: 44–54.

13. John Whittier Treat, ed., *Contemporary Japan and Popular Culture* (University of Hawai'i Press, 1996).

14. Miyoshi, Masao, "Japan is not interesting," *Trespasses: Selected Writings*, edited

by Eric Cazdyn (Duke University Press Books, 2010). Karatani, Kōjin, 1997, "Japan Is Interesting Because Japan is not Interesting" (http://www.karataniforum.org/index.html, accessed in 1997) still accessible on thewaybackmachine.org.

15. Faye Yuan Kleeman, *Under an Imperial Sun: Japanese Colonial Literature of Taiwan and the South* (University of Hawai'i Press, 2003); Edward Mack, *Acquired Alterity: Migration, Identity, and Literary Nationalism* (University of California Press, 2022), 185; Christina Yi, *Colonizing Language: Cultural Production and Language Politics in Modern Japan and Korea* (Columbia University Press, 2018); Christina Yi, Andre Haag, and Catherine Ryu, eds., *Passing, Posing, Persuasion: Cultural Production and Coloniality in Japan's East Asian Empire* (University of Hawai'i Press, 2023).

16. Japonisme as an aesthetic movement enabled Westerners to express non-normative sexual orientations in ways otherwise not permitted in their own societies. See, for instance, Christopher Reed, *Bachelor Japanists: Japanese Aesthetics and Western Masculinities*, First Edition (Columbia University Press, 2016). Particularly noteworthy literary figures with a deep interest in Japan were Arthur Waley and Virginia Woolf, as noted in John W. de Gruchy, *Orienting Arthur Waley: Japonism, Orientalism, and the Creation of Japanese Literature in English*, First Edition (University of Hawai'i Press, 2003). In her 1925 book review in *Vogue* on Waley's translation of the *Tale of Genji*, Woolf describes Murasaki Shikibu in terms of a transvestite and androgynous figuration that would later help to inspire her novel *Orlando: A Biography* (1928): "While the Aelfrics and Aelfreds croaked and coughed in England, this court lady [. . .] was sitting down in her silk dress and trousers with pictures before her and the sound of poetry in her ears [. . .] to tell the story of the life and adventures of Prince Genji." Andrew McNeillie, ed. *The Essays of Virginia Woolf*, vol. 4, 1925.

17. Jeffrey Angles, *Writing the Love of Boys: Origins of Bishōnen Culture in Modernist Japanese Literature* (University of Minnesota Press, 2011); Julia C. Bullock, *The Other Women's Lib: Gender and Body in Japanese Women's Fiction* (University of Hawai'i Press, 2019); Sharon Chalmers, *Emerging Lesbian Voices from Japan* (Routledge, 2003); Reginald Jackson, *A Proximate Remove: Queering Intimacy and Loss in The Tale of Genji* (University of California Press, 2021); Yoshiya Nobuko, *Forget Me Not Girls' Love: Mei Yumi's 1930s Japanese Literature*, Amazon Digital Services LLC—KDP Print US, 2019; Jim Reichert, *In the Company of Men: Representations of Male-Male Sexuality in Meiji Literature*, 1st edition (Stanford University Press, 2006); Paul Gordon Schalow, *A Poetics of Courtly Male Friendship in Heian Japan* (University of Hawai'i Press, 2006), Stephen D. Miller, ed., *Partings at Dawn: An Anthology of Japanese Gay Literature*, First Edition (Gay Sunshine Press, 1996); Suzuki, Michiko, *Becoming Modern Women: Love and Female Identity in Prewar Japanese Literature and Culture* (Stanford University Press, 2010); J. Keith Vincent, *Two-Timing Modernity: Homosocial Narrative in Modern Japanese Fiction* (Harvard University Asia Center, 2012); John Whittier Treat, "AIDS Panic in Japan, or How to Have a Sabbatical in an Epidemic," *positions: asia critique* 2, no. 3 (August 1, 1994): 629–79; Claire Maree, *queerqueen: Linguistic Excess in Japanese Media*. Studies in Language, Gender, and Sexuality (Oxford University Press, 2020).

18. Seth Jacobowitz, "Beyond Nation: Time, Writing, and Community in the Work of Abe Kōbō by Richard F. Calichman," *Monumenta Nipponica* 72, no. 2 (2017): 337–44.

19. Takeuchi Kayo, *Kuia suru gendai nihon bungaku: Kea dōbutsu katari* (Seikyu-sha, 2023); Iwakawa Arisa, *Monogatari to torauma: Kuia feminizumu hihyō no kanōsei* (Ōdzuchi-sha, 2022); Tamura Miyuki, *Kōjutsu hikki suru bungaku — kaku koto no daikō to jendā* (Nagoya daigaku shuppankai, 2023).

20. See Philip C. Brown's excellent "Summary of Discussions: The State of the Field in Early Modern Japanese Studies," *Early Modern Japan*, Spring 2003. See also Haruo Shirane, ed., *Traditional Japanese Literature: An Anthology, Beginnings to 1600* (Columbia University Press, 2012); David Lurie, Haruo Shirane, and Tomi Suzuki, eds., *The Cambridge History of Japanese Literature* (Cambridge University Press, 2015). This recent interest can also be seen in the New Horizons in Japanese Literary and Cultural Studies International Symposium organized by Columbia University and Waseda University March 13, 2015, accessed January 1, 2025, http://flas.waseda.jp/jcs-j/wp-content/uploads/sites/15/2015/07/symposium-summary-English.pdf

21. The editors of this volume have published elsewhere our own respective research monographs on formative relations between media and literature in modern Japan. See for instance Jonathan E. Abel, *Redacted: The Archives of Censorship in Transwar Japan* (University of California Press, 2012) and *The New Real: Media and Mimesis in Japan from Stereographs to Emoji* (University of Minnesota Press, 2023); and Seth Jacobowitz, *Writing Technology in Meiji Japan: A Media History of Modern Japanese Literature and Visual Culture* (Harvard Asia Center, 2016).

22. Gilles Deleuze and Félix Guattari, *A Thousand Plateaus: Capitalism and Schizophrenia* (University of Minnesota Press, 1987).

23. Earl Miner's *The Japanese Tradition in British and American literature* (Princeton University Press, 1958) and Jan Walsh Hokenson's *Japan, France, and East-West Aesthetics: French Literature, 1867–2000* (Farleigh Dickinson University Press, 2004) deserve special mention for their research into the ways modern Japanese literature has served as a touchstone for the British and French literary imagination, respectively.

24. It is noteworthy that students from China and South Korea are often among the most avid enrollees in Japanese language and literature courses, not only in the United States, but from around the world.

25. "Record 3.4 Million Foreign Residents in Japan as Work Visas Rise," *Kyodo News*, accessed October 22, 2025, https://english.kyodonews.net/articles/-/46780.

26. "The Nobel Prize in Literature 2017," accessed January 10, 2022, https://www.nobelprize.org/prizes/literature/2017/summary. See also Rebecca Suter, *Two-World Literature: Kazuo Ishiguro's Early Novels* (University of Hawai'i Press, 2020) and Yugin Teo, *Kazuo Ishiguro and Memory* (Palgrave Macmillan, 2014).

27. See Thu-huong Ha, "Akutagawa Prize Draws Controversy after Win for Work That Used ChatGPT," *The Japan Times*. January 19, 2024. https://www.japantimes.co.jp/culture/2024/01/19/books/akutagawa-prize-book-chatgpt/ and "Award-Winning Author's AI Use Revelation Roils Japan's Literary World," *Mainichi Daily News*, February 4, 2024. https://mainichi.jp/english/articles/20240204/p2g/00m/0et/001000c

28. Yoshimoto Mitsuhiro has written at length how Japanese film in North American academia has historically been relegated to the position of a token non-Western example for global film studies. He has also exposed the absence of film as a proper discipline in Japan. Here, along similar lines, we simply wish to acknowledge that in North American Japanese literature scholars, too, have often taken on the teaching of

Japanese film despite a lack of expertise in the medium. If film was initially used to broaden the appeal of Japanese literary and culture courses from the 1990s onward, this subsequently led decidedly to a salutary outcome: more rigorous training in Japanese film and visual studies. On the one hand, it also led to an attenuation of Japanese literary studies when film studies did not repay the favor. See Yoshimoto Mitsuhiro, "A Future of Comparative Film Studies," *Inter-Asia Cultural Studies* 14, no. 1 (March 1, 2013): 54–61; Yoshimoto Mitsuhiro, "Questions of Japanese Cinema: Disciplinary Boundaries and the Invention of the Scholarly Object," in *Learning Places* (Duke University Press, 2002), 368–402; and Yoshimoto Mitsuhiro, "The University, Disciplines, National Identity: Why Is There No Film Studies in Japan?" *South Atlantic Quarterly* 99, no. 4 (October 1, 2000): 697–713, which was reprinted in Harootunian and Yoda's *Japan After Japan*.

29. Norma Field, "The Way of the World: Japanese Literary Studies in the Postwar United States," 268–69.

30. *2020 MLA Newsletter* (Volume 54, issue 3), 6.

31. Hakui Yoshinori, Director-General, Higher Education Bureau, Ministry of Education, Culture, Sports, Science and Technology, on the MEXT Top Global University Japan website, accessed January 1, 2025, https://tgu.mext.go.jp/en/aftercorona/index.html

32. Reni Juwitasari, "'Kokusaika': Education Reform for Internalization in Japanese Universities," *Japan Watch* (2019), accessed January 1, 2025, http://japanwatch.today/th/blog/post/kokuisaka-education-reform-for-internalization-in-japanese-universities

33. Adam Kern, "Comixing Frameworks: Rethinking the Euroamerican Critical Paradigm from the Perspective of Manga Studies," 4.

34. Oguma Eiji, *A Genealogy of "Japanese" Self-Images*, trans. David Askew (Trans Pacific Press, 2002).

35. *Man'yōshū* scholar Ian Hideo Levy won the Noma Literary Award for New Writers in 1992 for his debut novel in Japanese *Seijōki no kikoenai heya* (A Room Where the Star-Spangled Banner Cannot Be Heard). More recently, Greg Khezrnejat, a literature professor at Hōsei University specializing in transnational and minority authorship in modern Japanese literature, won the Kyoto Literature Award in 2021 for his debut work of fiction, the novella *Kamogawa rannā* (Kamogawa Runner).

36. Matthew Fraleigh, "Modern Japanese Literature and Sinitic Literary Traditions," 166.

Bibliography

"Akutagawa Prize Draws Controversy after Win for Work That Used ChatGPT." *The Japan Times*. Accessed January 2, 2025. https://www.japantimes.co.jp/culture/2024/01/19/books/akutagawa-prize-book-chatgpt/

Angles, Jeffrey. *Writing the Love of Boys: Origins of Bishōnen Culture in Modernist Japanese Literature*. University of Minnesota Press, 2011. http://site.ebrary.com/id/10455040

Bourdaghs, Michael, ed. *The Linguistic Turn in Contemporary Japanese Literary Studies: Politics, Language, Textuality*. University of Michigan Center for Japanese Studies,

2010. https://doi.org/10.3998/mpub.9340192

Chalmers, Sharon. *Emerging Lesbian Voices from Japan*. RoutledgeCurzon, 2003. https://search.ebscohost.com/login.aspx?direct=true&scope=site&db=nlebk&db=nlabk&AN=93134

de Gruchy, John Walter. *Orienting Arthur Waley: Japonism, Orientalism, and the Creation of Japanese Literature in English*. University of Hawai'i Press, 2003. http://catdir.loc.gov/catdir/toc/fy041/2003001344.html

Deleuze, Gilles, and Félix Guattari. A *Thousand Plateaus*. A&C Black, 2004.

Field, Norma. "'The Way of The World': Japanese Literary Studies in the Postwar United States." In *The Postwar Developments of Japanese Studies in the United States*, edited by Helen Hardacre, 227–93. Brill, 1998. https://doi.org/10.1163/9789004644861_010

Hardacre, Helen, ed. *The Postwar Developments of Japanese Studies in the United States*. Brill, 1998.

Hokenson, Jan. *Japan, France, and East-West Aesthetics: French Literature, 1867–2000*. Fairleigh Dickinson University Press, 2004. http://catdir.loc.gov/catdir/toc/ecip048/2003019869.html

Iwabuchi, Koichi. "From Western Gaze to Global Gaze: Japanese Cultural Presence in Asia." In *Global Culture, edited by Diana Crane, Nobuko Kawashima, and Ken'ichi Kawasaki, 256–73*. Routledge, 2002.

Iwabuchi, Koichi. *Recentering Globalization: Popular Culture and Japanese Transnationalism*. Duke University Press, 2002. http://lib.myilibrary.com/browse/open.asp?id=306425&entityid=https://idp.brunel.ac.uk/entity

Jackson, Reginald R. *A Proximate Remove: Queering Intimacy and Loss in The Tale of Genji*. Joan Palevsky Imprint in Classical Literature. University of California Press, 2021. https://doi.org/10.1525/9780520382558

Jacobowitz, Seth. "Beyond Nation: Time, Writing, and Community in the Work of Abe Kōbō by Richard F. Calichman (Review)." *Monumenta Nipponica* 72, no. 2 (2017): 337–44.

Japan Watch. "'Kokusaika': Education Reform for Internalization in Japanese Universities." Accessed January 2, 2025. https://japanwatch.today/th/blog/post/kokuisaka-education-reform-for-internalization-in-japanese-universities

Karatani, Kōjin. *Architecture as Metaphor: Language, Number, Money*. Edited by Michael Speaks. Translated by Sabu Kohso. Writing Architecture. MIT Press, 1995.

Karatani, Kōjin. *History and Repetition*. Edited by Seiji M. Lippit. Weatherhead Books on Asia. Columbia University Press, 2012.

Karatani, Kōjin. *Isonomia and the Origins of Philosophy*. Translated by Joseph A. Murphy. Duke University Press, 2017. https://search.ebscohost.com/login.aspx?direct=true&scope=site&db=nlebk&db=nlabk&AN=1576853

Karatani, Kōjin. *Nation and Aesthetics: On Kant and Freud*. Translated by Jonathan E. Abel, Darwin H. Tsen, and Hiroki Yoshikuni. Global Asias. Oxford University Press, 2017.

Karatani, Kōjin. *Origins of Modern Japanese Literature*. Translation edited by Brett de Bary. Post-Contemporary Interventions. Duke University Press, 1993. http://www.gbv.de/dms/bowker/toc/9780822313120.pdf

Karatani, Kōjin. *Transcritique on Kant and Marx*. Translated by Sabu Kohso. MIT Press, 2003. https://search.ebscohost.com/login.aspx?direct=true&scope=site&db

=nlebk&db=nlabk&AN=100072

Karatani, Kōjin. *The Structure of World History: From Modes of Production to Modes of Exchange*. Translated by Michael K. Bourdaghs. Duke University Press, 2014. https://doi.org/10.1515/9780822376682

Katō, Shūichi. *A History of Japanese Literature*. Kodansha International, 1979.

Katō, Shūichi. *A History of Japanese Literature: The First Thousand Years*. Translated by David Chibbett. Kodansha International, 1981.

Keene, Donald. *Dawn to the West: Japanese Literature of the Modern Era, Fiction*. A History of Japanese Literature. Columbia University Press, 1998.

Keene, Donald. *Dawn to the West: Japanese Literature of the Modern Era, Poetry, Drama, Criticism*. A History of Japanese Literature. Columbia University Press, 1999.

Levy, Ian Hideo. *A Room Where the Star-Spangled Banner Cannot Be Heard: A Novel in Three Parts*. Translated by Christopher D. Scott. Japanese Studies Series. Columbia University Press, 2011.

Mack, Edward Thomas. *Acquired Alterity: Migration, Identity, and Literary Nationalism*. New Interventions in Japanese Studies. University of California Press, 2022. https://torl.biblioboard.com/content/d710c009-a3b6-477d-83f9-24155bc09100

Maeda, Ai, James A. Fujii, and 前田愛 (1932–1987). *Text and the City: Essays on Japanese Modernity*. Asia-Pacific. Duke University Press, 2004. http://libaccess.mcmaster.ca/login?url=http://catdir.loc.gov/catdir/toc/ecip0410/2003022708.html

Maree, Claire. *queerqueen: Linguistic Excess in Japanese Media*. Studies in Language, Gender, and Sexuality. Oxford University Press, 2020. http://search.ebscohost.com/login.aspx?direct=true&scope=site&db=nlebk&db=nlabk&AN=2503811

Miller, Stephen D., ed. *Partings at Dawn: An Anthology of Japanese Gay Literature*. First edition. Gay Sunshine Press, 1996.

Miner, Earl. *The Japanese Tradition in British and American Literature*. Princeton University Press, 1958.

Miyoshi, Masao, Eric M. Cazdyn, and Fredric Jameson. *Trespasses: Selected Writings*. Post-Contemporary Interventions. Duke University Press, 2010.

Miyoshi, Masao, and Harry D. Harootunian, eds. *Japan in the World*. Duke University Press, 1993. http://www.gbv.de/dms/bowker/toc/9780822313502.pdf

Miyoshi, Masao, and Harry D. Harootunian, eds. *Learning Places: The Afterlives of Area Studies*. Asia-Pacific. Duke University Press, 2002. https://doi.org/10.1215/9780822383598

Miyoshi, Masao. *Off Center: Power and Culture Relations between Japan and the United States*. Convergences. Harvard University Press, 1991. http://www.gbv.de/dms/bowker/toc/9780674631755.pdf

Miyoshi, Masao, and Harry D. Harootunian, eds. *Postmodernism and Japan*. Post-Contemporary Interventions. Duke University Press, 1989. http://site.ebrary.com/id/10195232

Muta, Orie. "Popular Literature." *Japanese Studies* 12, no. 2—Get Access. Accessed January 2, 2025. https://www.tandfonline.com/doi/pdf/10.1080/10371399208521904

"Navy Japanese Language School | Densho Encyclopedia." Accessed January 2, 2025. https://encyclopedia.densho.org/Navy_Japanese_Language_School/

NobelPrize.org. "The Nobel Prize in Literature 2017." Accessed January 2, 2025.

https://www.nobelprize.org/prizes/literature/2017/summary/

Nobuko, Yoshiya. *Forget Me Not Girls' Love: Mei Yumi's 1930s Japanese Literature*. Amazon Digital Services LLC—KDP Print US, 2019.

Oguma, Eiji. *A Genealogy of "Japanese" Self-Images*. English ed. Japanese Society Series. Translated by David Askew. Trans Pacific Press; Distributor, International Specialized Book Services, 2002.

"Record 3.4 Million Foreign Residents in Japan as Work Visas Rise." Kyodo News+. Accessed January 2, 2025. https://english.kyodonews.net/news/2024/03/d72c322 6dfb0-record-34-million-foreign-residents-in-japan-as-work-visas-rise.html

Reed, Christopher. *Bachelor Japanists: Japanese Aesthetics and Western Masculinities*. Modernist Latitudes. Columbia University Press, 2017. https://doi.org/10.7312 /columbia/9780231175753.001.0001

Reichert, Jim. *In the Company of Men: Representations of Male-Male Sexuality in Meiji Literature*. Stanford University Press, 2006. http://catdir.loc.gov/catdir/toc/ecip05 17/2005023284.html

Sakai, Naoki. *Translation and Subjectivity: On "Japan" and Cultural Nationalism*. Public Worlds. University of Minnesota Press, 1997. http://site.ebrary.com/id/1015 9599

Schalow, Paul Gordon. *A Poetics of Courtly Male Friendship in Heian Japan*. Book Collections on Project MUSE. University of Hawai'i Press, 2007. https://search .ebscohost.com/login.aspx?direct=true&scope=site&db=nlebk&db=nlabk&AN= 236672

Seidensticker, Edward. "The 'Pure' and the 'in-Between' in Modern Japanese Theories of the Novel." *Harvard Journal of Asiatic Studies* 26 (1966): 174–86. https://doi.org /10.2307/2718464

Sherif, Ann. "The Politics of Loss: On Eto Jun." *positions: east asia cultures critique* 10, no. 1 (2002): 111–39.

Shirane, Haruo. *Traditional Japanese Literature: An Anthology, Beginnings to 1600*. Abridged ed. Translations from the Asian Classics. Columbia University Press, 2012.

Shirane, Haruo, Tomi Suzuki, and David Barnett Lurie, eds. *The Cambridge History of Japanese Literature*. Hardback. Cambridge University Press, 2016.

Strecher, Matthew C. "Purely Mass or Massively Pure? The Division Between 'Pure' and 'Mass' Literature." *Monumenta Nipponica* 51, no. 3 (1996): 357–74. https://doi .org/10.2307/2385614

Suzuki, Michiko. *Becoming Modern Women: Love and Female Identity in Prewar Japanese Literature and Culture*. Stanford University Press, 2010. http://site.ebrary.com /id/10364957

Suzuki, Sadami. "Three Themes and a Few Points of View—for Rewriting of Japanese Modern and Contemporary Cultural and Literary History." *Japan Review*, no. 5 (1994): 125–44.

Szanton, David L. "The Politics of Knowledge: Area Studies and the Disciplines," 2002. https://escholarship.org/uc/item/59n2d2n1

Tansman, Alan. "Japanese Studies: The Intangible Act of Translation." In *Politics of Knowledge*, edited by David L. Szanton, 184–216. University of California Press, 2009. https://doi.org/10.1525/9780520932111-006

Tansman, Alan. *Japanese Literature: A Very Short Introduction*. Very Short Introductions. Oxford University Press, 2023.

Treat, John Whittier. "AIDS Panic in Japan, or How to Have a Sabbatical in an Epidemic." *positions: asia critique* 2, no. 3 (August 1, 1994): 629–79. https://doi.org/10.1215/10679847-2-3-629

Treat, John Whittier. "Japan Is Interesting: Modern Japanese Literary Studies Today." *Japan Forum* 30, no. 3: 421–40. Accessed January 2, 2025. https://www.tandfonline.com/doi/full/10.1080/09555803.2018.1441171

Treat, John Whittier, ed. *Contemporary Japan and Popular Culture*. ConsumAsiaN Book Series. University of Hawai'i Press, 1996. http://www.gbv.de/dms/bowker/toc/9780824818548.pdf

Treat, John Whittier. *The Rise and Fall of Modern Japanese Literature*. University of Chicago Press, 2018.

Vincent, J. Keith. *Two-Timing Modernity: Homosocial Narrative in Modern Japanese Fiction*. Harvard East Asian Monographs. Harvard University Asia Center: Distributed by Harvard University Press, 2012.

Whitman, John. "5. Kokugogaku versus Gengogaku: Language Process Theory and Tokieda's Construction of Saussure Sixty Years Later." In *The Linguistic Turn in Contemporary Japanese Literary Studies: Politics, Language, Textuality*, edited by Michael K. Bourdaghs, 117–32. University of Michigan Press, 2020. https://muse.jhu.edu/pub/166/edited_volume/chapter/2701375

Woolf, Virginia, and Andrew McNeillie. *The Essays of Virginia Woolf. Vol. 4, 1925–1928*. Hogarth Press, 1994.

Yi, Christina. *Colonizing Language: Cultural Production and Language Politics in Modern Japan and Korea*. Columbia University Press, 2017. https://doi.org/10.7312/yi--18420

Yi, Christina, Andre Haag, and Catherine Ryu, eds. *Passing, Posing, Persuasion: Cultural Production and Coloniality in Japan's East Asian Empire*. University of Hawai'i Press, 2023.

Yoda, Tomiko, Harry Harootunian, Rey Chow, and Masao Miyoshi, eds. *Japan After Japan: Social and Cultural Life from the Recessionary 1990s to the Present*. Duke University Press, 2006. https://doi.org/10.1515/9780822388609

Yoshimoto, Mitsuhiro. "A Future of Comparative Film Studies," Inter-Asia Cultural Studies 14, no 1. Accessed January 2, 2025. https://www.tandfonline.com/doi/abs/10.1080/14649373.2013.745972

Yoshimoto, Mitsuhiro. "Questions of Japanese Cinema: Disciplinary Boundaries and the Invention of the Scholarly Object." In *Learning Places: The Afterlives of Area Studies*, edited by Masao Miyoshi, Harry Harootunian, and Rey Chow, 368–402. Duke University Press, 2002. https://doi.org/10.1515/9780822383598-017

Yoshimoto, Mitsuhiro. "The University, Disciplines, National Identity: Why Is There No Film Studies in Japan?" In *Japan After Japan: Social and Cultural Life from the Recessionary 1990s to the Present*, edited by Tomiko Yoda, Harry Harootunian, Rey Chow, and Masao Miyoshi, 81–97. Duke University Press, 2006. https://doi.org/10.1515/9780822388609-004

Yū, Miri. *Tokyo Ueno Station*. Translated by Morgan Giles. First American edition. Riverhead Books, 2020.

Žižek, Slavoj. *The Parallax View*. Short Circuits. MIT Press, 2006. http://site.ebrary

.com/id/10173638

グレゴリー・ケズナジャット., and Gregory Khezrnejat. 鴨川ランナー. Tōkyō: 講談社, 2021.

九段理江. 東京都同情塔 / *Tokyo-to dojo-to* / *Qudan Rie* = トーキョートドージョートー / クダンリエ. Tōkyō [Japan]: 新潮社, 2024.

田村美由紀. 口述筆記する文学: 書くことの代行とジェンダー. Shohan. Nagoya: Nagoya Daigaku Shuppankai, 2023. Tamura, Miyuki. *Kōjutsu Hikki Suru Bungaku: Kaku Koto no Daikō to Jendā*. Nagoya: Nagoya Daigaku Shuppankai, 2023.

疋田 雅昭. "書評 岩川ありさ著『物語とトラウマ: クィア-フェミニズム批評の可能性』." 日本近代文学 = *Modern Japanese Literary Studies* / 日本近代文学会編集委員会 編. 108 (May 2023): 179. Hikida, Masaaki. "Shohyō Iwakawa Arisa Cho *Monogatari to Trauma: Kuia-Feminizumu Hihyō no Kanōsei.*" *Nihon Kindai Bungaku = Modern Japanese Literary Studies / Nihon Kindai Bungakukai Henshū Iinkai Hen*. 108 (May 2023): 179.

藤木 直実. "書評 岩川ありさ著『物語とトラウマ: クィア-フェミニズム批評の可能性』." 昭和文学研究 = *Showa Literary Studies* / 昭和文学会編集委員会 編 87 (September 2023): 261. Fujiki, Naomi. "Shohyō Iwakawa Arisa Cho *Monogatari to Trauma: Kuia-Feminizumu Hihyō no Kanōsei.*" *Shōwa Bungaku Kenkyū = Showa Literary Studies / Shōwa Bungakukai Henshū Iinkai Hen*. 87 (September 2023): 261.

藤木 直実. "書評 岩川ありさ著『物語とトラウマ: クィア-フェミニズム批評の可能性』." 昭和文学研究 = *Showa Literary Studies* / 昭和文学会編集委員会 編 87 (September 2023): 261. Fujiki, Naomi. "Shohyō Iwakawa Arisa Cho *Monogatari to Trauma: Kuia-Feminizumu Hihyō no Kanōsei.*" *Shōwa Bungaku Kenkyū = Showa Literary Studies / Shōwa Bungakukai Henshū Iinkai Hen*. 87 (September 2023): 261.

金井 景子. "書評 武内佳代著『クィアする現代日本文学: ケア-動物-語り』." 昭和文学研究 = *Showa Literary Studies* / 昭和文学会編集委員会 編 87 (September 2023): 270. Kanai, Keiko. "Shohyō Takeuchi Kayo Cho *Kuia Suru Gendai Nihon Bungaku: Kea-Dōbutsu-Katari.*" *Shōwa Bungaku Kenkyū = Showa Literary Studies / Shōwa Bungakukai Henshū Iinkai Hen*. 87 (September 2023): 270.

PART I

Negotiating Disciplinary Formation

CHAPTER 1

Between the Margins and the Mainstream

Modern Japanese Women Writers and Evolving Trends in North American Japanese Literature Scholarship

Rebecca Copeland

"Why must you women insist on studying each other so?" the middle-aged scholar sniffed contemptuously as I explained my writing project. He was then the editor of one of the few journals that published articles on Japanese literature. Still untenured, I was hoping for a sympathetic reaction to my proposed essay on the emergence of late 19th-century women writers. No one had yet tackled the topic in English. "I don't see why my studying women writers is any different from men studying men writers," I responded defensively. He softened somewhat, reaching over to tap my hand, "But you see, my dear, you study women as women; we study men as authors."

Of course, in an academy—and society—where a woman is constantly defined by her gender, how else should we study them? I was prepared to fire back, but I was too busy retrieving my hand from his touch. It didn't matter anyway. He would never "get it." He wasn't alone, of course. While a graduate student in Tokyo in the early 1980s I often had similar encounters. Scholars in conservative literature departments were nonplussed by my decision to focus on the notable if somewhat scandalous writer Uno Chiyo (1897–1996). With her highly publicized divorces and her penchant for confessional writing, she was more appropriate for sensational journalism than serious study, they argued. Many even tried to equate Uno's perceived licentiousness with my own personal values. It seemed I was frequently required to retrieve my hand from disapproving but lecherous men.

Fortunately, my graduate school mentors were more open-minded and encouraged their PhD students, most of whom were women, to pursue diverse subjects.[1] The late 1980s, in fact, saw a sharp rise in the number of dissertations at North American universities on the topic of modern Japanese women writers. When I completed my dissertation on Uno Chiyo in 1986, mine may have been the first at Columbia University to focus on a modern (in fact a living) woman writer, but I was not alone in my interests. My classmate Joan Ericson, for example, was beginning to work on Hayashi Fumiko (1903–1951), and Eileen Mikals-Adachi had already begun a project on Enchi Fumiko (1905–1986), which she would complete at a Japanese institution. Beyond Columbia there were others as well. Alan Tansman and Ann Sherif, each at different institutions, completed dissertations on Kōda Aya (1904–1990) in 1989 and 1991, respectively. In 1985 Phyllis Larson contributed a dissertation on the modern poet Yosano Akiko (1878–1942), and Jan Bardsley's 1989 dissertation focused on Hiratsuka Raichō (1886–1971) and the New Woman journal, *Seitō*. All this work, appearing at roughly the same time, led in turn to the simultaneous publication in the 1990s of books and articles on modern Japanese women writers. And so a new area of investigation opened in the larger field of Japanese literature.

What was it about the 1980s that encouraged this shift in subject matter? In this chapter, I survey the development of studies in North America on modern Japanese women's literature and the subsequent publications, translations, conferences, and classes in the late 20th century. Moving to the 21st century, I explore the influence these have had on today's academy. Although the evidence will show we have made significant strides since the nonplussed scholar challenged my choice of literary subjects, there remains much to do.

Japanese Literature Enters Academe

In order to get a sense of the way academic trends in Japanese literature developed over time, I analyzed the subjects of Japanese literature dissertations across the span of the twentieth century by using the online database Proquest.[2] I conducted my research with the following assumptions: Dissertations on Japanese literature were likely focused on the premodern "classics" of poetry, prose, and drama until the postwar, when studies of modern mainstream men novelists became popular. Whereas premodern women were often the subject of study (Murasaki Shikibu, Sei Shōnagon, etc.), modern women writers were not—and inquiries into premodern women were not framed by questions of gender. My hunch was that once Japanese Studies programs in the North American academy opened wide enough to allow consideration of modern women writers (encouraged by the pioneering efforts of progressive scholars in the 1970s), it was not long before the gates opened wider still to accommodate studies of other non-canonical categories, such as ethnic minorities in Japan (see, for example, Davinder Bhowmik's chapter in this volume on Okinawan literature), genre fiction (mystery fiction, science fiction, etc.) and greater interdisciplinarity overall. In other words, once Women's Studies programs began to advocate for greater inclusiveness, newer modes of seeing, and challenges to the politics of power, the doors opened to the kinds of Cultural Studies projects that John Treat describes in his chapter in this volume.

If Proquest is to be trusted, the earliest dissertations on "Japan" as a subject or area of study began in the late 1880s with topics that ran from industrialization, the silk trade, the constitution, and religion (mostly Buddhism and Christianity). Focus on modern Japanese literature did not begin until 1932 when a student at the University of Southern California, published a master's thesis on Kikuchi Kan (1888–1948), Kume Masao (1891–1952), Ogawa Mimei (1882–1961), and members of the Shirakabaha (or White Birch Society), with accompanying translations. All men, of course, and all entrenched in defining the parameters of a (masculinist) modern Japanese literature. This thesis was followed by studies of Natsume Sōseki (1867–1916) and later Arishima Takeo (1878–1923). Whereas the focus on Japanese literature prior to WWII seemed to have little pattern, scholars hewed closely to canonical men writers of more or less bourgeois taste. A notable exception was a curious fascination with the naturalized Japanese, Lafcadio Hearn (1850–1904), who by 1940 had been the subject of seven dissertations and/or theses.

The postwar saw new activity in Japanese literature, with scholars like Ivan Morris, Donald Keene, Donald Shively, P. G. O'Neill, Robert Brower, Howard Hibbett, Helen McCullough, and Edward McClellan (all who would become luminaries in the field) completing their dissertations in the 1950s. All but McClellan, who wrote on Natsume Sōseki, treated a premodern subject. The generation that was to follow in the 1960s continued the tilt toward the premodern. Makoto Ueda, Douglas Mills, Francis Motofuji, and Edwin Cranston wrote on premodern topics. But James O'Brien, devoted his 1969 dissertation to modern novelist Dazai Osamu (1909–1948), thus initiating a trend that would continue into the 1970s with studies of: Kunikida Doppo, Shiga Naoya, Akutagawa Ryūnosuke, Tanizaki Jun'ichirō, and Kawabata Yasunari, along with Mishima Yukio and Abe Kōbō. The list was all men all the time until Brett de Bary included Miyamoto Yuriko among her *Five Writers and the End of the War: Themes in Early Postwar Japanese Fiction* (Harvard University, 1978).

Things changed in 1980 when Robert Danly chose to focus his dissertation exclusively on Higuchi Ichiyō. Danly takes pains, however, to present her "as an author" and to minimize her gendered voice. Ichiyō is described, much as her pen name implies, as a singular phenomenon, nurtured by supportive men with little regard for the fact that she was writing within an active enclave of other women writers. Ichiyō *was* an extraordinarily talented writer, but this claim of singularity renders her "anomalous" and simultaneously erases other women writers, too. In turn, Ichiyō's apparent uniqueness (an attitude espoused in Japan) shaped anthologies, absolving the need for any other woman writer.

Perhaps the "first" dissertation on a modern Japanese woman writer was Victoria Vernon Nakagawa's *Three Japanese Women Writers: Higuchi Ichiyō, Sata Ineko, and Kurahashi Yumiko* (University of California, Berkeley, 1981). In her study, Nakagawa intentionally places these three writers in a feminist position vis-à-vis the masculine canon, cogently drawing on the pioneering work of Western feminist critics, such as Sandra M. Gilbert, Susan Gubar, and Rosalind Miles. More dissertations on women followed almost yearly. Bertha Lynn Burson's study of Kurahashi Yumiko (University of Texas-Austin, 1983), Phyllis Larson's work on Yosano Akiko (University of Minnesota, 1985), Janice Brown's exploration of Hayashi Fumiko that same year (University of British Columbia). And then my 1986 dissertation on Uno Chiyo was followed by studies of Enchi Fumiko, Oku Mumeo, Okamoto Kanoko, Hiratsuka Raichō, and Kōda Aya. Apart from Nakagawa's dissertation, the treatment of these women writers initially focused on "the life and the works," but gradually tilted toward "awakenings," "resistance," and patently feminist notions. (Jeffrey Angles, in his chapter on translation, also notes this shift away from single author studies and toward an "increasingly comparative perspective . . . of multiple authors, texts, and historical moments.") In other words, scholars began interpreting these writers' works against gender norms and patriarchal institutions, including the sexism of the literary world that defined public perception of their work and themselves as women writers. From 1988, with Maryellen Toman Mori's dissertation on Okamoto Kanoko, for example, we see the descriptor "women's studies" appearing on Proquest (in relation to Japanese literature).

In the Context of Women's Studies

In his chapter John Treat describes those of us in Japanese literature as being "[a]lways late to the party, we have a sadomasochistic relationship with any new trend in literary studies"). This is not wholly true when it comes to the incorporation of Women's Studies. During the 1970s, Women's Studies began to take root in North American academies with, as Jean Robinson has stated, "politics as its mid-wife."[3] Taking women's lives and work as worthy of academic exploration was in itself a political act.[4] By the late 1970s, Ellen Moers's analyses inspired awareness of the nineteenth-century tradition of women writers while Elaine Showalter pioneered the notion of "gynocriticism," soon to be followed by Gilbert and Gubar's landmark The *Madwoman in the Attic* (1979). These works posited the legitimacy of studying women's texts and advocated for the creation of a women's canon. More importantly, they encouraged scholars to mine works by women (indeed all works) for innovative channels of expression that subverted the status quo, which is precisely what we see in Victoria Vernon Nakagawa's above-mentioned 1981 study of Ichiyō, Sata, and Kurahashi.

Whereas there was a higher proportion of women attending PhD programs in the United States than in Japan, feminists in Japan were no less active. The 1970s in Japan was a decade known for visible feminist activism on several fronts, including Japanese participation in the 1975 UN-sponsored International Woman's Year. Women's studies centers and programs developed in Japan in the 1980s. Feminist literary critics such as Mizuta Noriko and Komashaku Kimi began actively publishing works at this time that spoke directly to the situation of women writers in Japan while simultaneously treating canonical men-authored works to feminist interpretations. Komashaku's *Majō no ronri* (Witch's Theory, 1978), a collection of essays she wrote between 1971 and 1977, and Mizuta's *Hiroin kara hiirō e* (From heroine to hero, 1982), essays written between 1970 and 1981, established the basic framework for feminist criticism in a Japanese literary world. Kitada Sachie has called these works "the origin of Japanese feminist criticism."[5]

As previously noted, most studies of modern Japanese women's writing in English that emerged in the decade of the 1980s cohered to the standard "life and works" type of investigation. Whereas perhaps not theoretically riveting, these dissertations served the purpose of making women authors worthy of consideration and proved the significance of social and cultural contexts to the understanding of their work. They were placed front and center as an object of study, thus resisting the typical subject approach in Japan and elsewhere that either ignored completely or shunted modern women writers to the corners of the canon. One finds this marginalization driving the large, omnibus anthologies of "modern Japanese literature" that relegated women authors to a few slim, collective volumes. For example, the 97-volume *Gendai Nihon bungaku taikei* (Outline of Contemporary Japanese Literature), published by Chikuma Shobō in the 1970s, includes only 12 or so volumes featuring a woman writer—and none of the volumes is devoted exclusively to one woman, as is the case for many men considered mainstream. In this respect, these mid-1980s dissertations in North America did much to insist on adding modern women writers to the Japanese literary canon—at least in English language studies.[6] Grounding the woman writer's work within the parameters of her social contexts established the inescapable effects of gender politics on her life—she was always and already a woman—and this fact would influence reception of her work, her choice of topics, her audience, and her public persona. Attending to this gendered grounding connected women writers to women active in other spheres and across regional boundaries. This approach also shed light on the alleged transcendence of gender afforded to literary men.

Translation as Canon Forming

Regardless how many dissertations "introduced" modern women writers to the North American academy, these writers could hardly leave the confines of the UMI microfilms without accompanying translations. Only translation would make their work available for cross-cultural comparison and classroom teaching. (See Angles's chapter for the importance of translation to the academic enterprise.) The 1980s, therefore, also saw a sharp rise in translations of works by modern women writers. Scholars, such as Angela Coutts and Sharalyn Orbaugh, have already provided nuanced analyses of the rate and placement of these translations—pointing to the fact that even while women's works were being translated in greater numbers, they were still being marginalized when anthologized alongside the "more important" men writers.[7] What is also notable is that when these translations were published in collections focused exclusively on women, those collections tended to be with either university presses or small publishing houses and thus easily went out of print. (*This Kind of Woman*, Stanford University Press, 1982; *Rabbits, Crabs, Etc.*, University of Hawai'i Press, 1982; *Stories by Contemporary Japanese Women Writers*, Routledge, 1982; *Unmapped Territories*, Women in Translation, 1991; *To Live and to Write*, Seal Press, 1993, are representative anthologies that were timely and significant but now largely unavailable.) Whereas in the more canonical anthologies with larger trade presses, such as Grove, Random House, Kodansha (which are still accessible), works by women receive only token attention. (See Angles's chapter for further discussion of the precarity of translation sales.)

Women's Studies as Cottage Industry

Academic journals and conferences, largely with international profiles, have done much to legitimize Japanese Women's Studies in the United States. Journals, such as the *US-Japan Women's Journal* established in 1988 has as its goal the promotion of scholarly exchange on social, cultural, political, and economic issues pertaining to gender and Japan. Initiated largely under the direction of above-mentioned feminist pioneer, Mizuta Noriko, the editorship was managed by historian, Sally Hastings, and later by Alisa Freedman, both of whom made the journal a lively, interdisciplinary space that allowed for the creation of important networks of scholars of Japanese women studies. Even so, the journal has mostly gone unrecognized in American academe—at least judging from the paucity of libraries that subscribe to it.

Women Studies conferences on Japanese literature began to take the stage a few years after the founding of the *US-Japan Women's Journal*, with the first one at Rutgers University in 1993. This conference was followed by an anthology of essays, *The Woman's Hand* (published by Stanford University Press), which made enormous strides in grounding the study of Japanese women's writing in North American academies, while simultaneously laying the groundwork for the creation of a woman's literature canon. While the conference and the volume offered the imprimatur of academic acceptability on the one hand, it also conferred on the conference attendees and others working on women's writing the more emotional sense of "legitimacy." It is essential to recognize how these conferences, panels, and book collaborations helped nurture those "dancing through the minefield" of American academe.[8]

Research on women's literature steadily gained ground. In 2001, "Across Time and Genre: Reading and Writing Women's Texts," a conference held at the University of Alberta, proved so popular and inclusive, the organizers, Sonja Arntzen and Janice Brown, were forced to run simultaneous panels and include two keynote speakers.[9] Slightly over ten years later, the 2013 Emory University conference, "Revisiting Japanese Feminisms," gave ample evidence of the richness of scholarship now available on Japanese women's writing and activism. The conference included second- and even third-generation scholars of Japanese women's writing who convened over a "reconsideration" of Japanese feminism. The resulting publication, edited by Julia C. Bullock, Ayako Kano, and James Welker, explored the dynamic intersection of gender, political action, and ethnicity in Japan. More recently scholars from both North America and Japan collaborated in 2019 on "The Woman in the Story: Female Protagonism in Japanese Narratives," a conference co-sponsored by UCLA and Waseda University through the Yanai Initiative, that explored the way "women" as a trans-historical category have been represented over time in Japan.[10]

By the second decade of the twenty-first century, we have seen an increase in monographs and translations meant to assist English-language readers in understanding the richness and depth of modern women's literature in Japan. In many, the goal has been to move us beyond comfortable assumptions about what Japanese literature is or who Japanese women are. Overturning stereotypes of Japanese fiction, and particularly, women's writing, as bland and passive has in some cases grown so pronounced that we may have produced an equally distorted view of Japanese writing as always deviant, dangerous, and twisted—or as Treat has described it "Japanese quirky" (Treat).[11]

And yet, through our innovation we have created, in a way, new mainstreams, new canons of authenticity and value, and new uses for Japanese literature. To some degree, this elasticity, as positive as it is in many respects, threatens to marginalize or at least distort, women's positionality even further. Those of us with interests in women's writing, therefore, feel required to remain vigilant, insisting on the relevance of our interests, and frustrated by the complacency that suggests our work is over, or worse, that it is regressive.

In Defense of Classes on Women Writers

Of late, different approaches to combating the marginalization of Japanese women's writing have emerged. One approach argues that courses focused exclusively on Japanese women writers are passé and threaten to do more harm than good. Bhowmik notes of approaches to Okinawan writing, "[o]ne effect of this concentration of Okinawa in edited volumes and certain journals is the exoticization of Okinawa" (Bhowmik). Similarly, courses devoted to women—as a category—serve to keep women separate, marginal, and "other." Rather than treating women this way, some prefer to work thematically, to get beyond the narrow constructions of canon and consider literary activity more conceptually. This approach allows us to offer courses on disaster, futurism, modernism, and so forth that fold both men and women writers into the discussion equally. Theoretically, at least. Unfortunately, as actual women, we do not have the luxury to experience gender theoretically. Even a skim of newspapers in Japan and the US shows how conservative forces are attempting to constrain women as a gender and a reproductive class ever more firmly in resistance against the gains of #MeToo and LBGTQ groups. Surely, this deployment of "woman" connects with past dynamics and attempts to write against it and out of it.

Broad intellectual categories and innovative frameworks offer attractive approaches to classes. But does that mean the "Woman Writer" class has no value or has been surpassed? The fact remains that women writers in most cultures are still perceived as "secondary." They may be "important," but when an instructor is faced with a limited schedule and the need to expose students to the broadest possible survey of historical movements, influential ideas, and high points, these "secondary" writers are often given short shrift—if they are given any shrift at all. Let's not forget that as recently as 2013 a Canadian professor proudly noted that he only taught the "best writers"—and never women "or Chinese."[12] When women writers are shoehorned into a schedule or sidelined, students are not allowed to appreciate them on their own merits or in light of their history. Either they are there to represent the "margins," in a practice that narrows the import and artistry of their works, or they are read "gender blind." The latter practice creates the artificial sense that the woman writer entered a level playing field, writing of universal (read masculine) concerns, and enjoyed collectively masculine experiences.[13]

Thinking back to the condescending editor who told me that he studied men as writers, I cannot miss the arrogance of his posture. According to him, I, a woman, did not belong and women writers did not belong, and of course, gender politics—which would have unseated his arrogant stance—was not relevant to literary study. I do not want to see us move into another space—concerned, for example, about the environment—in ways that dismiss the weight and history of gender. Indeed, looking at the future fully aware of gender dynamics illuminates the conservative bent in the way we have heretofore approached the environment, nuclear politics, and other issues of recent consideration.

A quick and informal survey of the field of Japanese literature—conducted through an email listserv for Japanese literature scholars—yielded information on who teaches courses on Japanese Women Writers. Most who responded were from either small liberal arts colleges or large state schools. And most considered the opportunity to teach "women writers" a luxury.

Many noted that they would like to teach such a class but were taxed with teaching required classes such as language, large survey courses, or "canonical" literature. They did not have the wherewithal to offer a specialty course. Those who were able to do so, however, acknowledged good enrollments and thoughtful participation. As Kimberly Kono, Professor of Japanese Language and Literature at Smith College wrote of her class:

> Teaching a class on Japanese Women Writers gives students the opportunity to problematize the category of *joryū bungaku* [women's literature]. I have several different days in my modern Japanese literature survey course, where we discuss *joryū bungaku* but I really feel like an entire semester of experiencing the diversity of women's writing is much more powerful for students. Reading Japanese women's writing from Meiji (1868–1912) to the present, students get to think about how this gendered category shaped not only how women wrote and how their work was received at different points in the modern period, but also which texts are translated and then included (or not) in anthologies.[14]

Early 21st-century gender politics are taking us in new directions as activism focuses on dissolving the gender binary. But I do not believe these advances supersede the need to be mindful of the way gender has been historically encoded, enforced, and often resisted in literature. In fact, tackling the politics of "women as women" historically in Japan illuminates the power of women's literary voices and simultaneously gives us a path for bringing in different identities. Additionally, women-focused classes allow the development of new interpretive strategies that take account of the past while opening the way for plurality in the future.

Side Benefits to Women Writers Courses

Women's Studies classes have evolved from the 1980s, just as Women's Studies programs have given way to Gender or Gender and Sexuality studies in most institutions. A course on the reading of women writers is not "just" premised on the fact that the writers are women. In other words, it is not just a corrective (although that is still important) but it also provides the opportunity to challenge students to think more broadly about gender, intersectional politics, and power. In such a course, students are allowed to appreciate the impact categorization has had on these writers over time and the fact that women writers in particular have had to navigate a different set of criteria in finding their passage to print. Their writing is almost always informed in some way by this experience. Because their works are frequently resistance pieces, understanding the contexts and assumptions under which they wrote allows students to better appreciate what they wrote as well as the courage and innovativeness these writers displayed in gaining access to print. Reading these works as a collective also permits students to see the rich versatility in the way these writers take on the challenge. There is no singular "woman's voice." And yet when studied collectively students find that their works, as divergent as they may be, speak to one another across time. Women writers often draw on the same themes and strategies earlier women used, augmenting, adapting, and intensifying the message as they go along.

Women writers, almost regardless of time and place, were troubled by strong patriarchal social systems that denigrated their efforts to write.[15] They were undermined as imitative, derided by critics as monkeys and plagiarist. Hampered by a language that only re-enforced a masculinist social order, women writers developed creative strategies to parody, subvert, and sidestep linguistic traps. Many resorted to re-writing myth and in doing so indulged their "mimic" nature (Ōba Minako, Tsushima Yūko, Kirino Natsuo, etc.). Another strategy of resistance becomes the use of taboo to disconcert and unsettle the reader in such a way as to get past social expectation (Kurahashi Yumiko, Kōno Taeko, Yamada Eimi, Kanehara Hitomi, etc.). Thus, we have celebrations of incest, the murder of children, cannibalism, bestiality, sadomasochism, and more. Moreover, there is a decided self-consciousness to the narrative that underscores the awareness of performance and foregrounds the subversion of gendered norms. Reading texts by women collectively accentuates these tropes and strategies in ways that are lost when a short selection of works by women are blended into a class with a larger framework. If anything, that short stint in the spotlight makes the lone writer's resistance seem all the more violent and "quirky."

The question then arises, what are we teaching when we teach women's texts? Certainly, we focus on the historical contexts that produced the author. Most students have had little access to women's history (in either their target or source culture) prior to taking a women-focused class, as these details are usually left out of larger historical surveys or civilization classes. Students gain a stronger understanding of those movements and moments related to women's lives. These understandings augment but also nuance the knowledge received in those other classes. More than factual information, students are also asked to hone their analytical skills and their ability to discuss the generic attributes of the texts under consideration. These classes draw attention to narrative voice and strategy, performance and authenticity, narrative time, linearity, and more. Finally, in a class that focuses on the construction of gender and the performance of identity, students naturally reflect on their own experiences. Many are surprised to learn that women's concerns along with their intrinsic power do not differ significantly across time and culture. This discovery makes them more attuned to questions of gender in their own current sphere of reference. In turn, the success of these women-focused classes argues that we need to step away from teaching the famed modern literary men as the universal norm and rather study them *as men*, asking similar questions that show how norms of masculinity and men's lives provide the backdrop against which they wrote. Scholarship in men's studies in recent years makes this possible.

Conclusion

Barely forty years have elapsed since modern Japanese women writers became a subject of study in the North American academy. Enormous strides have been made to integrate modern women's writing into the regular study of Japanese literature and culture. And yet, the results reveal more strides are still needed before the study of women achieves anything close to parity with men.

At the 2019 conference held at UCLA, "The Woman in the Story: Female Protagonism in Japanese Narratives," co-organizer Christina Laffin spoke to the ongoing need for women-focused classes, conferences, and contents to combat the institutionalized bias toward men (works by men and scholarship by men). Given the steady increase of women entering graduate programs, we may want to conclude that gender inequities are fading.[16] Perhaps they are, but the propensity to favor men and men-centered scholarship is still strong. Dr. Laffin underscored this point by presenting statistics on the percentage of representation women authors have received in recent literary histories. For example, *The Cambridge History of Japanese Literature*, edited by Haruo Shirane, David Lurie, and Tomi Suzuki and published in 2016 weighs in at 865 pages, of which only a little over 100 cover topics related to women writers. In Haruo Shirane-edited *Traditional Japanese Literature: An Anthology, Beginnings to 1600* (2007), out of 1288 pages, approximately 217 are devoted to women; and the Japanese section of the 2003 The *Columbia Companion to Modern East Asian Literature*, edited by Sharalyn Orbaugh, has about a quarter of its contents that is "woman specific."[17]

Not only are women writers given significantly less attention in Japanese literary histories in North America,[18] the number of courses with a decidedly "woman focus" lags far behind those with a "generalized" or "universal" interest. And, in most classrooms, the "universal" defaults to masculine, androcentric concerns. According to the *Directory of Japanese Studies* sponsored by the Japan Foundation and based on information collected from the Survey of Japan Specialists and Japanese Studies Institutions in North America in 2011–2012 (partially updated in 2015–16) there were 410 courses on Japanese literature at institutions of higher education across the US. Out of these, 12 were devoted to women writers; 3 focused on gender in literature; and 2 concerned the "feminine" in Japanese traditions.[19] Surely, more sustained focus on the works and contexts of women writers at the college level will produce more dissertations, in turn, producing publications that fully account for women's contributions as writers, editors, and readers.

Given institutional practices that still mitigate against adequate representation of women's creative endeavors, experiences, and contexts, it is important to continue working to help students appreciate the challenges women face and the strategies they have designed to combat the biases against them. Courses devoted to women writers have helped and will continue to help open the door to other "non-mainstream" courses and will serve to enrich the educational experiences of students who, thanks to the #MeToo and other movements, have become more attuned to appreciate the importance of gender and gender difference. Today, when we look at the kinds of dissertations scholars of Japanese literature are producing, we find that whereas few are devoted exclusively to a single woman writer, more and more focus on subsets of women's writing, such as women and science fiction or women and the colonial experience. Even topic-driven dissertations that deal primarily with men writers generally include a comparative look at a woman. Dissertations on proletarian writers or on Japanese modernism, for example, devote space to writings by women. The ground is shifting. Even so, with recent governmental challenges to DEI, even these modest gains to equity hang in the balance.

Thurgood Marshall was once asked why he still belonged to the black lawyers' association "at this late date," he replied "It's not that late yet." So, too, is it with women.[20]

Notes

1. Not all mentors (most of whom were men) were as encouraging. In a recent anthology of memoristic essays by women scholars who earned PhD degrees in Japanese studies between 1950 and 1980, many describe being deterred from working on

women subjects. Anne Walthall, for example, describes how angry her mentor, Tetsuo Najita, became when she asked to write on Hōjō Masako (1157–1225), the wife and spokesperson for the first shogun. Professor Najita denounced the interest in women as "a fad." See Anne Walthall, "I Owe My Career to Men," in Alisa Freedman, ed. *Women in Japanese Studies: Memoirs from a Trailblazing Generation*. Columbia University Press, 2023.

2. Unfortunately, the data that Proquest offers is only as reliable as what has been provided by degree-granting institutions over time. We cannot discover on Proquest what hasn't already been uploaded into the system. That doesn't mean it doesn't exist. So, whereas my overview was "exhausting" it is not "exhaustive," and many of the "discoveries" I made were made because I already knew to look for them.

3. As cited by Scott Jaschik in "The Evolution of American Women's Studies," *Inside Higher Ed.* 27 Mar 2009. Web. 16 July 2019.

4. Japan might be seen as something of an exception, since many of the celebrated premodern writers were women. But as noted above, in early studies of these women, scholars were intent on minimizing the role of gender in their works.

5. Kitada Sachie and Miya E. M. Lippit, "Contemporary Japanese Feminist Literary Criticism," *U.S.-Japan Women's Journal.* English Supplement, no. 7 (1994): 72–97.

6. Note that it was still a small portion of the canon. Others have written on the "token" approach to including women writers in encyclopedias of modern Japanese literature. Many point to Donald Keene's massive 1329-page study of modern Japanese fiction that sets aside 54 pages to discuss "The Revival of Writing by Woman." See Donald Keene, *Dawn to the West: Japanese Literature in the Modern Era* (History of Japanese Literature Vol. 3) (Holt, Rinehart and Winston, 1984).

7. See Angela Coutts, "The Gendering of Japanese Literature: The Influence of English-Language Translation on Concepts of Canon in the West," *Japan Forum* 14, no. 1 (2002): 103–25; and Sharalyn Orbaugh, "The Construction of Gendered Discourse in the Modern Study of Japanese Literature." *Across Time and Genre: Reading and Writing Japanese Women's Texts Conference Proceedings University of Alberta*, ed. Janice Brown and Sonja Arntzen, 1–9 (Department of East Asian Studies, University of Alberta, 2002).

8. In reference to Annette Kolodny's inspirational essay "Dancing through the Minefield: Some Observations on the Theory, Practice and Politics of a Feminist Literary Criticism," *Feminist Studies* 6, no. 1 (Spring, 1980): 1–25.

9. The event brought together generations of scholars, from the pioneers of the field to graduate students presenting on new dissertations.

10. Like the Alberta conference, this one too had a rich representation of scholars across generations, which unlike the earlier conference, led to contentious discussions both in the panels and behind the scenes. Whereas senior scholars appeared eager to celebrate milestones and the luxury of sharing scholarship in a safe, receptive space, newer scholars expressed frustration with the lack of greater attention to LGBTQ voices, lack of focus on the intersectionality of discrimination, or the lack of diversity among the invited speakers.

11. Among the deviant we can include the translations of works by Kirino Natsuo (b. 1951) that intentionally work against the image of Japanese women as gentle and submissive; or the 2005 translation of Kanehara Hitomi's shocking 2003 *Hebi ni piasu* (Snakes and Earrings), which inspired a number of analytical essays on Japan's vio-

lent "subcultures." Notably not translated are the works of Kirino's contemporary, the massively popular and prolific Hayashi Mariko (b. 1954). Perhaps her focus on the awkwardly single woman craving sex and going on shopping sprees is too lighthearted, even "ordinary." Conversely, award-winning writer, Kakuta Mitsuyo (b. 1967), though represented by translations, has not yet become the subject of academic scrutiny.

12. David Gilmour's comments were widely publicized and rebuked. See Liz Bury, "Canadian Author David Gilmour Sparks Furore Over Female Writers," *The Guardian*, 27 Sept. 2013. Web. 16 July 2019.

13. Chieko Ariga brilliantly made this point in reference to Japanese women writers and the way *kaisetsu* or commentaries (appended to the end of paperbacks in Japan)—frequently authored by men—erased the specifically gendered topics of their fictional works and tried to relate to them as "universal." See "Text Versus Commentary: Struggles over the Cultural Meanings of 'Woman,'" in *The Woman's Hand: Gender and Theory in Japanese Women's Writing*, eds. Paul Gordon Schalow and Janet A. Walker, 352–81 (Stanford University Press, 1996).

14. As per email exchange, June 3, 2019.

15. See, for example, Rebecca Copeland, ed. *Woman Critiqued: Translated Essays on Japanese Women's Writing* (University of Hawai'i Press, 2006) that provides numerous examples of the way Japanese critiques of women's writing easily adhered to each and every item in Joanna Russ's sarcastic guide *How to Suppress Women's Writing* (University of Texas, 1983).

16. According to Mark J. Perry: "2009 marked the year when men officially became the "second sex" in higher education by earning a minority of college degrees at all college levels from associate's degrees to doctoral degrees." In 2017, 56.2% of all Arts and Humanities PhD degrees were earned by women. See Perry, "What the Underrepresentation of Men in Graduate Programs Means for the Nation," *Spero News*, 4 Oct. 2018. Web. 16 July 2019.

17. Christina Laffin's opening remarks for *The Woman in the Story: Female Protagonism in Japanese Narratives*. UCLA, 13 Mar. 2019. Address.

18. The paucity of representation is certainly no better in Japan. In his paper "Literary Canon Formation in the Digital Age" Hoyt Long examined publisher Chikuma Shobō's 99-volume *Gendai Nihon bungaku zenshū* (Contemporary Japanese Literature Anthology 1968–1973) and found that of the 215 authors represented, only 16 were female (so 7%).

Examining the Nichigai Associates index of *zenshū* (literature anthologies or compendia) of 600,000 total entries covering 1,255 anthologies and 8,500 authors, he found that in omnibus zenshū, women and their works never represented more than 10% of the total content and that this changed little over time. See Long, "Literary Canon Formation in the Digital Age," *Association for Japanese Literary Studies*, University of California - Berkley, 9 Sept. 2018. [Thanks to Christina Laffin for this information.]

19. *Directory of Japanese Studies in the United States and Canada*. "Courses About Japan." 2015–2016. Web. 16 July 2019.

20. Grateful to Dr. Nancy Berg of Washington University in St. Louis for this statement from "Remembering Thurgood Marshall," Narr. Alex Chadwick. NPR. 25 Jan. 1993.

Bibliography

Ariga, Chieko M. "Text Versus Commentary: Struggles over the Cultural Meanings of 'Woman.'" In *The Woman's Hand: Gender and Theory in Japanese Women's Writing*, edited by Paul Gordon Schalow and Janet A. Walker, 352–81. Stanford University Press, 2022.

Brown, Janice, and Sonja Arntzen. *Across Time and Genre: Reading and Writing Women's Texts: Conference Proceedings, University of Alberta*. Department of East Asian Studies, University of Alberta, 2002.

Bury, Liz. "Canadian Author David Gilmour Sparks Furore over Female Writers." *The Guardian*, September 27, 2013, sec. Books. https://www.theguardian.com/books/2013/sep/27/author-david-gilmour-female-writers

Copeland, Rebecca L., ed. *Woman Critiqued: Translated Essays on Japanese Women's Writing*. University of Hawai'i Press, 2006.

Coutts, Angela. "The Gendering of Japanese Literature: The Influence of English-Language Translation on Concepts of Canon in the West." *Japan Forum* 14, no. 1 (January 1, 2002): 103–25. https://doi.org/10.1080/09555800120109050

"Directory of Japanese Studies > 2015–2016 Update." Accessed February 6, 2025. http://japandirectory.socialsciences.hawaii.edu/Update2015_2016.aspx

Freedman, Alisa, ed. *Women in Japanese Studies: Memoirs from a Trailblazing Generation*. Association for Asian Studies, 2023.

Jaschik, Scott. "'The Evolution of American Women's Studies.'" *Inside Higher Ed*. March 26, 2009. Accessed February 6, 2025. https://www.insidehighered.com/news/2009/03/27/evolution-american-womens-studies

Kanehara, Hitomi. *Snakes and Earrings*. Dutton, 2005.

Keene, Donald. *Dawn to the West: Japanese Literature of the Modern Era, Fiction*. Columbia University Press, 1998.

Kitada, Sachie, and Miya E. M. Lippit. "Contemporary Japanese Feminist Literary Criticism." *U.S.-Japan Women's Journal*. English Supplement, no. 7 (1994): 72–97.

Kolodny, Annette. "Dancing through the Minefield: Some Observations on the Theory, Practice and Politics of a Feminist Literary Criticism." *Feminist Studies* 6, no. 1 (1980): 1–25.

Orbaugh, Sharalyn. "The Construction of Gendered Discourse in the Modern Study of Japanese Literature." *Across Time and Genre: Reading and Writing Women's Texts*, 2002.

Russ, Joanna. *How to Suppress Women's Writing*. 1st edition. University of Texas Press, 1983.

CHAPTER 2

The Inclusion of Okinawa in Japanese Literary Studies

Davinder L. Bhowmik

I began my research on Okinawan literature in the early 1990s when little to nothing was available in English. While that has happily changed with an uptick in the number of monographs, edited volumes, and anthologies of literature, why, I wonder, does it remain still far easier for me to present in-depth research on Okinawa to an Okinawan studies audience than it is to a Japan Studies one? The waves of cultural and postcolonial studies that dominated my years in graduate school *did* result in welcome shifts in Japan Studies, making it more expansive and readier to entertain subnational concerns such as my own research interest in Okinawa. Yet, the gulf that persists whenever I present research to a non-specialist audience in "the field" suggests it is uneven at best. Perhaps, had Okinawa created its own written language, rather than utilizing Japanese, the requisite language for its modern literature, one could pursue studies of Okinawa without the constraints of operating through the nation-state framework of Japan in which Okinawa continues to occupy a tenuous place.[1]

The limitations of the nation-state framework have become increasingly obvious today. Climate change, among the most pressing of the sundry issues that now vex us, recognizes no state borders. Planetary wealth and its distribution seem unchecked by any national, political mechanism. The nation-state has taken a battering from global forces, ecological and otherwise. But where are we without it, and the formations of knowledge so rooted in the study of nations, Japan included? Prior work on Okinawa in the prewar period drew my attention away from Japan toward developments in Taiwan, Korea, and other of Japan's formal colonies,[2] and my current work, which considers Okinawa's long postwar, moves me again away from Japan proper to understand Okinawa and its heavy base burden in relation to military bases concentrated in countries such as Germany and South Korea. A singular focus on Japan can and does seem irrelevant for the study of Okinawa, which demands interdisciplinary breadth owing to its early history as part of an independent Ryūkyū kingdom that paid tribute to Japan and China and its Asia-Pacific wartime history in which the belatedly incorporated island prefecture was forced to assimilate to Japanese ways in the manner of formal colonies such as Korea and Taiwan, only then to be sacrificed in the Battle of Okinawa and severed from Japan during the long American occupation (1945–1972).

Allow me to relate a brief anecdote and a recent news incident to illustrate how, despite its return to national sovereignty in 1972, Okinawa continues to occupy a liminal space within Japan. Just before a recent research trip to Okinawa a colleague wished me safe travels to Okinawa *and* Japan. I righteously corrected said colleague by launching into a screed on Okinawa's legal status as a prefecture, which it attained first in 1879 and regained after the end of the American occupation in 1972. To my great chagrin, soon after my arrival in Okinawa, upon exclaiming to my local Airbnb host how happy I was to be back in Japan—*Nihon ni kite ite, ureshii desu*—she curtly corrected me, saying "*Okinawa desu.* (You're in Okinawa.)" Clearly, for her, and many others, Okinawa is not a part of Japan; it is a chain of more than 150 islands that stand decidedly apart from the nation. The Japanese government's treatment of Okinawans as second-class citizens in the prewar period and Abe's and Kishida's administration's disregard for Okinawans' overwhelming resistance to a military base relocation in once pristine Henoko, as demonstrated in the most recent prefectural referendum, show clearly how sovereignty—Japan's—rests on exceptionalism—Okinawa's.[3] So long as Japan's bases, dams, and nuclear plants are pushed to and remain in the nation's peripheries its urban centers and population will continue to flourish at the expense of those outside their view—the peripheral, the marginalized.

When my Okinawan Airbnb host claimed that Okinawa was not Japan, her assertion struck me as both issuing from a deeply held personal conviction and one that jibed with the hard won "all Okinawa" political consensus that held military base construction in Henoko was wrong.[4] Conversely, when in October 2016 a riot police member dispatched from Osaka and tasked with securing the controversial Henoko base called local protestors "natives" (*dojin*) time and space blurred.[5] The officer's ethnic slur, a speech act smacking of contemporary colonialism, harkened back to the prewar period when discrimination against Okinawans and Koreans was rampant. The Airbnb host's and the police officer's assertions alike pointed to Okinawa's difference, yet fierce pride fueled the host's statement, and barely-concealed contempt lay behind the officer's utterance. If the two decades I had previously spent doing research in Okinawa hadn't already driven home that Okinawa is part of an academic field where position matters these two recent incidents did.

Let's return now to the early 1990s when I first began to research Okinawa as a PhD student in Japanese literature. What little I found available in English amounted to works such as William Lebra's *Okinawan Religion*; George Kerr's problematic *The History of an Island People*;[6] Okinawa: *Two Postwar Novellas*, which contained translations by Steve Rabson of the Akutagawa Prize–winning novellas *The Cocktail Party* by Ōshiro Tatsuhirō and *An Okinawan Boy* by Higashi Mineo; a few scattered translations and articles; and the odd Tuttle Books volume on topics such as Okinawa's culture and customs.[7]

Fortunately, through a key professional introduction I met Professor Nakahodo Masanori, a leading scholar of Okinawan literature at the University of the Ryukyus in Okinawa in 1994. Not only did Professor Nakahodo's guidance lead me to rich source material in Japanese instrumental to completing a dissertation and authoring a book in English on literature from Okinawa,[8] but he in turn introduced me to several scholars working on Okinawa. These included Professors Okamoto Keitoku and Shinjō Ikuo, both of whom also taught literature at the University of the Ryukyus (Ryūdai); historian Yakabi Osamu from Okinawa University; and Kurosawa Akiko, a literary scholar from Okinawa International University. Professor Nakahodo's office was a hub of activity for faculty, graduate, and undergraduate students interested in Okinawa. The University of the Ryukyus, established in 1950 during the American occupation of Okinawa and designated as a national university in 1972 following Okinawa's return to Japan, draws researchers interested in Okinawa from all over the globe to its esteemed Okinawa collection.

Although I would return regularly to confer with Professor Nakahodo and others in Okinawa the critical mass assembled at Ryūdai in the early 1990s did not continue indefinitely. The robust hiring that followed Okinawa's reversion and peaked in the 1990s when Ryūdai boasted three full time professors of Japanese literature with major research interests in Okinawa (Nakahodo, Okamoto, and Shinjō) ended with the untimely deaths of Okamoto in 2006 and Yakabi in 2010 and the retirement of Nakahodo in 2009. Today, Ryūdai has only one Okinawan literature expert, Shinjō Ikuo. Although Shinjō's major publications focus on subnational literary issues pertaining to Okinawa, as the sole scholar of modern Japanese literature he is responsible for teaching students the whole of the modern literary tradition leaving scant opportunity to incorporate Okinawa into the curriculum.

After 1972 Ryūdai became the primary place to study Okinawan literature and some of the students taught by Professors Okamoto and Nakahodo have now become established scholars or literary authors in their own right. After studying at Ryūdai, Shinjō Ikuo pursued a PhD at Ritsumeikan before returning to Ryūdai where he has established himself as a prodigious scholar.[9] Gabe Satoshi received his PhD at Ryūdai and has since been appointed at Okinawa University where he teaches courses on Okinawan literature and publishes on the important postwar literary journal, *Ryūdai bungaku* (Ryūdai Literature). As an undergraduate Murakami Yōko studied in her native Hiroshima before pursuing graduate studies at Ryūdai. After receiving her PhD at the University of Tokyo she returned to Okinawa where she teaches Japanese literature at Okinawa International University. Murakami's 2016 monograph *Dekigoto no zankyō* (The Reverberation of Events) deftly combines her two primary research interests of atomic bomb literature and Okinawan literature.

In addition to the above-named scholars of Japanese literature whose primary research interest is Okinawa, Professors Nakahodo and Okamoto taught two of Okinawa's leading contemporary fiction writers: Sakiyama Tami and Medoruma Shun. Sakiyama and Medoruma have authored numerous essays and prize-winning works of fiction since the early 1980s. Readers eager for more writing by these two esteemed authors must bide their time, however. Sakiyama teaches Japanese full-time at a cram school and Medoruma is equally consumed by protests against the base in Henoko where he participates by surveilling and writing a blog[10] about construction activity as a member of a canoe brigade. The constraints of everyday life in Okinawa clearly impinge on these authors' literary output.

The Japanese gaze on Okinawa, which began as early as the 1920s when ethnologists such as Yanagita Kunio, Origuchi Shinobu, and Yanagi Muneyoshi turned to Okinawa in an attempt to locate the origins of Japanese culture, continues apace today as mass media promotes to tourists Okinawa's natural beauty even as the prefecture's heavy military base burden endangers biological diversity and has resulted in scores of sexual assaults, aircraft and vehicular accidents, incessant noise pollution, and other ills. Indeed, the

"Okinawa boom" that reared its head in mainland Japan in the early 1990s, when indigenous culture of Okinawa was all the rage, shows no signs of ending as demonstrated by the one million strong crowd that flocks to Shinjuku for Tokyo's annual Okinawa festival. James C. Fisher explains Japan's enduring gaze on Okinawa as follows:

> It is hard to deny that Japan's adoption of Okinawan culture is a textbook example of cultural appropriation. The "Okinawa boom" in Japanese popular media—and the cultural appropriation into which it has matured—fills the popular imagination with a particularly *Japanese* understanding of Okinawa and its relationship to the Japanese nation, an understanding often at odds with that of Okinawan people themselves, as reflected in their literature, political movements, and brave defiance of the combined interests of the Japanese government and U.S. military. In other words, it tells a story of Okinawa that Japan enjoys hearing, rather than the story that needs to be told.[11]

The story of Okinawa that needs to be told lies in the prefecture's literature, which, thanks to a number of recent anthologies, is far more accessible than in past decades. Published in 1989, Steve Rabson's translations of Ōshiro Tatsuhirō's *The Cocktail Party* and Higashi Mineo's *Child of Okinawa* were rare exceptions to the prevailing tendency to translate primarily writers from Tokyo. In 2000, Steve Rabson and Michael Molasky co-edited *Southern Exposure: Modern Japanese Literature from Okinawa*, an anthology of fiction and poetry. This was a singular achievement, for it more than doubled what had previously been available in English translation. After the University of Hawaiʻi held a conference to inaugurate its Center for Okinawan Studies in 2008, two more literary anthologies were published. The first was *Living Spirit*, edited by Frank Stewart, published in 2011. I edited, with Steve Rabson, the second, *Islands of Protest: Japanese Literature from Okinawa*, published in 2016. These anthologies of literature, together with a growing number of collected volumes of non-fiction writing on Okinawa such as *Resistant Islands: Okinawa Confronts Japan and the United States* (Gavan McCormack and Satoko Oka Norimatsu, eds.), *Rethinking Postwar Okinawa: Beyond American Occupation* (Pedro Iacobelli and Hiroko Matsuda, eds.), *Islands of Discontent* (Laura Hein and Mark Selden, eds.), and *Japan and Okinawa: Structure and Subjectivity* (Glenn Hook and Richard Siddle, eds.) now make it possible to teach substantial courses on Okinawa.

In addition to the edited volumes listed above, scholarly monographs and academic journals began to publish more scholarship on Okinawa in their pages beginning in the 1990s. In 1993 Norma Field's inclusion in her In *the Realm of a Dying Emperor* of a chapter on Chibana Shōichi, an Okinawan supermarket owner who protested the raising of the Japanese flag at an athletic meet in Okinawa, drew readerly interest in the complexity of everyday life in Okinawa. Also published in 1993 was historian Alan Christy's article "The Making of Imperial Subjects in Okinawa," which appeared in the first volume of *positions: east asia cultures critique* spearheading a stream of writing on Okinawa that focused on issues of relations of power germane to postcolonial studies. The rape of a 12-year-old schoolgirl by three US military servicemen in 1995 fueled politically engaged scholarship on Okinawa of which anthropologist Linda Angst's article "The Sacrifice of a Schoolgirl: Discourses of Power, and Women's Lives in Okinawa" is an exemplar (Angst 2001).

Among academic journals the Asia-Pacific Journal (APJ) provides award-winning, extensive coverage of topics related to Okinawa from its early history to its most recent gubernatorial election. The website of the APJ also includes an Okinawa course reader available for download. Titled "Putting Okinawa at the Center" the first of the reader's two parts covers historical topics such as the myth of Ryukyuan pacifism (Smits 2010), group suicides during the Battle of Okinawa (Aniya 2009), and postwar Okinawan migration to Bolivia (Iacobelli 2013). The second part of the reader focuses on contemporary subjects ranging from language loss and revitalization (Heinrich 2005), music and memory (Roberson 2010), and the politics of performance (Nelson 2013). The APJ also regularly includes translated pieces from Okinawa's two major newspapers the *Ryūkyū Shimpō* and the *Okinawa Times*, a welcome contribution given the frank reporting of these two dailies, which one senior scholar in Japan quipped to me that he considered "anti-Japan" (*han-Nichi*).

Challenges

Despite the welcome increase in academic scholarship on Okinawa in Japanese and English since the early 1990s there remain a number of constraints to studying Okinawa. One challenge is the overall decline in faculty positions that we have experienced after the 2008 global recession. At most universities the primary responsibility of scholars interested in Okinawa hired to teach Japanese literature, whether in Japan or elsewhere, is to teach undergraduates the broader canon. This leaves little time to introduce students to translations and scholarly work on Okinawa despite their growing number.

Another challenge is ghettoization. Many scholars with an interest in Okinawa publish their work in edited volumes whose focus is Okinawa or in journals that support research in the region. One effect of this concentration of Okinawa in edited volumes and certain journals is the exoticization of Okinawa. Recently the International Institute for Okinawan Studies, which publishes the International Journal of Okinawan Studies (IJOS), housed at the University of the Ryukyus, published its final issue. While some may well lament the loss of a valuable venue in which to publish international research in English on Okinawa, funding for IJOS has been converted to Research Institute for Islands and Sustainability (RIIS), which will publish a journal whose focus is on islandology and other regions of the world as well as Okinawa. This broadening of focus from a consideration of Okinawa exclusively to an examination of Okinawa not through a nation-state framework but rather within the framework of global islands may be one way to de-ghettoize Okinawan Studies, which is always already ghettoized within Japan Studies.

A final constraint, related to ghettoization, is the difficulty of accessing research materials on Okinawa. The Okinawa Research Institute at Hōsei University, established in 1972 to encourage comparative work in the culture, history, and linguistics of Okinawa continues to draw students and scholars from all over the world to its collection. Not all such collections endure. Inaugurated in 2006, the Institute for Ryukyuan and Okinawan Studies, housed at Waseda University, closed its doors in 2015 due to funding issues and the eminent retirement of director, Keiko Katsukata-Inafuku, a literary scholar with interests in American literature, Okinawan literature, and gender studies. The institutes at Hōsei and Waseda contain valuable resources difficult to obtain without traveling to Okinawa where an abundant amount of material published by regional publishers not often included in major research databases can be found. Today, the Center for Okinawan Studies at the University of Hawai'i is the only hub for Okinawa-related research activity outside of Japan.

New Trends

Despite dwindling faculty positions, ghettoization, and the difficulty involved in accessing research materials related to Okinawa I would like to introduce now some welcome trends that have emerged from the increase in publications on Okinawa in recent decades.

The dozens of recently published translations of poetry, drama, and fiction from Okinawa have and will continue to produce further writing on Okinawa. To give one unexpected example, consider *Above the East China Sea*, the 2014 novel by Sarah Bird. In this widely reviewed ninth novel of Bird's the author writes a somber narrative of war's effect on two young girls, one Okinawan, the other American. Given that the Battle of Okinawa is the uber-theme in postwar fiction from Okinawa, I found the opening line of Barbara Fisher's review of Sarah Bird's novel, which made the shortlist in the Sunday Book Review of the *New York Times* startling: "The Battle of Okinawa is a piece of World War II history rarely explored in fiction, especially from the points of view Bird has chosen" (Fisher 2014).

As I have explained above, in recent years literature from Okinawa has increased several folds in English translation, though to my knowledge, none depicts the so-called "Typhoon of Steel" and its aftereffect, the militarization of Okinawa, by employing a narrative that alternates between a young Okinawan girl and her American counterpart. And, while a few works written in Japanese feature well-depicted American characters, such as George in Matayoshi Eiki's "The Wild Boar that George Gunned Down," (in *Living Spirit*) most Americans make only cameo appearances in Okinawan fiction. *Above the East China Sea*, through alternating narratives of Tamiko and Luz, gives equal weight to Americans and Okinawans.

The fact that Sarah Bird has carefully read English translations of Okinawan fiction and poetry is clear from the start of *Above the East China Sea*. Not only is the novel prefaced by an excerpt of a poem by Yonaha Mikio entitled "Ocean of the Dead," but one half of the novel, Tamiko's story, takes the form of a dialogue between mother and unborn child that Yamanoha Nobuko adopts in her 1985 story "Will o' the Wisp" (both Yonaha's poem and Yamanoha's story appear in *Islands of Protest*). Indeed, the novel is replete with material the author surely gleaned from copious Okinawan studies reference material, from the island's history and culture to its language and politics. For the most part, Bird subtly incorporates her material into the novel's well rounded, believable characters, and avoids the pedagogic cast that runs through some works of Okinawan literature, particularly by Ōshiro Tatsuhirō. The palpable sense the novel exudes of being in Okinawa comes, perhaps, from Sarah Bird's own experience as a military brat in Okinawa, which baffled her, as she explains in her acknowledgments: "This novel began in 1970 when I was an Air Force dependent strolling around the vast green fairways of a golf course at Kadena Air Base, and I wondered, Why, do we get all this space to play a game?" (Bird 2014) Why, indeed.

Another trend in studies of Okinawa can be seen in transnational scholarship. Here, I will mention a few examples of recent scholarship that bridge concerns in Okinawa and South Korea. In *Okinawa and Jeju: Bases of Discontent* Donald Kirk writes about ordinary individuals caught in the contact zone between civilian and military life. Acknowledging the many differences between the two regions Kirk describes he nevertheless offers a compelling view of how Jejuans and Okinawans figure in a geopolitical arena dominated by the larger forces of Seoul, Tokyo, Washington, and Beijing. Matayoshi Eiki's 1980 prize-winning novella *The White Leadtree Mansion* (*Ginnemu yashiki*) set in 1953 tells the story of a Korean man who confesses to the Okinawan protagonist violence he inflicts on his girlfriend, a Korean "comfort woman." The theme of discrimination against Koreans that runs through the work has long interested scholars in Korea and in 2014 resulted in a first-time translation into Korean of Matayoshi's work. Just as translations into English of literature from Okinawa inspired Sarah Bird's novel, so too may the translation into Korean of a seminal work by Matayoshi lead to further writing and scholarship.[12]

Although the bulk of Okinawan studies to date has tended to remain within a Okinawa-Japan or Okinawa-United States framework, given the history of Okinawan migration pre- and post-WWII it is a welcome trend to see recent scholars turning their attention to issues of the Okinawa diaspora in places like Hawaii, The Philippines, and Brazil. Kawamura Minato's inclusion of Sakiyama Asao's 1997 Davao Pilgrimage (*Dabao junrei*) in a collection of Okinawan short stories he edited in 2003 no doubt contributed to Ryan Buyco's taking it up in his 2017 article on the story "Afterlives of the Okinawan Community in Davao, Mindanao." Recent scholarship by Pedro Iacobelli, author of *Postwar Emigration to South America from Japan and the Ryukyu Islands* and co-editor of *Rethinking Postwar Okinawa: Beyond American Occupation* is sure to stimulate further interest in intersections between South American and Okinawan studies. Nakahodo Masanori whose research interest spans from Okinawa, to the South Seas, and to Hawaii continues beyond retirement to publish voluminous research on poetry, fiction, and letters written by Okinawan emigrants to Hawaii as demonstrated in his 2012 study *Expressions of Migrants to Hawaii of Okinawan Descent* (*Okinawa-kei Hawaii imintachi no hyōgen*) and his 2019 study *Hawaii and Okinawa: Journals, Film, 2Gs, and POWs* (*Hawaii to Okinawa: nisshi, eiga, Nisei, horyōtachi*).

The ongoing challenges Okinawans face as their collective voice of protest against the military bases is routinely ignored by Tokyo and Washington D.C. have led to several scholars in the field of Okinawan Studies to combine their writing with on-the-ground activism as in the case of Medoruma Shun. Ethnic studies scholars Wesley Ueunten and Ariko Ikehara are but two examples. Ueunten who teaches at San Francisco State University publishes work on Okinawan identity and the diaspora in South America; participates actively in his local Okinawa prefecture association; performs the *sanshin*, a string instrument beloved in Okinawa; and travels the globe to engage communities in talk story (*yuntaku hintaku*), an ethnographic method to critique and discover knowledge of Okinawa and connect scholars to ordinary people. Ariko Ikehara who received her Ph.D. in Ethnic Studies at the University of California, Berkeley, as did Ueunten, specializes in performance studies and has recently created a space she calls Koza X MiXtopia Research Center in Okinawa City. Housed in Gintengai in the famed Teruya District, the Center is an experimental lab for art, events, and building archives in Okinawa City inspired in part by Ikehara's and others' combining theories of third, non-binary spaces drawn from performance art. This innovative new space brings together grassroots activism, culture, economic revitalization, and academic study.

A final example of innovation in scholarship in Okinawan Studies is the Okinawa Memories Initiative that grew out of the Gail Project directed by Alan Christy, Cowell Provost and professor of history at the University of California, Santa Cruz.[13] The project, inspired by a collection of photos taken in Okinawa in the early 1950s by serviceman Charles Eugene Gail, is a collaborative, international public history that focuses on the early years of the American military occupation of Okinawa. The project is comprised of the photos, key historical documents, oral histories by Americans and Okinawans, and undergraduate research and writing. The hands-on research and creation of stories and art by students involved in the Gail Project have sown seeds for the Okinawa Memories Initiative, a broader community history and dialogue project focusing on Okinawa that engages UC Santa Cruz with nearby academic institutions and ones in Okinawa.

Conclusion

The study of Okinawa continues to be done largely through Japan Studies. As I have demonstrated this presents scholars the dilemma of how to teach students about Okinawa responsibly while also covering essential knowledge of "the field." However, emerging scholarship on Okinawa taking place in Ethnic Studies, American Studies, Gender Studies, Postcolonial Studies, and Performance Studies is bringing the literature, history, and culture of Okinawa to a broader cross section of scholars and students. Okinawa's history as an island kingdom that paid tribute to Japan and China from the early

1500s to 1879; the colonial experience Okinawa endured in the prewar and wartime period; and the postcolonial condition that exists today where the preponderance of Japan's military bases with their attendant risks remain in Okinawa demands scholars eschew the nation-state framework and adopt a global perspective. Finally, interdisciplinarity is not only critical, but it may also free Okinawan Studies from the ghetto of Japan Studies.

Acknowledgments

This article has benefited from conversations with Kyle Ikeda, Kina Ikue, Nakahodo Masanori, Christopher Nelson, Annmaria Shimabuku, and Victoria Young among others.

Notes

1. I am grateful to Nakahodo Masanori for his insight on the constraints of Japanese language in Okinawan literature and to Victoria Young for raising a similar point that the study of Okinawa is largely conducted through the framework of Japan studies.

2. See my *Writing Okinawa: Narrative Acts of Identity and Resistance.*

3. Annmaria Shimabuku writes about this state of exception in her monograph *Alegal: Biopolitics and the Unintelligibility of Okinawan Life.*

4. Despite his conservative stance Takeshi Onaga, Okinawa's former Governer, managed to unite various factions in Okinawa through his "All Okinawa" campaign against military base construction while in office. See Gavan McCormack, "'All Japan' versus 'All Okinawa'—Abe Shinzo's Military-Firstism," *The Asia-Pacific Journal* 13, issue 11, no. 3, March 16, 2015.

5. See editorial in the *Ryūkyū Shimpō* on the "Dojin Incident", accessed September 15, 2019, http://english.ryukyushimpo.jp/2016/10/25/25930/

6. Interestingly, when Kerr's book is mentioned in Ōshiro's *The Cocktail Party* the narrator muses that the book, which emphasizes Okinawa's cultural divergence from other parts of Japan, served to justify the American occupation of Okinawa.

7. In his tripartite overview of ethnographic writing on Okinawa in English James Roberson (2015) includes more examples of research focusing on traditions of Okinawa, which he argues typified the occupation period.

8. Key among this material was the 20-volume *Okinawa bungaku zenshū* published in 1990.

9. Although the only scholar of Okinawan literature at Ryūdai, Shinjō Ikuo has contributed as tirelessly to literary criticism on Okinawa as did his predecessors Okamoto Keitoku and Nakahodo Masanori. Shinjō's monographs on Okinawa's literature include *Tōrai suru Okinawa* (The Arrival of Okinawa); *Okinawa o kiku* (Listening to Okinawa); *Okinawa no kizu to iu kairo* (The Circuit of Okinawa's Wound); and *Okinawa ni tsuranaru* (Connected to Okinawa).

10. Medoruma's blog is titled "From an Island where the Ocean Roars." https://blog.goo.ne.jp/awamori777

11. James C. Fisher, "The Dark Side of Japan's 'Okinawa Boom,'" accessed September 15, 2019, https://www.tokyoreview.net/2017/08

12. I should mention here, too, a 2019 publication by Oh Sejong, a professor of Japanese literature at Ryūdai whose research specialty is Zainichi Korean writing: *Okinawa to Chōsen no hazama de* (In Between Okinawa and South Korea).

13. See https://gailproject.ucsc.edu/, accessed September 15, 2019.

Works Cited

Angst, Linda. "The Sacrifice of a Schoolgirl: The 1995 Rape Case, Discourses of Power, and Women's Lives in Okinawa." *Critical Asian Studies* 33, no. 2 (2001): 243–66.

Bhowmik, Davinder L. *Writing Okinawa: Narrative Acts of Identity and Resistance*. Routledge, 2008.

Bhowmik, Davinder L., and Steve Rabson, eds. *Islands of Protest: Japanese Literature from Okinawa*. University of Hawai'i Press, 2016.

Bird, Sarah. *Above the East China Sea*. Knopf, 2014.

Buyco, Ryan. "Afterlives of the Okinawan Community in Davao, Mindanao: Sakiyama Asao's 'Davao Pilgrimage.'" *IJOS: International Journal of Okinawan Studies* 8 (2017): 27–41.

Christy, Alan S. "The Making of Imperial Subjects in Okinawa." *positions: east asia cultures critique* 1, no. 3 (1993): 607–39.

Field, Norma. *In the Realm of a Dying Emperor*. Pantheon Books, 1991.

Fisher, Barbara. "Sarah Bird's 'Above the East China Sea.'" *New York Times Book Review*, August 8, 2014. Accessed January 21, 2025. https://www.nytimes.com/2014/08/10/books/review/sarah-birds-above-the-east-china-sea-and-more.html

Fisher, James C. "The Dark Side of Japan's 'Okinawa Boom.'" Accessed January 21, 2025. https://www.tokyoreview.net/2017/08

Hein, Laura, and Mark Selden, eds. *Islands of Discontent: Okinawan Responses to Japanese and American Power*. Rowman & Littlefield, 2003.

Hook, Glenn, and Richard Siddle, eds. *Japan and Okinawa: Structure and Subjectivity*. Routledge, 2014.

Iacobelli, Pedro, and Hiroko Matsuda, eds. *Rethinking Postwar Okinawa: Beyond American Occupation*. Lexington Books, 2017.

Kawamura Minato. *Gendai Okinawa bungaku sakuhinsen* (Selected works of Contemporary Okinawan literature). Kōdansha bungei bunko, 2011.

Kerr, George H. *Okinawa, the History of an Island People*. 1st ed. Charles E. Tuttle, 1958.

Kirk, Donald. *Okinawa and Jeju: Bases of Discontent*. Palgrave Pivot, 2013.

Lebra, William P. *Okinawan Religion: Belief, Ritual, and Social Structure*. University of Hawai'i Press, 1966.

McCormack, Gavan, and Satoko Oka Norimatsu, eds. *Resistant Islands: Okinawa Confronts Japan and the United States*. Rowman & Littlefield, 2012.

Matayoshi Eiki. *Ginnemu yashiki* (White Leadtree Mansion). Shūeisha, 1981.

Medoruma Shun. (blog) *Umi nari no shima kara* (From an Island where the Ocean Roars). Accessed January 21, 2025. https://blog.goo.ne.jp/awamori777

Molasky, Michael, and Steve Rabson, eds. *Southern Exposure: Modern Japanese Literature from Okinawa.* University of Hawai'i Press, 2000.

Murakami, Yōko. *Dekigoto no zankyō: Genbaku bungaku to Okinawa Bungaku.* Inpakuto Shuppankai, 2015.

Nakahodo Masanori. *Okinawa-kei Hawaii imintachi no hyōgen* (Expressions of Migrants to Hawaii of Okinawan Descent). Bōdaainku, 2012.

Nakahodo Masanori. *Hawaii to Okinawa: nisshi, eiga, nisei, horyotachi* (Hawaii and Okinawa: Journals, Film, 2Gs, and POWs). Bōdaainku, 2019.

Nelson, Chris. *Dancing with the Dead: Memory, Performance, and Everyday Life in Postwar Okinawa.* Duke University Press, 2008.

Oh, Sejong. *Okinawa to Chōsen no hazama de: Chōsenjin no "Kashika/Fukashika" o meguru rekishi to katari.* Akashi shoten, 2019.

Okinawa bungaku zenshū. Henshū Iinkai. *Okinawa Bungaku zenshū.* Kokusho kankōkai, 1990.

Onishi, Yuichiro. *Transpacific Antiracism: Afro-Asian Solidarity in 20th-Century Black America, Japan, and Okinawa.* New York University Press, 2013.

Rabson, Steve, ed. and trans. *Okinawa: Two Postwar Novellas.* University of California Center for Japanese Studies, 1989.

Shimabuku, Annmaria M. *Alegal: Biopolitics and the Unintelligibility of Okinawan Life.* 1st ed. Fordham University Press, 2019.

Shinjō Ikuo. *Tōrai suru Okinawa* (The Arrival of Okinawa). Inpakuto shuppan, 2007.

Shinjō Ikuo. *Okinawa wo kiku* (Listening to Okinawa). Misuzu shobō, 2010.

Shinjō Ikuo. *Okinawa no kizu to iu kairo* (The Cycle of Okinawa's Wound). Iwanami shoten, 2014.

Shinjō Ikuo. *Okinawa ni tsuranaru* (Connected to Okinawa). Iwanami shoten, 2018.

Stewart, Frank, and Katsunori Yamazato, eds. *Living Spirit: Literature and Resurgence from Okinawa.* University of Hawai'i Press, 2011.

CHAPTER 3

Do Black Lives Still Matter to Japanese Literary Studies?

William H. Bridges IV

I am an optimist. Mine is a peculiar predicament. To be Black and American and an optimist is to navigate the world as a living contradiction, the realities of your existence a perpetual reminder that you must sacrifice one of the three if the other two are to survive. It is easy to be American and optimistic. And one can survive as a Black American, if one is not too naïve. But to be Black and American and optimistic? One of the three is bound to be broken, shattered under the weight of cognitive dissonance.

How can you remain optimistic when you have, in theory, done everything right but things keep going wrong? Yes, you have your shiny PhD in Japanese literary studies, but a scholar of Japanese literature is not what the world sees when it looks at you. Your new colleague sees a janitor, and he will ask if you are in the classroom to pick up the trash. (To be clear, sanitation is a noble profession. It is not, however, the profession for which you trained.) Your students see an anomaly, and they will drop your class in droves after they see a Black face at the front of their introductory Japanese classroom. (The students who remain will not hesitate to tell you why their peers dropped.) So too will their parents see you as anomalous, and, during your office hours, their children—your students—will relay their parents' curiosity concerning why a Black man is teaching their child Japanese. Your senior colleague will see an epistemological threat to the paradigms of the Japanese literary studies of yesteryear: *You don't really*, this colleague will ask rhetorically, *think what our department needs is another scholar of Afro-Japanese studies*? These are the selfsame colleagues who will peer review your work and deem your writing too "hyperbolic" or "energetic" or "rhythmic" or "figurative" or some other euphemism for "too Black," too informed by a life spent listening to the poetry and prose of Black life. (These colleagues have yet to see that, if Black voices matter to Japanese literary studies, they must matter no matter the voice in which they are written, or, more accurately, their mattering must supersede any yesteryear notions of how a scholar of Japanese literary studies "should" sound. They must matter, in a word, unconditionally. The scholar who imbues Japanese literary studies with the epistemological insights of Black thought will speak in a different voice precisely because their cadence is a testament to the work required—the experiences both lived and learned—to provide those insights, the Afro-Japanese literary scholar's belonging to and travels between two epistemic communities. Japanese literary studies cannot receive this gift without the package.) The Tokyo Metropolitan Police Department sees a face reminiscent of one of the boogeymen in their counter-terrorism training videos, and they will detain you regularly as you make your way to the National Diet Library. Your banker sees a risk to be redlined, and he will reject your home loan application. Your family sees a desperately needed source of income, and they will ask not about your research but about how much money you can spare. Seemingly no one will see a scholar of Japanese literary studies, except you when you look at yourself in the mirror.

But, even in the face of the world's unimaginative visions of blackness, I maintain a sense of optimism, of possibility. My optimism is not to be confused with naivete. I realize the price we pay for optimism is the last 8 minutes and 46 seconds of George Floyd's life, a timespan which serves as a microcosmic compression of centuries of black oppression and bloodshed. But I remain optimistic because our cultural moment has given us the opportunity to shift the parameters of the possible.

For example, it is now possible to see that, if Japanese literary studies is to be done with intellectual and ethical integrity, it must understand that Black lives matter, that Black existence has long been an integral component of the histories, presents, and futures of our object of study. This is not a moment to beg for anything, questions included, because it is not that Black life needs Japanese literary study to do it some favor, but rather that Japanese literary studies needs Black intellects (ways of knowing the world) and intellectuals for the sake of its own epistemological wholeness. So, let's ask and reckon with, rather than presume the veracity of, this question: Do Black lives still matter to Japanese literary studies?

If we are serious about answering this question, it is helpful to begin by dispelling the obvious answers, the truisms that might help us sleep (or keep us up) at night but do relatively little to further our thinking. The first truism is this: Yes, it is undeniably clear that Black lives matter to Japanese literary studies. To say that Black lives matter to Japanese literary studies is simply a matter of knowing one's literary history: Kanagaki Robun writes of "darkies from the African states hired on the cheap,"[1] Nagai Kafu and the "mass of hideous negroes"[2] surrounding his depiction of Washington D.C., the intertextual gestures toward African princes in Natsume Sōseki's coming-of-age novel,[3] the references to Othello and Redcap porters in Miyamoto Yuriko's nonfiction,[4] the analogies of black brotherhood in Ema Shū's short fiction,[5] the rhetoric of blood quantums and justified racial self-loathing in Tanizaki's praise of shadows,[6] Ariyoshi Sawako's transpacific travels from Tokyo to Harlem,[7] Tawada Yōko's time travel between the corporeal theft of slavery and the homelessness of the émigré,[8] and the sisterhood developed by (Japanese) Sayuri and (Nigerian) Salimah—the heroines of Iwaki Kei's *Farewell, My Orange* (2013)—after they, like Iwaki herself, migrate to Australia.

This is an inexhaustive list (for it seems almost impossible to exhaust the importance of Black lives to Japanese literature), one which cuts through the heart of the modern Japanese literary canon. If we are to understand modern Japanese literature—a body of literature born in the wake of America's forced opening of Japan and periodized by what John Dower calls a race war[9]—we will have to understand how Black lives matter to this body.

So, yes, Black lives obviously matter to modern Japanese literature. But it is also true that Black lives do not matter to Japanese literary studies. This is simply a matter of pragmatic linguistics. When lives truly matter, we do not need to protest their mattering. They simply matter. We hold the truth of their mattering to be self-evident. "A tiger," Wole Soyinka once wrote, "does not stand in the forest and say 'I am a tiger.' . . . He pounces. . . . When you pass where the tiger has walked before, you see the skeleton of the duiker, [and] you know that some tigritude has emanated there."[10] So too with those lives that matter. Their mattering is emanant. In my studies of Japanese culture, I have yet to come across the expressions "imperial lives matter" or "ministerial lives matter," because when a life genuinely matters its profundity is not up for debate. The lives matter. That is a statement. Do Black lives still matter to Japanese literary studies? This is an interrogative, an interrogation. And when under interrogation it becomes clear how little Black lives matter.

So Black lives obviously matter (to Japanese literary history) and obviously have not mattered (historically to the institution of Japanese literary studies in the American academy). For the sake of expediency, let us agree to set aside these two axiomatic answers. When we set aside the axiomatic, here is what we are left with: in its current configuration, there are occasions—or we might say conditions—in which Black lives matter to Japanese literary studies. In other words, *when* Black lives matter to Japanese literature and literary studies, they tend to matter *conditionally*.

An example of one of the conditions under which Black lives begin to matter can be found in a possible counterargument to the case I made above concerning the importance of Black lives to Japanese literary history. One might make the counterargument that there are no Black lives in any of the works of literature referenced above. Rather than Black lives, what one has is Black characters, textual proxies of Black life. (For the sake of counterargument, we will momentarily table the inspiration actual Black lives have been to the production of works of Japanese literature—Abe Tomoji's ode to Stepin Fetchit, Kijima Hajime's correspondences with Langston Hughes, Ōe Kenzaburō's meeting with Ralph Ellison and commenting on Toni Morrison, Yamada Eimi reading James Baldwin, and so on.) Michael Bourdaghs writes that the 1970s and '80s linguistic turn in Japanese literary criticism "continue[s] to reverberate today, shaping the way Japanese literature is studied both at home and abroad."[11] This shaping might obfuscate the way Black lives have mattered to Japanese literature.

For Black lives to truly matter to a given branch of literary studies, it can be productive to think less in terms of textuality and more along the lines of the aesthetic as Katya Mandoki understands the term. Mandoki proposes analysis of the aesthetic in the etymological sense of the term. In this light, the aesthetic is the study of sensation, and aesthetic experience is predicated on "the condition of being alive" in ways that "consists of openness and permeability to the world. There is no aesthesis," Mandoki continues, "without life, and no life without aesthesis. What is at stake for aesthetic studies is the basic condition of any live being."[12] In this view, "aesthetic experience" is not an honorific reserved for encounters with works of fine art or natural beauty: it is an everyday inevitability for any living thing that is vulnerable to and receptive of the environment in which it lives.

Caroline Levine has recently written of what she categorizes as the "aesthetic humanities," which include literary studies in its fold.[13] What would it mean to understand the "aesthetics" of the aesthetic humanities in Mandoki's sense of the term, or the aesthetic as the spectrum of experiences by which vulnerable, living beings make sense of things? I ask this question not to answer it here, but to suggest one of the conditions under which Black lives begin to matter to Japanese literary studies: namely, a re-imagining of the terminologies, methodologies, and epistemologies by which we study Japanese literature, one by which, for example, the aesthetics of Japanese literary blackness speak to and help make sense of the aesthetics of blackness and the mattering of Black lives writ large wherever the sensations of Black life make themselves palpable.

Although I hope the emphasis above falls on the condition (an openness to methodological transformation) rather than the example (the possibility of "aesthetic" readings alongside textual readings of blackness in Japanese literature) by which Black lives begin to matter to Japanese literary studies, I do find this particular example to be revelatory. For another condition under which Black lives have traditionally mattered to Japanese literature is as an object of misery. If we are willing to entertain aesthetic approaches to the blackness of Japanese literature, there is something we must confront. Here is the confrontation: although a work of literature can be many things, one of the things it can be is a record of and response to human suffering. Modern Japanese literature often makes a self-soothing turn of this confrontation, with Black lives mattering not on their own terms, but only under the condition that its simulation of Black pain somehow speaks to Japan's cultural concerns and anxieties. Modern Japanese literature is replete with examples of opportunistic aesthetics of Black pain and suffering—the hatchet through the skull in Ōe Kenzaburō's "Shiiku"; the neo-slavery of Numa Shōzō's *Kachikujin Yapū*; the cirrhotic livers of Rick and William and the other Black alcoholics of Yamada Eimi's oeuvre[14]; the martyrdom of the Black mother, Sister Krone, who is eaten alive by ravenous demons in Shirai Kaiu and Demizu Posuka's *The Promised Neverland*. On the terms of this trope, Black lives matter only as a kind of synecdochal reminder of the limits of human cruelty and capacity to suffer, with Japanese bodies buffered just beyond the imagined suffering.

I am interested here, however, less in the yesteryear tropes by which Black lives have conditionally mattered and more in the possibility of Black lives mattering *unconditionally*. That is to say, what would Japanese literary studies look like if Black lives mattered even when they do not adhere to the methodological mandates of the discipline, or when they are simply being rather than suffering? How might we reconfigure and reimage our fields of study such that Black lives matter unconditionally, both to Japanese literary studies and beyond? Is such reconfiguration possible?

Let me be clear here. Unconditional mattering is more of an ideal than an actuality. In practice, unconditional mattering is—like unconditional love and other such unconditionals—predicated on the unspoken condition of continued existence. Even our unconditional lovers cannot love us in death, hence death doing us part. We might think here of the promise of the title (rather than the content) of author Murakami Ryū's writings of blackness, which calls for *kagirinaku tōmei ni chikai* imaginaries, or imaginaries as asymptotically close to the things we imagine as possible. In this light, the things we refer to as unconditionals are the alignment of a set of conditions as asymptotically close to unconditionality as the realities of a moment in history can bear. In other words, unconditional mattering occurs conditionally, with the first of these conditions being the survival of the thing that matters. There are relatively few things that can be done both unconditionally and posthumously. So too with the mattering of Black lives: Black lives cannot truly matter once they have passed away, for once they have passed these lives are no longer lives. To say that Black lives matter is to (among other commitments) make a commitment to their ongoing vitality and existential flourishing: life is one of the conditions upon which the mattering of Black lives is predicated.

To ask, then, if it is possible for Black lives to matter unconditionally to Japanese literary studies is, from a theoretical standpoint, a kind of shorthand. The longhand question is this: how might we reconfigure and reimage our fields of study such that Black lives both continue to flourish existentially and matter unconditionally to our studies? Under which conditions might the mattering of Black lives to Japanese literary studies come as asymptotically close to unconditional significance as possible?

The first thing to note here is that reimaging and reconfiguration is possible. The organization of academic units are reflections of the people, institutions, and logics in power at the time of their organization. I have written elsewhere on what I call fragmented epistemologies, by which I mean the ways in which the parallel post-World War II formations of area studies and ethnic studies in the American academy disconnected the cognitive labor of race and ethnic studies from that of area and Asian studies.[15] This configuration—which naturalizes the epistemological severing of the cognitive labor of a field such as Black studies from a field such as Asian studies—is a reflection of the people, institutions, and logics in power at the time of the organization of these fields. In turn, this historical formation emerges as a present in which, to borrow Shu-mei Shih's articulation, Asian Studies rarely investigates its racial unconscious, or what Shih calls the "open secret"—"that there is a dearth of African American or other non-Asian minority scholars in Asian studies"[16]—underwritten by the unspoken racial logic by which Asian Studies organized itself.

But other histories, and, as such, other unactualized possibilities for our present configuration of Japanese literary studies are available to us. I have in mind here the model provided by Black studies in Japan. The first meeting of the *Kokujin kenkyū no kai* (The Japanese Association for Negro Studies, now the Japanese Black Studies Association) was held on June 22, 1954. Gathered at their headquarters at the Kobe City University of Foreign Studies, the original eight members of the Association were adamant that their view be transnational, that they study the conditions of Black life not only in America—conditions which they saw as consonant with their own given the Allied occupation—but that they study Black life unconditionally, in the Americas, Africa, Asia, Europe and any place Black life might flourish.

This vision was led by Nukina Yoshitaka, professor of American literature and culture and the founder of Japan's Association for Negro Studies. Nukina's organization of the Association for Negro Studies was predicated on his understanding that an attempt to ensure the existence of a democratic Japan (read: a Japan whose future would not look like its fascist past) required the nation to turn its attention toward Black studies. Nukina had seen the atrocities of occupied Java as a conscript of the Imperial Japanese Army, and he had read the 1944 Japanese translation of Du Bois's *The Negro*, in which Du Bois reminds us that "there were half a million slaves in the confines of the United States when the Declaration of Independence declared 'that all men are created equal.'"[17] In his history of the formation of the Japanese Association for Negro Studies, Furukawa Hiromi (a former student of Nukina, founding member of the Association, and prolific scholar of Afro-Japanese history in his own right) noted that the Association took up "Black studies in an age when the field had yet to be inaugurated in the United States" because the field offered "a kind of metric for the attainability of American democracy."[18] And this metric, in turn, provides an invaluable measurement not just for postwar Japan, but for the world. This is why, as Furukawa notes elsewhere, the Association's charter did not include "any limitation on the geographical reach of its object of study," which both "positioned the association to respond flexibly" to the question of blackness the world over and to grow the Association's circle of members limitlessly.[19]

In thinking toward the possibility of a historical precedent for the unconditional mattering of Black lives to Japanese literary studies, it is important to recall this: the Association's refusal to place limiting conditions on its geopolitical configuration and requirements for membership was informed by Nukina's near lifelong dedication to Esperanto. Nukina began teaching himself Esperanto at age 12. Five years later, he joined the Osaka Esperanto Study Group, and he would join Japan's national Esperanto society, *Nihon Esperanto Gakkai*, in 1935. Esperanto in Japan had long held a kind of gravitational pull for Japan's intellectual left and its vision of a *lingua franca* of worldwide peace and solidarity, but, in the war's aftermath, and with the Allied opening of political discourse, the Japanese Communist Party (JCP) took an acute interest in Esperanto. The postwar Esperantists attracted by this gravitational pull formed the Japan Esperanto Association, which was affiliated with the Party by way of the Japan Democratic Culture League, an umbrella organization for the JCP's network of popular front cultural activities and associations. In the immediate postwar years, Nukina was the head of his prefectural branch of the Japan Esperanto Association in Hyogo. And, when a red purge culminated in the dissolution of the Japan Esperanto Association in 1950, Nukina was a founding force and inaugural head of the Kansai Esperanto League in 1951.

Nukina's stewardship of the Kansai Esperanto League, then, occurred concomitantly with his work to establish the Association for "Negro" Studies. The very formation of the Association for Negro Studies in Japan is shot through with Esperantist sensibility. The Association's very organization as an "association" (*kai* in Japanese) open to the public and anyone interested in Black studies rather than as a purely scholastic society, its lack of an official director during its inaugural years, its focus on collaborative translations of works of Black literature into Japanese—in both logistics and logics, the Association for Negro Studies was informed by a JCP-style vision of Esperanto.

The importance of this piece of history is right there in the language's name: etymologically, the Esperantist is one who hopes, one who speaks hope into being by way of the imagining of new languages and the creation of new communities. The creation of an association for Black studies in Japan, then, was intertwined with a desire for a universal language of hope, an open-door, transnational community of those longing for a way to articulate our shared humanity. This is precisely the hope harbored by Ludwik Zamenhof, the initiator of Esperanto. The objective of Esperanto was, in Zamenhof's vision, never to achieve the perfect language. Rather, the objective was to create a community of radical cosmopolitanism around the shared project of the democratic creation of a universal language. Esperanto was "only a fraction of a larger project," a project toward, in Zamenhof's words "the unification of humanity in one fraternal family."[20] This project is what Zamenhof called in his opening address to the Second Esperanto Congress the "inner idea" of Esperanto. Those hoping for this inner idea "will not be afraid when the world jeers at them and calls them utopian . . . They will be proud to be called utopians. At every new congress, their love for the internal idea of Esperantism will be stronger, and little by little our annual congress will be a constant celebration of humanity and of human brotherhood."[21]

For even someone with an understanding of Esperanto as rudimentary as mine, it is clear that the lexicology of the language itself is imbued with this inner idea. One *has* a mother tongue, an organic language claimed as possession and personal property on the condition of *jus sanguinis*. One *participates* in Esperanto, a cyborganic, modular language whose only condition for participation is that very participation itself. This participation entails learning roots, but also realizing that these roots are almost infinitely recombinable. After this realization, one attaches grammatical endings, prefixes, and suffixes to these roots pragmatically, creating a potentially endless flow of neologisms in order to meet the ever-evolving communicative needs of the language community as they expand eternally into unknown futures. This design is proffered in hope of a universal language with the flexibility to accept any new member, foreseen or unforeseen, whom the community might encounter unconditionally.

If I see the "inner idea" of Esperanto at the rudimentary level, I can only assume that Nukina envisioned it with his mastery, and that his vision is in part why he modeled the Association for Negro Studies on Esperanto circles. We might call this Nukina's Esperantic (read: hopeful) vision for Black studies in Japan. The unconditional hope of the Esperantist—or more accurately, a hopefulness predicated only on the condition of the ongoing existence of the hopeful and those for whom one holds hope—reverberates. It reverberates across the new languages and communities it creates. Such reverberations channel the mattering of Black lives through the Japanese Association of Black Studies and to modern Japanese literature. When a young Ōe Kenzaburō speaks at an Association conference on the "qualitative similarities"[22] of Black and Japanese literatures, or when Kojima Nobuo imbues his writing of the fraught dynamics of US–Japanese race relations with the lessons he learned with Association interlocutors, or when the poetry of Kijima Hajime resonates with his friendship with and epistles to and from and translations of Langston Hughes, or when the authors who collaborated on *Mayonaka no toritachi*, a collection of Japanese translations of Black women's literature, return to their own writing in Japanese—each of these are the precedent of the possibility of the unconditional mattering of Black lives reverberating from the Association to Japanese literature.

Some readers might wonder if the precedent I point to here is too utopian. Perhaps they are right. But I understand Zamenhof's notion of utopia by way of Ruth Levitas. For Levitas, "utopia is . . . necessarily characterized by failure—but this is a feature in its favour, not an argument against it. *Utopia is a method rather than a plan, a process rather than a goal.*"[23] Rather than an idealized vision of perfection, utopia here is the method by which collectives imagine, critique, and work toward possible futures, futures which have the potential to be better than our present realities.

It is with this in mind—namely, that "utopia" as I understand it gestures not toward a state of being but a method of channeling desire for better ways of being together into transformative action, that is, of guiding labor practices (intellectual or otherwise)—that I have asked the question I ask. Do Black lives *still* matter to Japanese literary studies, with emphasis now on "still," or the ongoing work that remains to be done? In the wake of the murder of George Floyd, their mattering seemed undeniable. But do they *still* matter today, as the BLM lawn signs fade away and our collective attention turns to the multiple crises before us? If they do still matter, we should ensure their longevity with systemic reconfiguration, by writing the ways in which they matter into the very structures and foundations of our institutional organizations. In a word, if Black lives still matter to Japanese literary studies, we should instill their mattering.

Della Mosley and her colleagues have written of what they call radical hope, which entails "envisioning equitable possibilities, and understanding histories of oppression along with the actions of resistance taken to transform these conditions."[24] If Black lives matter unconditionally to Japanese literature, we are in need of radical hope coupled with the radical action and transformations such hope inspires. Wendy Wheeler writes that "meaning is always a kind of doing. The meaning of a sign is to be found in the changes . . . it brings about."[25] What is true of Wheeler's sign is true of the signs of blackness in Japanese literature. To interpret is to act: one measure of the meaning of a sign is the transformations it inspires.

My emphasis here is on action and transformation: if Black lives matter unconditionally to Japanese literary studies, this mattering should reconfigure the very research, curricula, and institution practices of Japanese literary studies. One might imagine any number of transformations, from requirements to take race and ethnicity proseminars in Japanese studies doctoral programs (I fulfilled a doctoral requirement by taking a course in French; I can only imagine that theoretical literacy in conceptualizations of race and ethnicity is at least as beneficial to the intellectual formation of a Japanese literary scholar as French literacy) to commitments to support the growth of Japanese studies programs at HBCUs and recruit students and scholars from this newly formed pipeline. These are simply examples. I will leave the imagining of the particulars of such programmatic transformation to the communities who agree to take up the work of instilling the mattering of Black lives. For my aim here is not to set the conditions upon which Black lives matter to Japanese literary studies. It is instead to adumbrate—an adumbration which is one-part historical reminder and one-part open invitation—the possibility that Black lives have long mattered to Japanese literary studies, and that one day, depending on our action, they might still matter simply on the condition of their ongoing survival.

Notes

1. Kanagaki Robun, *Seiyō dōchū hizakurige*, 254.
2. Nagai Kafū, *Amerika monogatari*, 209–10.
3. See Natsume Sōseki, *Sanshirō*.
4. See Miyamoto Yuriko, "Watashi no mita Beikoku no shounen" and "Desudemouna no hankachiifu."
5. Ema Shū, "Kokujin no kyōdai."
6. See Tanizaki Jun'ichirō, *In'ei raisan*.
7. See Ariyoshi Sawako, *Hishoku*.
8. See Tawada Yōko, "Kageotoko."
9. See John Dower, *War Without Mercy: Race and Power in the Pacific War*.
10. Wole Soyinka, as cited in Janheinz Jahn, *Neo-African Literature: A History of Black Writing*, 265–66.
11. Michael Bourdaghs, ed., *The Linguistic Turn in Contemporary Japanese Literary Studies*, dust jacket.
12. Katya Mandoki, *Everyday Aesthetics: Prosaics, the Play of Culture and Social Identities*, 48.
13. See Caroline Levine, *The Activist Humanist: Form and Method in the Climate Crisis*.
14. See Yamada Eimi, *Torasshu* and *Payday!!!*
15. See "Introduction: Do Black Lives Matter for Asian Studies?" in *Who Is the Asianist? The Politics of Representation in Asian Studies*.
16. Shu-mei Shih, "Racializing Area Studies, Defetishizing China," 45.
17. W. E. B. Du Bois, *The Negro*, 110, 146.
18. Hiromi Furukawa and Tetsushi Furukawa, Nihonjin to Afurika-kei Amerikajin: Nichi-Bei kankeishi ni okeru sono shosō, 13.
19. Hiromi Furukawa, "Sōsetsu 40 shūnen ni mukete: Kaiko to kadai," 2.
20. Roberto Garvía, *Esperanto and Its Rivals: The Struggle for an International Language*, 88–89.
21. Garvía, 90.
22. Ōe Kenzaburō, "Konnan no kankaku nitsuite—Wa ga sosaku taiken," 94.
23. Ruth Levitas, "Where There Is No Vision, the People Perish: A Utopian Ethic for a Transformed Future," 9, my emphasis.
24. Della Mosley, "Radical Hope in Revolting Times: Proposing a Culturally Relevant Psychological Framework," abstract.
25. Wendy Wheeler, "The Lightest Burden: The Aesthetic Abductions of Biosemiotics," 22.

References

Ariyoshi, Sawako. *Hishoku*. Kadokawa, 1999.

Bourdaghs, Michael, ed. *The Linguistic Turn in Contemporary Japanese Literary Studies: Politics, Language, Textuality*. University of Michigan Press, 2010.

Bridges, Will, Marvin Sterling, and Nitasha Sharma, eds. *Who Is the Asianist? The Politics of Representation in Asian Studies*. Columbia University Press, 2022.

Dower, John. *War Without Mercy: Race and Power in the Pacific War*. Pantheon Books, 1993.

Du Bois, W. E. B. *The Negro*. Cosimo Classics, 2007.

Ema, Shū. "Kokujin no kyōdai." *Nihon puroretaria bungakushū*, vol. 16, 319–38. Shin Nihon Shuppansha, 1984.

Furukawa, Hiromi. "Sōsetsu 40 shūnen ni mukete: Kaiko to kadai." *Kokujin kenkyū*, vol. 63, 1992.

Furukawa, Hiromi, and Tetsushi Furukawa. *Nihonjin to Afurika-kei Amerikajin: Nichi-Bei kankeishi ni okeru sono shosō*. Akashi Shoten, 2004.

Garvía, Roberto. *Esperanto and Its Rivals: The Struggle for an International Language*. University of Pennsylvania Press, 2015.

Iwaki, Kei. *Sayonara, Orenji*. Chikuma shobo, 2013.

Jahn, Janheinz. *Neo-African Literature: A History of Black Writing*. Grove Press, 1968.

Kanagaki, Robun. *Seiyō dōchū hizakurige*. In *Kanagaki Robun*, edited by Tsubouchi Yūzō, 3–266. Chikuma Shobo, 2002.

Levine, Caroline. *The Activist Humanist: Form and Method in the Climate Crisis*. Princeton University Press, 2023.

Levitas, Ruth. "Where There Is No Vision, the People Perish: A Utopian Ethic for a Transformed Future." Accessed February 12, 2024. https://cusp.ac.uk/wp-content/uploads/05-Ruth-Levitas-Essay-online.pdf

Mandoki, Katya. *Everyday Aesthetics: Prosaics, the Play of Culture and Social Identities*. Ashgate, 2007.

Matsuoka, Kazuko, ed. *Mayonaka no toritachi: Onnatachi no dōjidai*. Asahi Shinbunsha, 1982.

Miyamoto, Yuriko. "Desudemōna no hankachiifu." *Aozora Bunko*. Accessed February 12, 2024. www.aozora.gr.jp/cards/000311/files/2985_10087.html

Miyamoto, Yuriko. "Watashi No Mita Beikoku No Shōnen." *Aozora Bunko*. Accessed February 12, 2024. www.aozora.gr.jp/cards/000311/files/3693_13081.html

Mosley, Della, et al. "Radical Hope in Revolting Times: Proposing a Culturally Relevant Psychological Framework." *Social and Personality Psychology Compass* 14, issue 1, 2019.

Murakami, Ryū. *Kagirinaku tōmei ni chikai burū*. Kōdansha bunko, 1978.

Nagai, Kafū. *Amerika monogatari. Gendai Nihon bungaku zenshū* (*Nagai Kafū shū*), vol. 22, 175–280. Kaizōsha, 1927.

Natsume, Sōseki. *Sanshirō*. Iwanami Shoten, 1938.

Numa, Shōzō. *Kachikujin Yapū*. Gentōsha, 2014.

Ōe, Kenzaburō. "Konnan no kankaku ni tsuite—Wa ga sosaku taiken." *Bungaku* 31, no. 11 (1963): 1267–72.

Ōe, Kenzaburō. "Shiiku." *Shisha no ogori, Shiiku*, 89–160. Shinchōsha, 2013.

Shih, Shu-mei. "Racializing Area Studies, Defetishizing China." *positions: asia critique* 27, no. 1 (2019): 33–65.

Shirai Kaiu. *The Promised Neverland.* Viz Media, 2017.

Tanizaki, Jun'ichirō. *In'ei raisan.* Chūkō, 1933.

Tawada, Yōko. "Kageotoko." *Futakuchiotoko, 59–108.* Kawade shobo, 1998.

Wheeler, Wendy. "The Lightest Burden: The Aesthetic Abductions of Biosemiotics." In *Handbook of Ecocriticism and Cultural Ecology*, edited by Hubert Zapf, 19–44. De Gruyter, 2016.

Yamada, Eimi. *Payday!!!.* Shinchōsha, 2003.

Yamada, Eimi. *Torasshu.* Bungei Shunju, 1991.

CHAPTER 4

Ecocritical Precedent, Present, and Possibility in Japanese Literary Studies

Jon L. Pitt

Introduction

The year 2018 saw the publication of *Ecocriticism in Japan*, a collected volume edited by Hisaaki Wake, Keijiro Suga, and Yuki Masami. As the first book-length collection to announce itself as an ecocritical study of Japanese literature and visual media writ large, *Ecocriticism in Japan* is a convenient starting point to discuss the status of ecocriticism within the bilateral field of Japanese literary studies (both in the US and Japan). In his review, Gregory Golley claims that *Ecocriticism in Japan* answered "a growing need in Japan studies."[1] As a graduate student trying to conceptualize an ecocritical project in 2018, I felt this "growing need" acutely.

As I entered graduate school, ecocriticism felt alive and well in disciplines around me. Exciting things were happening in the 2010s. Multispecies ethnographies like Eduardo Kohn's *How Forests Think* (2013) and Anna Tsing's *The Mushroom at the End of the World* (2015) signaled a turn toward the more-than-human world in Anthropology. The emergence of the Anthropocene as a framework to rethink humans as geological agents pointed toward an interdisciplinary approach that could help bridge the gap between literary studies and the physical sciences, as seen in works like Rob Nixon's *Slow Violence and the Environmentalism of the Poor* (2011). Media studies were also experiencing an environmental turn, led in part by John Durham Peters's *The Marvelous Clouds: Toward a Philosophy of Elemental Media* (2015).

I read these works and attempted to use their insights in my own research, but I had the sense that Japanese literary studies was perhaps not as invested in ecocritical/environmental questions as were these other disciplines. To be sure, there *was* an active ecocritical scene developing in Japanese literary studies in the mid- to late-2010s, but it was almost entirely focused on the March 11, 2011 triple disaster of earthquake, tsunami, and nuclear meltdown at Fukushima Daiichi Nuclear Power Plant ("3.11" for short). While I was drawn to this new ecocritical turn in Japanese literary studies after 3.11, I struggled to find scholars working on environmental approaches outside of a 3.11 framework. Critical scholarship on 3.11 was (and remains) vital, but was it, I wondered, the only viable environmental topic in the study of Japanese literature?

Around the same time, I witnessed what felt like a renaissance in Japanese environmental history. Between Brett Walker's *Toxic Archipelago* (2010), the 2013 collected volume *Japan at Nature's Edge* (co-edited by Walker, Ian Miller, and Julia Adeney Thomas), and Robert Stolz's *Bad Water* (2014), historians of Japan were increasingly embracing non-anthropocentric modes of interpretation beyond the scope of 3.11. Historians of Japan had Conrad Totman's 1989 classic *The Green Archipelago*—an environmental history of forestry in Japan stretching back to the 7th century—as a kind of guiding star. I longed for something similar in Japanese literary studies, but nothing seemed to hold the kind of esteem and influence that Totman's work held over environmental historians of Japan.

But *Ecocriticism in Japan* signaled that a broader environmental turn could be just around the corner. Its publication made visible a concerted effort by scholars from both Japan and North America to address the urgent need for more ecocritical work on Japanese literature (and media more broadly). This effort is ongoing. Although significant efforts are being made to bring the study of Japanese literature into the fold of the environmental humanities, there is much more work to be done.[2] I agree with John Whittier Treat's claim in his chapter in this volume that "Eco-criticism is the most promising area of Japanese literary studies today," and so I intend to point to some ecocritical possibilities that remain un- or under-explored in our field. But I also want to show that, indeed, much more ecocritical work already *has been done* than I had realized at the time of *Ecocriticism in Japan*'s publication. While that volume was the first to adopt the words "ecocriticism" and "Japan" in its title, it was far from the first work of ecocritical scholarship on Japanese literature. In what follows, I offer a partial genealogy of works that predated and that have since followed its publication. Although incomplete, I hope such a genealogy can offer insight onto where Japanese literary studies has been, where it is currently, and where it could end up in terms of ecocritical approaches.

Ecocritical Precedent

Ecocriticism emerged as a viable approach to the study of literature in the 1990s, largely in response to a growing concern over environmental crisis. In *The Ecocriticism Reader* (1996), Cheryll Glotfelty points to the creation of the Association for the Study of Literature and Environment (ASLE), which she co-founded in 1992, as evidence of ecocriticism's newfound status as "a recognizable critical school."[3] ASLE-Japan—ASLE's first international branch—was formed only two years later, in 1994. By 1998, ASLE-Japan was publishing its own journal, *Literature and Environment* (*Bungaku to kankyō*), featuring articles that applied an ecocritical lens to literatures both Euroamerican and Japanese. It would appear, then, that Japanese literary studies was an early adopter of ecocriticism. But according to Yuki Masami, one of Japan's foremost ecocritics, this was not the case. In the *Oxford Handbook of Ecocriticism* (2014), Yuki claims that "it has taken a long time for ecocriticism to spread its roots deeply in Japan's literary and cultural soil" and suggests this is "because the distinction between ecocriticism and thematic literary studies concerning nature has not been clearly perceived" in Japan.[4] Her point is that precisely because Japan has "a thousand-year-old literary tradition of paying attention to nature," scholars are apt to mistake conventional approaches to Japanese literature as "ecocritical" even if they do not adopt ecocritical frameworks.[5] Such is the case with Haruo Shirane's *Japan and the Culture of the Four Seasons* (2012)—a work unquestionably concerned with the writing of nature in Japanese literature, but one that is not invested in making an ecocritical intervention per se.

Yuki identifies three stages in the development of ecocriticism in Japan: an initial stage from the early 1990s to 2000 in which foundational texts of ecocriticism were translated into Japanese, a second, "comparativist" phase in the 2000s where scholars of non-Japanese literature applied ecocritical theories to Japanese literature, and a third phase beginning in the late aughts "characterized by a cross-fertilization between ecocriticism and Japanese literary studies."[6] In her introduction to *Ecocriticism in Japan*, Yuki notes that the essays collected in that 2018 volume "materialize" the third phase in her historiography. While I do not intend to challenge Yuki's timeline, I do wish to highlight several works that fall outside these parameters to demonstrate that scholars in Japanese literary studies have had an investment in ecocriticism for decades.

The first text that deserves attention as an early work of ecocriticism on Japanese literature is Karen Colligan-Taylor's *The Emergence of Environmental Literature in Japan* (1990).[7] Colligan-Taylor was ahead of the curve. Her book features a chapter on Miyazawa Kenji, who has become a mainstay of ecocritical scholarship, and includes a translation of Kenji's "Wolf Forest, Basket Forest, Thief Forest" (*Oinomori to zarumori, nusutomori*), which went on to receive ecocritical treatment by Kota Inoue and Gregory Golley in the following decade. Eight years after her book, Colligan-Taylor would revisit Kenji's work in "Miyazawa Kenji's Work Invites Ecocriticism"—the first article in the first issue of ASLE-Japan's *Literature and Environment* journal. Colligan-Taylor also includes, in her book, a chapter on "environmental consciousness" in Japanese science fiction, demonstrating an early awareness that Sci-Fi has important things to say about environmental crisis—a claim currently being explored in research on Climate Fiction.

Perhaps the most forward-thinking element of Colligan-Taylor's book is its attention to environmental destruction vis-à-vis the 19th century Ashio Copper Mine disaster and the industrial methyl mercury poisoning of the Minamata Bay. The book devotes a chapter to Ishimure Michiko's *Paradise in the Sea of Sorrow: Our Minamata Disease* (*Kugai jōdo: waga Minamatabyō*, 1969), a work that continues to draw significant attention in ecocritical scholarship for its poetic documentation of Minamata Disease. Twenty-six years after the publication of Colligan-Taylor's book, and only two years before the publication of *Ecocriticism in Japan*, Yuki Masami would publish, with co-editor Bruce Allen, a collected volume titled *Ishimure Michiko's Writing in Ecocritical Perspective: Between Sea and Sky* (2015). The following year, Christine Marran published her excellent monograph *Ecology Without Culture: Aesthetics for a Toxic World* (2017), which discusses Ishimure at length. The fact the Marran's book stands as one of the best works of ecocriticism in the field to date speaks to the importance of Ishimure's work as a lasting generative force.

Colligan-Taylor was not alone in her interest in Ishimure in the late 1980s. In 1989, Livia Monnet published a lengthy examination of Ishimure in her two-part essay in *Japan Forum* on autobiographical texts by modern Japanese women writers. While not as obviously ecocritical as her later work, Monnet's reading of Ishimure in this early essay draws significant attention to the intersection of gender and environment. And even before this essay, Monnet was helping shape the direction of ecocriticism in Japanese literary studies by translating Ishimure's work into English. In 1982, Monnet published her translation of Ishimure's *Story of the Sea of Camellias* (*Tsubaki no umi no ki*, 1976). Eight years later, she would publish her groundbreaking full translation of *Paradise in the Sea of Sorrow*.[8]

We can see Monnet's work as part of Yuki's "first phase" of ecocriticism in Japan, the one defined by translation. But what makes Monnet's translation of *Paradise in the Sea of Sorrow* so significant is that it subverts Yuki's timeline by bringing a work of Japanese ecocriticism into English language scholarship, rather than the other way around. For *Paradise in the Sea of Sorrow* is an ecocritical text in its own right, in much the same way that Rachel Carson's *Silent Spring* is considered a work of ecocriticism. It's no surprise, then, that Ishimure is often referred to as "Japan's Rachel Carson." Monnet's work bringing Ishimure into translation (and thus into classrooms for decades now) has had a lasting impact on later generations of ecocritical scholars working on Japanese literature, illustrating Jeffrey Angles's point in his chapter in this volume that "translations can reshape the entire field by providing readers, students, and budding scholars with new forays into authors, subject matter, and issues." Japanese literary studies may not have had its own Conrad Totman, but it has had its own Ishimure Michiko, thanks in part to Monnet.

And if we grant translation of ecocritical texts the status of ecocritical scholarship, then Kyoko and Lili Selden's 1994 translation of Kayano Shigeru's autobiography *Our Land Was a Forest* (*Ainu no ishibumi*, 1990) also fits within the early period of ecocritical precedent. *Our Land Was a Forest* depicts Kayano's experience growing up on Japan's northernmost main island of Hokkaido as a member of the island's Indigenous people, the Ainu. Kayano's attention to the relationship between Japanese settler colonialism and environmental exploitation aligns with the current environmental humanities interest in TEK (or Traditional Ecological Knowledge). Although it has not had the kind of impact on ecocritical scholarship that Ishimure's work has, the importance of *Our Land Was a Forest* is only becoming more evident as anthropologists like ann-elise lewallen bring scholarly attention to the consequences of settler colonialism on Hokkaido.

While it would take years for another ecocritical monograph to appear in Japanese literary studies, journal articles and conferences devoted to ecocriticism and Japanese literature appeared throughout the early to mid-2000s. Of particular importance to Yuki's timeline were the 2003 international symposium in Okinawa and the 2007 Japan-Korea joint symposium in Kanazawa, both hosted by ASLE-Japan. Publications emerged from both events: *Dialogue between Nature and Literature* (*Shizen to bungaku no daiarōgu*, 2004) from the former and *Poetics of Place* (*Basho no shigaku*, 2008) from the latter.

The following decade saw ASLE-Japan continuing this trend; in 2014 it published *Thinking the Environment through Literature: an Ecocriticism Guidebook* (*Bungaku kara kankyō wo kangaeru: ekokuriteishizumu gaidobukku*), a wide-ranging collection of essays, translations, and scholarly conversations (or *taidan*) that commemorated the 20th anniversary of the organization's founding and featured selected essays previously published in ASLE-Japan's journal, including Colligan-Taylor's essay on Miyazawa Kenji.

If Colligan-Taylor's attention to Kenji in the 1990s marked one of Japanese literary studies' first forays into ecocriticism, then Gregory Golley's treatment of Kenji's writing in his *When Our Eyes No Longer See: Realism, Science, and Ecology in Japanese Literary Modernism* (2008) marks an important step forward in the field. Golley's project rethinks the meaning of "realism" in Japanese modernist literature through a deep engagement with contemporaneous science. Three of the book's six chapters are devoted to Kenji, and each one discusses the writer's work through a different scientific lens. Some may take issue with my calling Golley's work ecocritical. Yuki, for example, has argued that "ecocriticism characteristically accompanies a concern about environmental crises, while literary study of nature does not necessarily imply such awareness."[9] Yuki is right in asserting that ecocriticism developed in response to environmental crisis, but it has, in my estimation, moved beyond this paradigm to challenge anthropocentric views of the environment that fall outside the realm of crisis. *When Our Eyes No Longer See* is an example of such a work. And as it argues outside the characteristic frame of environmental crisis to make an environmental argument about the relationship between literature and science, it anticipates the interdisciplinary work currently being done in the environmental humanities.

The last monograph I wish to highlight in this period of ecocritical precedent is Karen Laura Thornber's *Ecoambiguity: Environmental Crises and East Asian Literatures* (2012). Thornber's scope is staggering; at nearly 700 pages, the book discusses literary texts not only from Japan, but also from Korea, China, and Taiwan. The Japan portion reads like an "ecocriticism guidebook" of its own and covers everything from poetry of the 8th century *Man'yōshū* to Nitta Jirō's historical fiction to the Sci-Fi of Tsutsui Yasutaka. As such, it is a valuable resource for anyone looking to explore Japanese environmental literature. It also does important work in disabusing readers of the trenchant notion that Japan has long maintained a harmonious relationship to the natural world—a misconception that scholars have been attempting to correct for decades, from Pamela Asquith and Arne Kalland in their 1996 volume *Japanese Images of Nature* to Yuki Masami herself, in her introduction to *Ecocriticism in Japan*, which is titled "On Harmony with Nature: Toward Japanese Ecocriticism."

Published only one year after 3.11, *Ecoambiguity* makes references to the triple disaster but does not discuss what has since been theorized as "Post-3.11 Literature." For this reason, I have chosen Thornber's book as the end of the "precedent" period. *Ecoambiguity* reads like a text right on the cusp of a major change—one ushered in by significant and pervasive ecocritical responses to 3.11. It is this change that marks our arrival at the "ecocritical present."

Ecocritical Present

3.11 has had a major impact on the field of ecocriticism in Japanese studies. Worldwide attention to the environmental devastation and irradiation of Northeastern Japan spurred many scholars to adopt ecocritical methodologies to help make sense of the unfolding crises. The insights gained by several decades of ecocritical work were suddenly, and tragically, made visible in the aftermath of 3.11, and Japanese literary studies found a new focus in its wake. *Ecocriticism in Japan*, for example, features several chapters devoted to 3.11, including essays by Margherita Long on Ōe Kenzaburō's post-Fukushima activism and Doug Slaymaker on Furukawa Hideo's 2011 novel *Horses, Horses, in the End the Light Remains Pure* (*Umatachi yo, sore demo hikari wa muku de*). And *Ecocriticism in Japan* was only one of several volumes to feature responses to 3.11. Other examples include the Roy Starrs-edited *When the Tsunami Came to Shore* (2014) and *Literature and Art After "Fukushima": Four Approaches*, also published in 2014 and co-edited by Yuki Masami and Lisette Gebhart. In 2014 there was also a special issue of *Japan Forum* titled "Beyond Fukushima: Culture, Media, and Meaning from Catastrophe." Edited by Jonathan Abel, the issue included essays by William Gardner on Komatsu Sakyō and Rachel DiNitto on post-Fukushima literature more generally. DiNitto appeared again in a 2017 volume titled *Fukushima and the Arts* (edited by Barbara Geilhorn and Kristina Iwata-Weickgenannt), which includes contributions from leading scholars working on 3.11, foremost among them Kimura Saeko.

Kimura has arguably contributed the most significant scholarship on literary responses to 3.11 to date. In 2013, she published *A Theory of Post-3.11 Literature: Toward a New Japanese Literature* (*Shinsaigo bungakuron: Atarashii Nihon bungaku no tame ni*) and followed it up in 2018 with *A Theory of Post-3.11 Literature After That* (*Sono go no shinsaigo bungakuron*). Kimura argues that far from (eco)ambiguity toward the crisis, literature written in response to 3.11 is infused with anxiety over radiation and its unknowability. She identifies a new genre of post-disaster literature in Japan, and I suggest, in turn, that 3.11 has likewise ushered in a new field: "Post-3.11 Literary Studies." The above-mentioned volumes belong to this field, as do several full-length monographs, including DiNitto's *Fukushima Fiction: the Literary Landscape of Japan's Triple Disaster* and Koichi Haga's *The Earth Writes: The Great Earthquake and the Novel in Post-3/11 Japan*, both published in 2019.

Post-3.11 Literary Studies has been aided by several translations into English, including Ted Goosen and Motoyuki Shibata's translation of Kawakami Hiromi's "God Bless You, 2011" (*Kamisama 2011*), a short story about a talking bear that Kawakami rewrote after 3.11. The story is included in *March Was Made of Yarn: Reflections on the Japanese Earthquake, Tsunami, and Nuclear Meltdown* (2012), a volume that also includes translations of prominent writers like Yōko Tawada, Kawakami Mieko, and Murakami Ryū. In the July 2011 issue of *Asia-Pacific Journal*, Jeffrey Angles published his translation of Wagō Ryōichi's "Pebbles of Poetry" (*Shi no koishi*, 2011), a poetry collection written in response to 3.11 via Twitter. Raj Mahtani's translation of Taguchi Randy's *Riku and the Kingdom of White* (*Riku to shira no ōkoku*, 2015), about a young boy who moves to Fukushima after the disaster, was published in 2016. In 2019, Doug Slaymaker published a collection of two 3.11-related novellas by Kimura Yūsuke titled *Sacred Cesium Ground and Isa's Deluge: Two Novellas of Japan's 3/11 Disaster*. Three years earlier, in 2016, Slaymaker and Akiko Takenaka published their translation of Furukawa Hideo's *Horses, Horses, in the End the Light Remains Pure*—the novel Slaymaker discusses in his chapter in *Ecocriticism in Japan*. A fierce and complex work, *Horses* reads the events of 3.11 into a deeper history of economic marginalization of Japan's Tōhoku region. Yū Miri's *Tokyo Ueno Station* (*JR Uenokōen-guchi*, 2014) does something similar, but casts its tale through the eyes of a ghost reflecting on a life lived among crises. The success of Morgan Giles's 2019 translation of *Tokyo Ueno Station* demonstrates that there is international interest in 3.11 literature.

There are promising new interventions into the field of Post-3.11 Literary Studies. The "Imagining Post 3.11 Futures and Living with Anthropogenic Change" conference, organized by Daniel O'Neill at UC Berkeley in 2020, brought together an interdisciplinary group of scholars that included Livia Monnet, Toshiya Ueno, Kimura Saeko, and Margherita Long. Long's forthcoming monograph on 3.11 literature, documentary film, and activism takes Post-3.11 Literary Studies into new ground, away from the conventional biopolitics that have dominated previous scholarship. Kimura, in turn, continues to push things in new directions, even as she expresses concern over the state of the field. In 2021, Kimura co-edited a volume with Anne Bayard-Sakai titled *"Post-3.11 Literature" as World Literature* (*Sekai bungaku toshite no "Shinsaigo bungaku,"* 2021). The book contains essays from scholars like O'Neill, Long, and DiNitto, along with prominent novelist Itō Seikō. Kimura's introduction to the volume questions whether Post-3.11 Literature, both as a genre and a critical field, may be settling into a fixed form that no longer "shakes" existing frameworks.[10] Kimura intends *"Post-3.11 Literature" as World Literature* to be a provocation that effects change, writing that she "thinks the book variously demonstrates the diversity of ecocriticism as a form of critical theory, and how its implementation can lead to new modes of reading."[11] Just as I used *Ecocriticism in Japan* to mark a break between precedent and present, so too do I see *"Post-3.11 Literature" as World Literature* as marking a new era in the development of ecocriticism in Japanese literary studies. And just as Kimura and the contributors to her volume invite readers to imagine new ecocritical possibilities, I now wish to highlight some possible directions in which the field could advance.

Ecocritical Possibilities

Now that Post-3.11 scholarship has helped ecocriticism gain significant traction in Japanese literary studies, the time is right for a further diversification of environmental topics and approaches. The first area I wish to highlight is Critical Plant Studies (CPS), where I situate my own research. Kimura discusses CPS (*shokubutsuron*) in her introduction to *"Post-3.11 Literature" as World Literature*, explaining how CPS grows out of Animal Studies—a field that looks at how humans theorize and treat more-than-human animals, often in relation to Foucauldian biopolitics. While Animal Studies has done much to combat anthropocentricism, CPS thinkers believe it ends up regulating plant life to the margins of "otherness"—a position once held by more-than-human animals themselves. Kimura points to the potential for CPS to intervene into Post-3.11 Literary Studies and mentions how Emanuele Coccia's CPS text *The Life of Plants: A Metaphysics of Mixture* (*La Vie des Plantes: Une Metaphysique du Mélange*, 2017) has been translated into Japanese. In fact, Coccia's book is only one of several works of CPS to have been translated into Japanese; works by Robin Wall Kimmerer and Stefano Mancuso are available as well.

Plants feature prominently in Japanese literature, and the range of texts awaiting a CPS approach bridges the premodern/modern divide. Fujihara Tatsushi's *Thoughts on Plants* (*Shokubutsukō*, 2022) engages directly with CPS theorists and can be considered the first Japanese academic book to enter the CPS corpus. However, in my opinion, several contemporary Japanese literary writers should also be considered among the ranks of CPS theorists. Itō Seikō, for example, writes philosophically about plants in several of his works, including his 1999 collection *Botanical Life* (*Botanikaru raifu: shokubutsu no seikatsu*). So, too, does Itō Hiromi, in works like *Wild Grass on the Riverbank* (*Kawara arekusa*, 2004) and *Tree Spirits Grass Spirits* (*Kodama kusadama*, 2014).[12] Azuma Chigaya, author of *Human Composting Project* (*Jinrui taihika keikaku*, 2020), straddles the line between CPS and Animal Studies, fostering a unique environmental philosophy that embraces the productive qualities of decomposition (on both literal and figurative levels). One historically important figure of Japanese botany whose naturalist writings have been overlooked in literary studies is Makino Tomitarō, the "Father of Japanese Botany." While nature writers like John Muir and Aldo Leopold where among the first objects of ecocritical scholarship in the US, Japanese nature writers like Makino and Hoshino Michio have received little attention thus far in Japanese literary studies.[13]

A critical focus on plant life in Japanese literature could likewise help the field embrace emergent theories of queer ecology, which Catriona Sandilands defines as "a loose, interdisciplinary constellation of practices that aim, in different ways, to disrupt prevailing heterosexist discursive and institutional articulations of sexuality and nature, and also to reimagine evolutionary processes, ecological interactions, and environmental politics in light of queer theory."[14] As Stella Sanford's *Vegetal Sex: Philosophy of Plants* (2022) lucidly demonstrates, plants' complex biological processes of reproduction defy rigid, heteronormative notions of gender and sexuality, and the work of many Japanese authors, such as Hoshino Tomoyuki and Itō Hiromi, for example, explore the potential for new, queer articulations of human gender and sexuality that draws from the botanical realm. Eiko Honda's research on the "queer nature" of the idiosyncratic polymath/scientist Minakata Kumagusa and his writings on microbes further demonstrates how queer ecologies can be articulated by looking toward "ecological interactions" with other more-than-human beings, be they microbe, fungus, or, indeed, animal.[15]

Because while CPS is positioned as a corrective to Animal Studies, the latter is by no means a fading field. Post-3.11 scholarship has been particularly sensitive to more-than-human animals, as more-than-human characters appear often in Post-3.11 literature, from *God Bless You 2011*'s talking bear, to the cattle at the heart of Kimura Yūsuke's *Sacred Cesium Ground*, to the cats of Kobayashi Erika's *Breakfast with Madame Curie* (*Madamu Kyurii to chōshoku o*, 2014). But there are also many Japanese writers who have engaged with more-than-human animals before 3.11, like Togawa Yukio, one of the founders of "Animal Literature" (*Dōbutsu bungaku*) in Japan. No major research on Togawa's work (or the literary genre he helped create) currently exists in English-language scholarship.

Environmental historians have been more attuned to Animal Studies; Brett Walker's *The Lost Wolves of Japan* (2005) and the collected volume he co-edited with Greg Pflugfelder the same year, *JAPANimals: History and Culture in Japan's Animal Life*, speak to the historical interest in more-than-human animals. Jakobina Arch's *Bringing Whales Ashore* (2018) is yet another example, and it signals a turn to another new field of ecocritical scholarship: the Blue Humanities. Blue Humanities theorist Steve Mentz argues that literary studies have largely neglected the "blue," i.e., the ocean, and I think this is true of Japanese literary studies, as well. Despite the Japanese archipelago being surrounded by the sea, and despite the central role the ocean plays in many works of Japanese literature, ecocriticism has remained largely land-locked. Popular works of historical fiction that focus on whaling, like Itō Jun's 2013 novel *Sea of the Leviathan* (*Kyogei no umi*) and works of proletarian literature like Kobayashi Takiji's *The Crab Ship Cannery* (*Kani kōsen*) are examples of inroads by which the Blue Humanities could find its way into Japanese literary studies.

Japanese literary scholars *have* paid close attention to the ocean in the realm of Science Fiction; Thomas Schnellbächer, for example, has written on the ocean in Japanese Sci-Fi and its relation to naval militarism. Images of rising seas and sinking islands have been commonplace in Japanese Sci-Fi since at least the publication of Abe Kōbō's *Inter Ice Age 4* (*Daiyon kanpyōki*, 1959) and continue to make frequent appearances in contemporary manga and anime, including in Shinkai Makoto's *Weathering With You* (*Tenki no ko*, 2019), which ends with Tokyo underwater. These works speak to the recent theorization of Climate Fiction (Cli-Fi), a genre that imagines the effects of climate change to often catastrophic extremes. Several literary works of Japanese Cli-Fi have been translated into English: Ueda Sayuri's "Fin and Claw" (*Uobune, kemonobune*, 2009), Yōko Tawada's *The Emissary* (*Kentōshi*, 2014), and Dempow Torishima's *Sisyphean* (*Kaikin no tō*, 2013). But Japanese literature is significant in its early examples as well, including Abe Kōbō's aforementioned *Inter Ice Age 4* and Satō Haruo's "A Record of Nonchalant" (*Nansharan no kiroku*), a 1929 short story that imagines a future where the elite live aboveground with access to air and sunlight and the masses live underground and consume "edible gas" through pipes. The poor underground dwellers are given the opportunity to live aboveground only if they are willing to become plants, as plants "abandoned this earth two or three centuries ago."[16]

In its prescient anxiety over resource scarcity, "Record of Nonchalant" also points us toward the last "ecocritical possibility" I discuss here: the Energy Humanities. In their introduction to *Energy Humanities: An Anthology* (2017), Imre Szeman and Dominic Boyer write how recent works of literature, film, and visual art have "explored the character of our energy epistemologies, with the aim of grasping the curious invisibility of such a powerful substance as oil, while also trying to render fuels nameable, readable, and visible."[17] The applicability of an Energy Humanities intervention into Post-3.11 literature is clear, given the extent to which many writers (like Kobayashi Erika) seek to better understand the "energy epistemologies" tied to Japan's reliance on nuclear power. But Energy Humanities can speak to Japanese literature more broadly. How would our readings of canonical works change if we looked at them from the perspective of energy use? There is much to say about resource use and energy demand in the works of Natsume Sōseki, for example. In turn, approaching literature from an Energy Humanities perspective moves us from the metropole of Tokyo into spaces of colonial resource extraction, giving us new ways to put works of canonical literature into conversation with works of colonial literature.

An important question remains: what about premodern literature? Does the Japanese poetic tradition, with its centuries of intense focus on nature, have anything to add to ecocriticism? So far, I have focused on modern and contemporary Japanese literature because, by and large, there has not been much ecocritical scholarship on classical Japanese literature. I believe there are a few reasons for this. The first can be seen in Yuki Masami's argument that ecocriticism and "thematic literary studies concerning nature" have been confused due to Japan's "thousand-year-old literary tradition of paying attention to nature." Ecocritics of Japanese literature have needed to situate themselves *against* the premodern canon in order to find critical purchase. After all, as Haruo Shirane has argued, the classical tradition is not *really* talking about the natural world, but rather a "secondary nature" (one "re-created or represented") that "became a substitute for a more primary nature that was often remote from or rarely seen by the aristocrats" who composed poetry.[18] If we accept Shirane's proposition (as ecocritics like Yuki Masami have), then it is hard to imagine how classical Japanese poetics could inform non-anthropocentric modes of reading. Premodern nature poetry thus becomes a kind of straw man—perhaps a necessary one—against which an ecocritical reading of modern and contemporary literary texts gains immediacy. Modern and contemporary literature, the argument goes, deals much more directly with the real material world, often through the lens of environmental crisis.

Therefore, the second reason I believe the classical canon has been neglected in ecocriticism stems from the field's focus on environmental degradation and 3.11. Christine Marran, for example, forcefully argues, in reference to Murakami Haruki's invocation of classical poetics in response to 3.11, that "classical poetics simply does not have . . . any language to describe how more than 160,000 environmental refugees would survive the loss of homes, farms, and schools to radiation fallout."[19] Marran (rightly, I believe) takes issue with Murakami's mention of the cherry blossom within a speech dedicated to his conviction that Japan will naturally recover from 3.11. Murakami opines: "Before our eyes, evanescent cherry blossoms scatter, the fireflies' will-o'-the-wisp vanishes, and the bright autumn leaves are snatched away. We recognize these events and we find in these changes a certain relief. Oddly, it brings us a certain peace of mind that the height of beauty passes and fades away."[20] For Marran, the cherry blossom is an "ethnic nationalist biotrope" that is inseparable from an ideology in which "Japan is ethnically homogenous, a nation that shares an 'ethnic mentality' and finds spiritual peace in the four seasons."[21] How could such an overdetermined tradition (one mobilized to militaristic ends in the 20th century) have anything to contribute to an ecocriticism concerned with the real-world effects of radiation?

Perhaps it cannot. But as I have been arguing, there exist possibilities beyond Post-3.11 Literary Studies. Classical Japanese poetry and narrative tales (*monogatari*) could well contribute to CPS, for example. Japan's oldest extant *monogatari*, *The Tale of the Bamboo Cutter* (*Taketori monogatari*, 9th or 10th century), begins with an old man finding a mysterious young girl inside a glowing stalk of bamboo. If one of the aims of CPS is to minimize the ontological distance between humans and plants, then a closer look at *The Tale of the Bamboo Cutter* feels warranted. As does a closer look at traditional *waka* poetry. Yes, the cherry blossom is an overdetermined, nationalistic image (as Emiko Ohnuki-Tierney explains in her 2002 book *Kamikaze, Cherry Blossoms, and Nationalisms*), and yes, Heian-era aristocratic poets were more concerned with the *idea* of nature than the natural world itself, but surely there is more to say about plants and more-than-human animals in the classical canon beyond the conventional tropes they have helped solidify.

Conclusion

In 2020, I began teaching Japanese environmental humanities at the University of California, Irvine. As far as I know, this position was the first of its kind in the United States. At UCI, I found a community of Japanese studies scholars invested in environmental research and graduate students doing research on ecocritical projects. I found an environmental humanities reading group (now a proper Research Center) that brought those of us in Japanese studies into dialogue with ecocritical thinkers from across the school. All of this speaks to the fact that ecocritical scholarship is growing and finding new relevancy with each passing year. But more than anything else, the interest and enthusiasm I have witnessed among students in my undergraduate classes has shown me just how deeply their generation cares about environmental issues. When I teach classes on Japanese environmental literature and visual media, many students come not specifically for the Japanese cultural content, but for the ecocritical content. Some of these students are inevitably STEM majors, and their insights into Japanese literature are unconventional and insightful. This cross-disciplinary engagement can help introduce new life into Japanese literary studies.

Returning one last time to Yuki Masami's timeline of ecocriticism in Japanese literary studies, I wish to conclude by paying attention to the language she invokes for her third phase, the one "characterized by a cross-fertilization between ecocriticism and Japanese literary studies." In using the biological language of "cross-fertilization," Yuki portrays this third phase not as the final step in the integration of ecocriticism and Japanese literary studies, but rather as the point of conception. This means that we are actually in a fourth phase—ontogeny. This developmental phase can be a collaborative project in which we all contribute to the outcome of the field. Following the metaphor, our various research projects and courses help the process of differentiation. Collectively, they could come together to distinguish Japanese literary studies within the environmental humanities and demonstrate that there is ample ground from which to grow, adapt, and bloom.

Notes

1. Gregory Golley, "*Ecocriticism in Japan* ed. by Hisaaki Wake, Keijiro Suga and Yuki Masami (review)," *The Journal of Japanese Studies* 45, no. 2 (Summer 2019): 494–98.

2. I differentiate between "ecocriticism" and "environmental humanities" as follows: I see the former as a critical mode of interpretation that can cut across disciplines, while I see the latter as the wide, interdisciplinary field that is made possible by ecocriticism, along with other modes of interpretation that stem from environmental/ecological thinking that may be less environmentalist in nature than ecocriticism.

3. Cheryll Glotfelty, "Introduction: Literary Studies in an Age of Environmental Crisis," in *The Ecocriticism Reader*, ed. Cheryll Glotfelty and Harold Fromm (University of Georgia Press, 1996), xviii.

4. Masami Yuki, "Ecocriticism in Japan," in *The Oxford Handbook of Ecocriticism*, ed. Greg Garrard (Oxford University Press, 2014), 519.

5. Yuki, "Ecocriticism in Japan," 519.

6. Yuki, "Ecocriticism in Japan," 519.

7. Yuki mentions *The Emergence of Environmental Literature in Japan* in her essay in *The Oxford Handbook of Ecocriticism*, pointing out that "discussions regarding literary environmentalism in Japan began outside the country as early as 1990" but that in Japan, "ecocriticism did not really begin to be discussed by scholars of Japanese literature until the late 2000s." Yuki, "Ecocriticism in Japan," 523.

8. A portion of *Paradise in the Sea of Sorrow* had been published as early as 1971, when part of the third chapter appeared in *Japan Quarterly* in translation by James Kirkup and Nakano Michio.

9. Yuki, "Ecocriticism in Japan," 519.

10. Kimura Saeko, "*Shinsaigo bungaku no genzaichi*," in *Sekai bungaku toshite no "Shinsaigo bungaku,"* ed. Kimura Saeko and Anne Bayard-Sakai (Akashi Shoten, 2021), 11.

11. Kimura Saeko, "*Shinsaigo bungaku no genzaichi*," 35. My translation.

12. My translation of *Tree Spirits Grass Spirits* was published by Nightboat Books in 2023.

13. Hoshino Michio is known outside of Japan primarily as a photographer. In Japan, however, his writing is equally well-celebrated, in particular his 1994 essay collection *The Traveling Tree* (*Tabi o suru ki*), a few portions of which were published in translation by Karen Colligan-Taylor in the photobook *Hoshino's Alaska* (2007).

14. Catriona Sandilands, "Queer Ecology," in *Keywords for Environmental Studies*, ed. Joni Adamson, William A. Gleason, and David Pellow (New York University Press, 2016), 169.

15. Eiko Honda, "Minakata Kumagusu and the emergence of queer nature: Civilization theory, Buddhist science, and microbes, 1887–1892," *Modern Asian Studies* 57, no. 4 (July 2023): 1105–34.

16. Satō Haruo, "A Record of Nonchalant," in *Three-Dimensional Reading: Stories of Time and Space in Japanese Modernist Fiction, 1911–1932*, trans. Angela Yiu (University of Hawai'i Press, 2013), 211–39.

17. Imre Szeman and Dominic Boyer, "Introduction: On the Energy Humanities," in *Energy Humanities: An Anthology*, ed. Imre Szeman and Dominic Boyer (Johns Hopkins University Press, 2017), 1–13.

18. Haruo Shirane, *Japan and the Culture of the Four Seasons: Nature, Literature, and the Arts* (Columbia University Press, 2012), 4.

19. Christine L. Marran, *Ecology Without Culture: Aesthetics for a Toxic World* (University of Minnesota Press, 2017), 7.

20. Murakami Haruki, "Speaking as an Unrealistic Dreamer," trans. Emanuel Pastreich, *Asia-Pacific Journal* (2011): 1–8.

21. Marran, *Ecology Without Culture*, 9.

Works Cited

Abe, Kōbō. *Inter Ice Age 4*. Translated by E. Dale Saunders. Perigee Trade, 1981.

Arch, Jakobina K. *Bringing Whales Ashore: Oceans and the Environment of Early Modern Japan*. University of Washington Press, 2018.

Azuma Chigaya. *Jinrui taihika keikaku*. Sōgensha, 2020.

"Basho" no shigaku: kankyō bungaku to wa nani ka? Edited by Ko Un et al. Fujiwara Shoten, 2008.

"Beyond Fukushima: Culture, Media, and Meaning from Catastrophe." Edited by Jonathan Abel. Special Issue, *Japan Forum* 26, issue 3 (2014).

Bungaku kara kankyō wo kangaeru: ekokuriteishizumu gaidobukku. Edited by Yuki Masami et al. Bensei Shuppan, 2014.

Coccia, Emanuele. *The Life of Plants: A Metaphysics of Mixture*. Translated by Dylan J. Montanari. Polity, 2019.

Colligan-Taylor, Karen. *The Emergence of Environmental Literature in Japan*. Garland, 1990.

DiNitto, Rachel. *Fukushima Fiction: The Literary Landscape of Japan's Triple Disaster*. University of Hawai'i Press, 2019.

Ecocriticism in Japan. Edited by Hisaaki Wake, Keijiro Suga, and Yuki Masami. Lexington Books, 2018.

Fujihara Tatsushi. *Shokubutsukō*. Ikinobiru Books, 2022.

Fukushima and the Arts: Negotiating Nuclear Disaster. Edited by Barbara Geilhorn and Kristina Iwata-Weickgenannt. Routledge, 2017.

Furukawa Hideo. *Horses, Horses, in the End the Light Remains Pure: A Tale That Begins with Fukushima*. Translated by Doug Slaymaker with Akiko Takenaka. Columbia University Press, 2016.

Glotfelty, Cheryll. "Introduction: Literary Studies in an Age of Environmental Crisis." In *The Ecocriticism Reader*, edited by Cheryll Glotfelty and Harold Fromm. University of Georgia Press, 1996.

Golley, Gregory. "*Ecocriticism in Japan* ed. by Hisaaki Wake, Keijiro Suga and Yuki Masami (review)." *The Journal of Japanese Studies* 45, no. 2 (Summer 2019): 494–98.

Golley, Gregory. *When Our Eyes No Longer See: Realism, Science, and Ecology in Japanese Literary Modernism*. Harvard University Press, 2008.

Haga, Koichi. *The Earth Writes: The Great Earthquake and the Novel in Post-3/11 Japan*. Lexington Books, 2019.

Honda, Eiko. "Minakata Kumagusu and the emergence of queer nature: Civilization theory, Buddhist science, and microbes, 1887–1892," *Modern Asian Studies* 57, no. 4 (July 2023): 1105–34.

Ishimure Michiko. *Paradise in the Sea of Sorrow: Our Minamata Disease*. Translated by Livia Monnet. University of Michigan Press, 2003.

Ishimure Michiko's Writing in Ecocritical Perspective: Between Sea and Sky. Edited by Bruce Allen and Yuki Masami. Rowman and Littlefield, 2015.

Itō Hiromi. *Wild Grass on the Riverbank*. Translated by Jeffrey Angles. Action Books, 2015.

Itō Jun. *Kyogei no umi*. Kōbunsha, 2013.

Itō Seikō. *Botanikaru raifu—shokubutsu seikatsu*. Shinchōsha, 1999.

Japan at Nature's Edge: The Environmental Context of a Global Power. Edited by Ian Jared Miller, Julia Adeney Thomas, and Brett L. Walker. University of Hawai'i Press, 2013.

JAPANimals: History and Culture in Japan's Animal Life. Edited by Gregory M. Pflugfelder and Brett Walker. University of Michigan Press, 2005.

Kayano Shigeru. *Our Land was a Forest: An Ainu Memoir.* Translated by Kyoko Selden and Lili Selden. Routledge, 1994.

Kimura Saeko. "*Shinsaigo bungaku no genzaichi.*" In *Sekai bungaku toshite no "Shinsaigo bungaku,"* edited by Kimura Saeko and Anne Bayard-Sakai. Akashi Shoten, 2021.

Kimura Saeko. *Shinsaigo bungakuron: Atarashii Nihon bungaku no tame ni.* Seidosha, 2013.

Kimura Saeko. *Sono go no shinsaigo bungakuron.* Seidosha, 2018.

Kimura Yūsuke. *Sacred Cesium Ground and Isa's Deluge: Two Novellas of Japan's 3/11 Disaster.* Translated by Doug Slaymaker. Columbia University Press, 2019.

Kobayashi Erika. *Madamu Kyurii to chōshoku o.* Shūeisha, 2018.

Kobayashi Takiji. *The Crab Cannery Ship and Other Novels of Struggle.* Translated by Željko Cipriš. University of Hawai'i Press, 2013.

Kohn, Eduardo. *How Forests Think: Toward an Anthropology Beyond the Human.* University of California Press, 2013.

Literature and Art after "Fukushima": Four Approaches. Edited by Lisette Gebhardt and Yuki Masami. EB Verlag, 2014.

March Was Made of Yarn: Reflections on the Japanese Earthquake, Tsunami, and Nuclear Meltdown. Edited by Elmer Luke and David Karashima. Knopf Doubleday, 2012.

Marran, Christine L. *Ecology Without Culture: Aesthetics for a Toxic World.* University of Minnesota Press, 2017.

Murakami Haruki. "Speaking as an Unrealistic Dreamer." Translated by Emanuel Pastreich. *Asia-Pacific Journal* (2011): 1–8.

Nixon, Rob. *Slow Violence and the Environmentalism of the Poor.* Harvard University Press, 2011.

Peters, John Durham. *The Marvelous Clouds: Toward a Philosophy of Elemental Media.* University of Chicago Press, 2015.

Sandford, Stella. *Vegetal Sex: Philosophy of Plants.* Bloomsbury, 2022.

Sandilands, Catriona. "Queer Ecology." In *Keywords for Environmental Studies,* edited by Joni Adamson, William A. Gleason, and David Pellow. New York University Press, 2016.

Satō Haruo. "A Record of Nonchalant." In *Three-Dimensional Reading: Stories of Time and Space in Japanese Modernist Fiction, 1911–1932.* Edited by Angela Yiu. University of Hawai'i Press, 2013.

Sekai bungaku toshite no "Shinsaigo bungaku." Edited by Kimura Saeko et al. Akashi Shoten, 2021.

Shinkai, Makoto, dir., *Weathering With You.* 2019. SHOUT! FACTORY, 2020.

Shirane, Haruo. *Japan and the Culture of the Four Seasons: Nature, Literature, and the Arts.* Columbia University Press, 2012.

Shizen to bungaku no daiarōgu. Edited by Yamazato Katsunori. Sairyūsha, 2004.

Stolz, Robert. *Bad Water: Nature, Pollution, and Politics in Japan, 1870–1950.* Duke University Press, 2014.

Szeman, Imre, and Dominic Boyer. "Introduction: On the Energy Humanities." In *Energy Humanities: An Anthology*. Edited by Imre Szeman and Dominic Boyer. Johns Hopkins University Press, 2017.

Taguchi, Randy. *Riku and the Kingdom of White*. Translated by Raj Mahtani. Balestier Press, 2016.

Tawada, Yōko. *The Emissary.* Translated by Margaret Mitsutani. New Directions, 2018.

Thornber, Karen. *Ecoambiguity: Environmental Crises and East Asian Literatures*. University of Michigan Press, 2012.

Torishima, Dempow. *Sisyphean. Translated by* Daniel Huddleston. Haikasoru, 2018.

Totman, Conrad. *The Green Archipelago: Forestry in Preindustrial Japan*. University of California Press, 1989.

Tsing, Anna Lowenhaupt. *The Mushroom at the End of the World: On the Possibility of Life in Capitalist Ruins*. Princeton University Press, 2015.

Ueda Sayuri. "Fin and Claw." In *Speculative Japan 3: "Silver Bullet" and Other Tales*. Kurodahan Press, 2020.

Wagō Ryōichi. "Pebbles of Poetry: The Tōhoku Earthquake and Tsunami," trans. Jeffrey Angles. *Asia-Pacific Journal* 9, issue 29, no. 4 (2011).

Walker, Brett. *Toxic Archipelago: A History of Industrial Disease in Japan*. University of Washington Press, 2010.

When the Tsunami Came to Shore: Culture and Disaster in Japan. Edited by Roy Starrs. Brill, 2014.

Yu Miri. *Tokyo Ueno Station*. Translated by Morgan Giles. Tilted Axis Press, 2019.

Yuki, Masami. "Ecocriticism in Japan." In *The Oxford Handbook of Ecocriticism*, edited by Greg Garrard. Oxford University Press, 2014.

CHAPTER 5

Comixing Frameworks

Rethinking the Euroamerican Critical Paradigm from the Perspective of Manga Studies

Adam L. Kern

The Japanese comic books known around the world as *manga* are often referred to in Japanese writing with Sinified graphs and in speech as *komikkusu*, a loanword from English signifying "comics," though not the double of co-mixing. Yet in the West, it is precisely this "comix" of word and image that for some theorists defines comics. The majority opinion, acknowledging the presence of words and images, nonetheless tends to define comics primarily as sequential visual narrative.[1] Such a definition takes as its unacknowledged model the Euroamerican multipanel though linear comic strip, with its ready assimilability into Western narratological and critical theory. Accordingly, single-panel comics are afforded scant attention. As are comics from other times and places. Hence, most Japanese comics are either squeezed into this Western cookie cutter, the excess discarded, or else left out of the recipe completely.

The presumption of a Japanese postwar deferential imitation of American culture and technology runs rampant throughout Western pop scholarship and journalism covering Japan. "With manga, the Japanese have demonstrated the same facility as with the automobile or the computer chip," writes Paul Gravett. "They have taken the fundamentals of American comics, the relationships between picture, frame, and word, and, by fusing them with their own traditional love for popular art that entertains, have 'Japanized' them into a storytelling vehicle with its own distinctive form" (Gravett 2004, 10). Similarly, in an article on the history of *manga* abroad, in *manga* form no less, titled "How Manga Conquered America," Jason Thompson and Okura Atsuhisa suggest that Japan may have lost the war, but won the peace (*Thompson* 2007).

Such accounts ignore non-Western comics. The Japanese themselves had their own longstanding comics tradition prior to exposure to Western strip-based comics, even well before Tezuka Osamu (1928–1989) supposedly "invented" *manga*. The notion of *manga* as Japanized comics, then, neglects this rich history, abiding by the narrative of the postwar Japanese "economic miracle," moving from ground zero to G-6 within a few decades. Still, the transformation was "miraculous" only if Japanese civilization and technology are assumed to have been backwards. Nothing could be further from the truth.

From a Japanese perspective, there has been a keen awareness of *manga* breaking into larger overseas markets. "World comics," as Tezuka himself put the matter. "That's how the Japanese thought about it. They told me that their goal was to create a comic style that would be universal, the style of the 21st century" (Gravett 2004, 157). This attitude is anything but obsequious.

The awareness of *manga* as *komikkusu* is all the more striking, then, since Japanese comics by whatever name represent the most venerable, most widely read, most profitable, and arguably most influential comics tradition in the world. Dwarfing its next two rivals, the Anglo-American and Franco-Belgian traditions, *manga* is a cultural juggernaut. Yet in the West, while many Japanese Studies programs offer dedicated courses on *manga*, and scholarship continues to bourgeon, Manga Studies as a field has not exactly prospered within the neoliberal university. There are many contributing factors. One is the dominance of the Euroamerican critical framework, particularly within literary studies. As Emily Apter has observed, "The nations that name the critical lexicon are the nations that dominate the classification of genres in literary history and the critical paradigms that prevail in literary world-systems" (Apter 2013, 58). The domination of Euroamerican paradigms does not mean that other paradigms should be neglected.

In this context, the very marginality of Manga Studies in the United States can be flipped into an advantage, to rethink the Euroamerican critical framework that privileges certain texts, authors, theories, methodologies, and practices that largely monopolize the academy. Manga Studies can provide a constructive critique of the ethnocentrism, chronocentrism, and ocularcentrism engendered by the critical framework that has come to dominate

Western Comics Studies. This critique is timely given the perception of the present crisis of literature. As some commentators have declared: "It is difficult to dispute, nonetheless, that literature has lost its hegemonic role as a provider of models and resources for making sense of human experience" (Even-Zohar, Feijó, and Monegal 2019, 13–14).

This loss is inevitable. It may ultimately even be for the best. Comics is swiftly gaining recognition, along with other media, as a major alternative to literature. While cinema and TV have obvious visual and other sensory appeal, comics, by virtue of its comixing of word and image, approximates how we human beings largely experience the world through a commixture of hearing and seeing. Understanding how and why this comixing has finally made comics ascendant may prove helpful in rethinking literature and its study within the humanities.

Comics themselves have drawn inspiration from literature, not just with the phenomenon of graphic novelization of classic novels (like Nancy Butler and Hugo Petrus's adaptation of Jane Austen's *Pride & Prejudice*), but with the way that the comics' appropriation of such works mirrors the way that Western literary studies tend to colonize other disciplines. World Literary Studies—under which Japanese Literary Studies too often gets pigeonholed—is habitually blighted by Anglophone and Eurocentric critical frameworks. To the extent that the usual Western paradigms that have subjugated literary studies and the humanities have already encroached upon Comics Studies, Manga Studies may be able to resist from within.

Admittedly, *manga* may not seem a likely candidate through which to explore all comics as a paradigm of human experience. In Japan, the weekly *manga* magazines are in decline. Sales peaked in 1995 and have been freefalling ever since. Nevertheless, reports of the death of *manga* are exaggerated. *Manga* resides at the core of the Japanese pop culture industry, one of the most vibrant in the world, the Uncola to America's Cocacolonization. Digital games and *anime* are more profitable, but as a medium *manga* is the cheapest to produce and thus will continue to serve as an indispensable feeder. Whether drawn by hand or designed digitally, *manga* provides the format of storyboards and dummy books that serve as blueprints for producing films and animation. Moreover, as Aaron Kashtan observes, comics is "even more curiously resistant to replacement by digital equivalents than other genres of books" (Kashtan 2018, 3). This resilience has to do with how its physical layout is pinned to the materiality of codex-form books in a way that digital versions cannot readily accommodate. Kashtan concludes "if we want to know where the printed book is going and where it ought to go, we need to think about comics" (4).

Comics Studies and the Verbovisual Turn

And yet Manga Studies has gained little traction in the Western neoliberal university, even as Comics Studies has made gains, particularly in the fields of education, medicine, and public health. The success of the new comics subfield of graphic medicine—"the intersection of the medium of comics and the discourse of healthcare" (Czerwiec 2015, 1)—suggests that one way forward for literary studies and the humanities is to build meaningful bridges with the sciences. Above and beyond the instrumentalism of using comics to disseminate medical discourse, or of "data visualization," word-image texts can more fundamentally serve to model scientific and medical theorization.

Comics has also been garnering critical acclaim, specifically in the form of the so-called "graphic novel." This backhanded term, lamentably putting comics down by holding it up to "literary" standards instead of accepting comics *for what it is*—neither art, nor literature, but its own thing—has nonetheless helped establish a subcategory of comics. The usual suspects here include Art Spiegelman's Pulitzer Prize-winning *Maus*, Chris Ware's Guardian Award-winning *Jimmy Corrigan*, and the works of MacArthur "Genius" Award-winners: Alison Bechdel's *Fun Home*, Gene Luen Yang's *American Born Chinese*, and Lynda Barry's *What It Is*.

Ratified in part by these "literary" comics, Comics Studies is gaining ground within the academy. Comics is presumed to be a form of Western graphic literature, to be approached from the perspective of Euroamerican theory and methodologies. Accordingly, *manga*—although relegated to Japanese or Asian area studies—is still reflexively treated as a Japanized version of Western comics. These assumptions are by no means universal. In Japanese cultural production, word and image have, until the twentieth century, traditionally overlapped. For one thing, the nature of Sinified graphs and their use in Japanese writing entail a comixing and streamlining of pictures, represented sounds, and abstract concepts. For another, calligraphic inscription plays on the homology between these qualities and various visual and latent verbal elements of the pictures framing the calligraphy.

In the Western world, by contrast, words and images have tended to be separated, their comixing eschewed as a kind of miscegenation. Abrahamic cultures have long privileged *logos* over *pictura*: the Mosaic injunction against graven images; the Muslim predilection for representing the infinite through the design of the mosaic; and the Christian exaltation of the word of God. In the West, not only ocularcentrism, but specifically *logocentrism* has reigned supreme. "Pictocentrism," as Japanologist Charles Inouye has termed it (Inouye 1992), has fared less well.

Granted, the undeniable power of the image means that there has always been a subterranean stratum of religious figuration. Consider the depiction of the saints and biblical characters within the stained-glass windows of the great European cathedrals. Or the illuminated manuscripts of the middle ages. Or, in the eastern Islamic world, "illustrations of poems depict[ing] the Prophet, usually with his face veiled, ascending to heaven on the winged horse Buraq" (Marks 2010, 49). Rejecting the word-image binary should not necessitate re-inscribing an equally problematical Orient-Occident binary.

Even so, the Western neoliberal university has tended to follow Abrahamic rhetoric, bifurcating word and image. Although there has been a Visual Turn, and a Spatial Turn, there has yet to be what might be termed a "Verbovisual Turn." Such a turn would focus on texts that are less logocentric or pictocentric than pictologocentric. Acknowledging this mode would help reconfigure the relationships among literary studies, art history, critical cartography, visual culture studies, and other disciplines in a radically new light.

And defining comics as any comixing of word and image without subordinating comics to the Euroamerican comic strip-based model would allow comics to assume its rightful place alongside literature and art as a major mode of human communication that encompasses a staggering range of overlapping media, formats, and genres across time and space. Under such a view, *manga* would be regarded as Japanized comics only to the extent that comics were regarded as Westernized *manga*. Accordingly, Manga Studies could move beyond the Western comic-strip model that exalts sequentiality, visuality, and narrativity while pitting word *against* image. As the comixing of word and image, comics including *manga* could be seen as a definitive mode of human communication. We are, after all, the only animal to represent our primary verbal and gestural modes of communication with the secondary mode of inscription, meaning not only written words and images, but also their comixing.

Such comixing has been with us since time immemorial. Some scholars maintain that comics originated earlier than Egyptian hieroglyphics, in the prehistoric painted rock art of Africa or Aboriginal Australia. The comixing of word and image is so prevalent throughout human history, it may well be the *rule* of inscribed human communication, with pictureless inscription the exception. "Written texts have been the preferred medium for the transmission of literature only during a relatively short period in the history of humanity," observes Even-Zohar et al., though seemingly oblivious to comics: "Before them were oral literature, both poetry and narrative, and eventually theater" (Even-Zohar et al., 2019, 16).

The notion that comics poses an existential threat to serious literature is vexed not because comics will somehow supersede literature, but because the assumption that pictureless literature is the norm and comics the deviation is itself suspect. The term "pictureless" here assumes a clean demarcation between word and image when no such thing can be said to exist universally. The borderline varies culturally and historically and linguistically. No educated Japanese or Chinese person, given the traditional centrality of calligraphy, would maintain that their writing system is sequestered from visual art. Only in recent Abrahamic cultures has such a myth of sequestration arisen.

Furthermore, the very act of inscribing words lends them visual form. Written words always have a pictorial dimension. Conversely, images, when presented on their own, typically evoke a verbal response, even if only "inside one's head." The fourteen hundred relief panels gracing the Buddhist temple at Borobudur in central Java, for instance, refer to well-known episodes from sutras that were available in multiple languages. Pilgrims to the monument must have produced the same overall verbal narrative to themselves in their own tongues. An image of Adam and Eve in the Garden of Eden evokes the same narrative regardless of whether rendered in Hebrew, Greek, or the English of King James. A narrative consisting of images alone can still be comix, then, so long as the verbal narrative produced in one's head is shared by others.

The Ghettoization of Manga Studies within Japanese Studies

One underlying reason for the marginalization of Manga Studies in the West beyond the denigration of comics has to do with persistent cultural assumptions within the neoliberal university that deny the "global history" of comics and other cultural forms.[2] Another reason, not unrelated, has to do with the mostly latent persistence of colonial racism known as Orientalism. Asian Studies programs tend to be underfunded compared to those of European and American studies. Yet the second and third largest economies in the world are those of China and Japan. The most widely spoken language in the world is Mandarin. In terms of global human population, the top half dozen countries in Europe and the Americas make up less than 10%, whereas the top half dozen countries in Asia make up nearly 50%.[3]

Too often, Anglophone Manga Studies is subsumed to a partnership between Literary Studies and Art History, but unlike Comics Studies, it is quarantined to Japanese Studies. Catherine Belsey warns "If cooperation with another discipline promises no more than a refuge from our own, our contribution will be lost among more powerful analyses. Interdisciplinarity will work best as an exchange between equal disciplines" (Belsey 2016). Just as Manga Studies has not fared well within Comics Studies, so too is Comics Studies not likely to fare well under literary studies, which has suffered its own power inequity with more powerful STEM disciplines. As Neil Vallelly has put the matter: "This downgrading also means that literary studies must justify [its] existence in the neoliberal university by proving [its] relevance to the more profitable disciplines, often under the umbrella term interdisciplinarity" (Vallelly 2019, 68).

Hence, Anglophone Manga Studies has been ghettoized within the neoliberal university. When departments and disciplines in the humanities are pitted against each other for resources in a kind of *battle royale*, Comics Studies and even Asian Studies regard *manga* gladiatorially.[4] What is startling, however, is that Manga Studies has its detractors even within Japanese Studies *itself*. One of the dirty secrets of the field is that some scholars look askance at *manga* as a necessary evil to draw students into the fold, but once there, something to be rejected for its simplemindedness relative to the supposedly great works of literature. Japanese Studies programs have benefited tremendously from *manga* and *anime*. Programs that refrain from offering coursework on these pop culture forms risk irrelevance or obsolescence.

Manga Studies has much to overcome within Japanology. Simon Grennan writes: "Fundamentally, [*manga*] is a popular visual literature of escapism" (Grennan 2018, 321). Similarly, John Treat avers: "manga seldom addresses real life" (Treat 2018, 209). It is true that much mainstream fare is escapist. Yet escapism per se appeals to people only if its ultimate foil is real life. At best, such works defamiliarize issues that are otherwise too painful to gaze upon directly. Moreover, many *manga* genres engage directly with real life. To name a few: educational *manga*, like Yoshida Sarasa's *Yasashii Bukkyō* (*Buddhism Made Easy*, 2016); autography, like Kobayashi Eriko's *Eriko no shippai nikki* (*Diary of My Daily Failures*, 2017); graphic medicine, like Nogizaka Tarō and Nagai Akira's *Iryū chīmu medikaru doragon* (*Medical Team Dragon*, 2002–2011); and gritty real-life works, such as Tatsumi Yoshihiro's classic *Tōkyō ubasuteyama* (*Abandon the Old in Tokyo*, 1971).

Even mainstream escapist entertainment can delve into matters of social significance: Inoue Takehiko's bestselling series *Riaru* (*Real*, 1999–present) addresses disability issues through the vehicle of wheelchair basketball. Tatsuta Kazuto's *Ichi-efu* (*Ichi-F*, 2014) is an exposé of Tokyo Electric Power Company's coverup of the nuclear meltdown that was part of Japan's triple disaster in March of 2011. And Nakazawa Keiji's *Hadashi no Gen* (*Barefoot Gen*, 1973–1987) provides a frank account of the atomic bombing of Hiroshima and its aftermath.

That said, *manga* is not really "uniquely Japanese" in the first place. In

Japan, many works are decidedly multinational in their production, as well as content, and reception, if not impact. A surprising number of *manga* are created by non-Japanese, printed elsewhere in Asia, and feed into overseas markets, where translated versions of these works interact in complex ways with other indigenous comics traditions. A growing number of *manga* originally conceived of in English or German or French masquerade as translations of Japanese-language works by supposed Japanese creators who turn out to be fictional alter-egos of the actual creators, whose names sometimes grace works as fictional "translators."

Manga might be better conceived of as Japanese-*styled* comics, a visual if not verbal style that can be learned by anyone, not just the Japanese. The distinction is rarely made in commercial publishing and bookselling, mass media, and popular journalism. In higher education, this distinction is downplayed, even within Japanese Studies, a field whose entire *raison d'être* is to treat things Japanese as unique objects of specialized knowledge. Thus, Japanese Studies itself tends to define and even isolate *manga* as Japanese comics, without a more global purview.

The Ghettoization of Manga Studies within Comics Studies

The situation with Comics Studies is not much better. In spite of the popularity of comics and graphic novels, Comics Studies programs are few and far between. As an emerging field, it is still struggling to find its place. Until Comics Studies is more firmly rooted within the academy, its support of Manga Studies will remain nominal. The failure of Comics Studies to fully admit Manga Studies into its ranks may also be a matter of Orientalism; for the "relationship between Occident and Orient," as Edward Said memorably observed, "is a relationship of power, of domination." (Said 1979, 5).

To be fair, most scholars of Comics Studies would dispute this characterization. Charles Hatfield, one of the disciplinary pioneers and founding members of the Comics Studies Society, denies this ghettoization (private communication, June 2019). *INKS*, the Society's journal, runs articles and includes editorial board members outside of Western Comics Studies. Still, most Comics Studies scholarship treats *manga* as the exception that proves the rule of Euroamerican primacy. Too often Comics Studies scholars seem oblivious to the role of Japanese comics in the history of comics worldwide. Moreover, while the CSS claims to be the first in the world, having been founded in 2016, it is first only in the *Western* world; in Japan, the Nihon Manga Gakkai (the Japan Society for Studies in Cartoons and Comics) was established in 2001, some 15 years earlier.

The worst preconception in Comics Studies, however, is the belief that comics is originally a Western artform. Who invented what, when, where, and why is ultimately a definitional shell game. Generally speaking, Comics Studies has set the terms of the debate as a simple binary choice: comics either arose in *fin-de-siècle* America, with works like Richard F. Outcault's (1863–1928) *Yellow Kid*, or else earlier in Europe, with the mid-nineteenth century works of Swiss creator Rodolphe Töpffer (1799–1846). Or even, perhaps, in the early eighteenth-century works of British creator William Hogarth (1697–1764).

This debate also routinely presumes that comics must be *mass-produced* in printed form, typically meaning Western metal-plate print, as with newspaper comic strips. By this logic, Hogarth's A *Rake's Progress* would qualify as comics only in its engraved form, not its original paintings. Nor would the original cartoons of Saul Steinberg, for that matter. Nor the original drawings (*genga*) and one-off commissioned works (*kakioroshi*) of legion *manga* creators today. Nor webcomics. Here, we are confronted with the question of materiality, not to mention where to draw the line between mere and mass dissemination. In the age of the internet, would small print-run "fanzine" comics—like John Porcellino's critically acclaimed *King-Cat Comics*—no longer be considered "comics" merely because its circulation pales in comparison to South Korean creator SIU's massively popular webcomic *Sin-ui Tap* (*Tower of God*)?

More significantly, non-Western sequential graphic narratives are still denied consideration as "real" comics on the grounds that they are not Western. The most conspicuous case in point being the woodblock-printed comic books of early modern Japan (1600–1868). These comic books, called *kusazōshi* ("grass-script booklets"), were mass produced in multiple print runs, sometimes totaling thousands of copies. Although in the West mass printing is often dated to Guttenberg's fifteenth-century Bible, in point of fact the Chinese developed mass woodblock-printing over a millennium earlier. The Japanese adapted this technology hundreds of years before Guttenberg. By the turn of the eighteenth century, woodblock-printing technology allowed not only faster production, but also the comixing of word and image far more seamlessly than anything possible in metal-plate printing.

Being mass-produced sequential visual narratives, *kusazōshi* satisfy the prevailing definition of comics in the West, except that their printing is not Western metal-block printing. Moreover, being produced in hundreds of titles per year, they were arguably the first major form of comic book in world history. Their existence has long been known within Japanese Studies in the West (Zolbrod 1968; Araki 1970). More recently, scholars writing in English have endeavored to spread word of these comic books beyond Japanese Studies (Shiokawa 1996; Shimizu 2001; Kern 2006; Koyama-Richard 2007; Ito 2008). Nevertheless, Comics Studies has paid little attention. Almost all scholars writing about comics as a mass-produced, sequential, pictorial narrative take it for granted that comics is European or American, not Asian.

This stubborn obliviousness can be seen within *The Routledge Companion to Comics* (Bramlett, Cook, and Meskin 2016). One chapter argues that the modern Japanese *manga* emanated not as a postwar imitation of Western comics, but as a result of the transnational encounter, during the late nineteenth century, between *kusazōshi* and Western political cartoons (Kern 2016). Another chapter by co-editor Aaron Meskin, titled "Defining Comics," treats *kusazōshi* as a "hard case" on the grounds that they are supposedly both more "illustrated literature" than real comics per se and also "Non-Western" (Meskin 2016, 222).

Laudably, Meskin's aim is to interject skepticism into the definitional project of comics. Yet tellingly, when addressing another hard case of "premodern comics," Meskin treats only Hogarth's engravings, ignoring earlier "Non-Western" Japanese comic books completely. This selectivity mirrors the consensus within Comics Studies that Japanese *kusazōshi* are "illustrated literature" or "picture books," anything but "authentic" comic books. This move seems to assume that *kusazōshi* lack multiframe pages, as in Western strip-based comics, instead presenting a single scene on a single page, as though a contemporary children's picturebook, like Margaret Wise Brown and Clement Hurd's *Goodnight Moon*.

Such a position is problematical for at least two reasons beyond the objection that the picturebook, as a kind of text comixing word and images, is a subcategory of comics. First, even if true that all *kusazōshi* present a single scene per page, such "scene-to-scene" transitions are acceptable within the theory of comics as sequential visual narratives. That is, strip-based comics themselves are not limited to moment-to-moment transitions, which are common to comics in the age of cinema. Just because cinema was not available in eighteenth-century Japan, however, does not mean that Japanese comics were *not* comics. The main visual regime of the day was the kabuki theater, where illustrated backdrops marked individual scenes within the plays. No wonder scene-to-scene transitions predominate within *kusazōshi*. Thus, to insist that comics be defined by a cinematic visuality rather than a theatrical one is *chronocentric*, privileging modern regimes over less familiar earlier ones. It also is *ethnocentric*, privileging specifically Western scopic regimes over all others.

Second, while most *kusazōshi* take the single page or even double-page spread as a single panel, it is also true that many such comic books contain at least one page with two or more panels. These panels typically present a different moment in time than that of the main panel. Such panels often assume the form of separate rooms within a building, or of "dream balloons" presenting words and images dreamed by a character. One famous example falls within Koikawa Harumachi's (1744–1789) *Kinkin sensei eiga no yume* (*Master Flashgold's Splendiferous Dream*, 1775), an influential bestseller said to have proverbially raised the price of paper. Simply put, to insist that panelization must assume a Euroamerican *framework*, when other kinds of framework exist even within the Western tradition, let alone other traditions, is blinkered.

Thus are the boundaries of Euroamerican comics—and Comics Studies—policed. As is the understanding of *manga* and comics. Acknowledging common terrain allows us to break down the walls that have been erected to separate Western comics from other comics that do not superficially resemble them. Conversely, a transnational approach to comics reveals that *manga* itself is not a "purely Japanese" form of comics. The putative "Japaneseness" of the modern Japanese *manga* is false, since *manga* is above all a transnational blending of Japanese and Western comics. What is more, labeling modern *manga* as Japanese obscures the Western imperialism that not only introduced Western comics into Japan, but also continues to ghettoize Japan as exotic Other.

The Ghettoization of Manga Studies within Manga Studies

Generally speaking, scholars of Japanese literary studies in Japan pay little to no heed to Japanese literary studies outside of Japan. This may owe to the myth of Japanese uniqueness. It is widely assumed that those raised outside of Japan can never acquire the same fluency in the language and literature as those raised domestically. Similarly, Japanese scholars of Manga Studies in Japan tend to pay little heed to Manga Studies—let alone Comics Studies—outside of Japan.

Professor Jaqueline Berndt, formerly of Kyoto Seika University, during her tenure as head of the affiliated Kyōto Kokusai Manga Myūjiamu (Kyoto International Manga Museum), endeavored to foster an annual international dialogue between Japanese and outside scholars of *manga*. Regrettably, the battle was uphill. When national newspapers in Japan covered a conference in 2014, only Japanese scholars like Natsume Fusanosuke and Shimizu Isao were featured, neglecting mention of the non-Japanese conference organizer and major *manga* scholar. Berndt eventually resigned her appointments and returned to Europe.

In her keynote address, delivered at an international symposium in 2019 associated with the British Museum's "Manga" exhibition, Berndt argued that Manga Studies, being primarily concerned with semiotics, narratology, and genre theory, completely encases Comics Studies, overlaps ever-so-slightly with Japanese Studies and Cultural Studies (which is concerned with users, fandoms, power relations, intersectionality), and overlaps more obviously with Media Studies (including aesthetics, tech, and economics).[5] While her point about the disjunction in content of Manga Studies and Comics Studies is well taken, and in spite of her own heroic efforts to span the divide, the assumption that Manga Studies is a single, unified field seems problematic. The chasm between Japan and elsewhere is gaping.

Fortunately, there are positive signs among younger scholars in Japan, who are conversant with non-Japanese scholarship on *manga*. And younger scholars in the West are becoming well versed in Japanese-language Manga Studies. Crossover work is being increasingly undertaken. A recent example of the kind of collaborative effort among Japanese and Western scholars is *Women's Manga in Asia and Beyond: Uniting Different Cultures and Identities* (2019), edited by Ōgi Fusami, Rebecca Suter, Nagaike Kazumi, and John A. Lent.

Conclusions

The marginality of Manga Studies within the Western neoliberal university allows it the necessary elbow room to generatively critique other fields and disciplines. Manga Studies can provide a much-needed corrective to the tendency within Comics Studies to define comics as sequential graphic narrative, a perspective that is steeped in both Euroamerican comic strips and narratological theory. The minority opinion, that comics should be defined as the comixing of words and images, not only is assimilated into the majority opinion, where it is regularly minimized, but also is based on the Abrahamic bifurcation of word and image. The worldwide predominance of *manga*, therefore, can help interrogate some of Euroamerican assumptions as ethnocentric, chronocentric, and logocentric.

Granted, many mainstream *manga* themselves uphold Eurocentric frameworks. However, many other comics in Japan and elsewhere, including the West, do not. In the contemporary US, for instance, the works of Chris Ware regularly play with space and time in a way that troubles overly simplistic strip-based models. In Japan, the phenomenally popular *kusazōshi* are another case in point. But even within contemporary *manga* there are significant counterexamples.

Ultimately, in spite of the reasons for the ghettoization of Manga Studies, overcoming this ghettoization itself should not be the goal. The very project of Manga Studies is too narrow; being limited to *manga*, it is too easily consigned to Japanese Studies and thus closed off to a global consideration of comics. The ultimate goal should be to ensure that Manga Studies and Comics Studies tend to their various cultural histories while contributing to a larger discussion of comics as a major mode of human communication in a transnational context. This reevaluation of comics broadly defined could then be extended back into various areas of cultural production, even within Japanese Studies.

For instance, *The Tale of Genji* (*Genji monogatari*, c. 1000) has typically been extolled as the world's first novel. While the impact of this masterpiece on later Japanese cultural production is undeniable, identifying *Genji* as a "novel" centuries earlier than that form was conceived is dubious. To the extent that *Genji* can be called a novel, though, it was only transposed into that Western literary form a millennium after the work's *début*, as a result of Japan's transnational encounter with the West during the late nineteenth and early twentieth centuries. When *Genji* was translated into Western languages, as a Japanized prose novel, its poetry and pictures were mostly jettisoned. Yet throughout its first millennium in Japan, it was often circulated, read, and conceived of largely as an illustrated tale. *Genji*'s longstanding affinity for illustration would seem to suggest, if one must deal in the terms of Euroamerican categories, that it was less the world's first novel than the world's first *graphic* novel.

It may be more difficult to reevaluate Western cultural history through the lens of comics, in the context of the Abrahamic logocentrism of the Western neoliberal university, than it is for Japanese Studies. As overall sales of literary books decline and *manga* books increase, however, there may be an opportunity to reevaluate the situation. A Comics Studies fully enriched by *manga* can help rethink literature itself as the exception that proves the rule of comics as a major mode—if not *the* major mode—of human communication across time and space. Just as the Japanese in the late nineteenth century began looking to Western models of literature, it may be time for the West—as well as the Japanese *themselves*—to become more open to comics including *manga* as a new model for human expression. The future of the humanities may well depend on it.

Notes

1. Robert Harvey defines comics as "the blending of verbal and visual content" (Harvey 2009, 25). Scott McCloud influentially writes of "juxtaposed pictorial and other images in deliberate sequence, intended to convey information and/or to produce an aesthetic response in the viewer" (McCloud 1993, 25).

2. For more on global studies and Japanese literature, see Tsuboi Hideto's contribution to this volume.

3. These percentages are based on the *United Nations Population Division* estimates for 2019.

4. For more on this sense of crisis, see the chapter by Jeffrey Angles in this volume.

5. Jaqueline Berndt, "Manga Studies' 'Manga' and the Outsider Perspective: Intercultural Observations." Talk delivered at the symposium "What is Manga? Exploring Japanese Manga and the Visual Narratives in Context through the British Museum's Manga Exhibition and Beyond." The British Library, August 23, 2019.

Works Cited

Apter, Emily. *Against World Literature: On the Politics of Untranslatability*. Verso, 2013.

Araki, James. "The Dream Pillow in Edo Fiction: 1772–81." *Monumenta Nipponica* 25, no. 1 (1970): 43–105.

Belsey, Catherine. "Interdisciplinarity." *Textual Practice* 30, no. 7 (2016): 1170–71.

Berndt, Enno, and Jaqueline Berndt. "Mangazines and Books: Changes in the Manga Market." In *Manga: Medium, Kunst und Material/Media*, edited by Jaqueline Berndt, 227–39. Leipzig University Press, 2015.

Bramlett, Frank, Roy T. Cook, and Aaron Meskin, eds., *The Routledge Companion to Comics*. Routledge, 2016.

Czerwiec, Mary Kay, et al., "Introduction: Welcome to the Graphic Medicine Manifesto." In *Graphic Medicine Manifesto, by* Mary Kay Czerwiec, Ian Williams, Susan Merrill Squier, Michael J. Green, Kimberly R. Myers, and Scott T. Smith, 1–20. Penn State Press, 2015.

Even-Zohar, Itamar, Elias J. Torres Feijó, and Antonio Monegal. "The End of Literature; or, What Purposes Does It Continue to Serve?" *Poetics Today* 40, no. 1 (March 2019): 7–31.

Gravett, Paul. *Manga: Sixty Years of Japanese Comics*. Laurence King Publishing, 2004.

Grennan, Simon. "The Influences of Manga on the Graphic Novel." In *The Cambridge History of the Graphic Novel, edited by* Jan Baettens, Hugo Frey, and Stephen E. Tabachnick, 320–36. Cambridge University Press, 2018.

Inouye, Charles Shirō. "Pictocentrism." *Yearbook of Comparative and General Literature* 40 (1992): 23–39.

Ito, Kinko. "*Manga* in Japanese History." In *Japanese Visual Culture: Explorations in the World of Manga and Anime, edited by* Mark MacWilliams, 26–47. M. E. Sharpe, 2008.

Kashtan, Aaron. *Between Pen and Pixel: Comics, Materiality, and the Book of the Future (Studies in Comics and Cartoons)*. Ohio State University Press, 2018.

Kern, Adam L. "East Asian Comix: Intermingling Japanese *Manga* and Euro-American Comics." Invited chapter for *The Routledge Companion to Comics, edited by* Frank Bramlett, Roy T. Cook, and Aaron Meskin, 106–15. Routledge, 2016.

Kern, Adam L. *Manga from the Floating World: Comicbook Culture and the* Kibyōshi *of Edo Japan.* Harvard East Asian Monographs, no. 279. Harvard University Asia Center, 2006.

Koyama-Richard, Brigitte. "The Magic of the Scroll: From the Earliest Caricatures to the Onset of the Comic Strip" and "The Birth of the Japanese Print: The Golden Age of Caricature." In *One Thousand Years of Manga, by Brigitte Koyama-Richard,* 8–35 and 36–98. Flammarion, 2007.

Marks, Laura. *Enfoldment and Infinity: An Islamic Genealogy of New Media Art.* MIT Press, 2010.

Meskin, Aaron. "Defining Comics." In *The Routledge Companion to Comics, edited by* Frank Bramlett, Roy T. Cook, and Aaron Meskin, 221–29. Routledge, 2016.

Ōgi, Fusami, Rebecca Suter, Nagaike Kazumi, and John A. Lent, eds. *Women's Manga in Asia and Beyond: Uniting Different Cultures and Identities.* Palgrave Macmillan, 2019.

Said, Edward. *Orientalism.* Random House, 1979.

Shimizu, Isao. "Red Comic Books: The Origins of Modern Japanese *Manga.*" In *Illustrating Asia: Comics, Humor Magazines and Picture Books, edited by John Lent, 137–50.* University of Hawai'i Press, 2001.

Shiokawa Kanako. "'The Reads' and 'Yellow Covers': Pre-Modern Predecessors of Comic Books in Japan." *Journal of Asian Pacific Communication* 7, nos. 1 and 2 (1996): 19–29. Special Issue: *Comic Art in Asia: Historical, Literary and Political Roots.*

Thompson, Jason. "How Manga Conquered America." Illustrated by Okura Atsuhisa. *Wired* (November 2007): 223–33.

Treat, John. *The Rise and Fall of Modern Japanese Literature.* The University of Chicago Press, 2018.

Vallelly, Neil. "From the Margins of the Neoliberal University: Notes Toward Nomadic Literary Studies." *Poetics Today* 40, no. 1 (March 2019): 59–79.

Zolbrod, Leon. "*Kusazōshi*: Chapbooks of Japan." *Transactions of the Asiatic Society of Japan* 3, no. 10 (1968): 116–47.

CHAPTER 6

Approaches to Researching and Teaching Manga as Literature

Deborah Shamoon

Manga occupies an uneasy space in Japanese literary studies. The development of modern Japanese literature was central to the formation of Japan as a modern nation in the Meiji period, alongside other domesticated, hybridized art forms such as *yōga* (Western-style oil painting), *shintaishi* (modern-form poetry), and *shinpa* (modern theater), but the same was never true for manga. Although Charles Wirgman brought European-style cartooning to Japan in the early Meiji period, and although Wirgman was also instrumental in the introduction of oil painting and photography, cartoons or comics were never high-status art forms.[1] To the contrary, throughout the decades in which manga developed, it was considered childish and trashy. Manga was considered harmful to children, subject to periodic censorship, and banned in many schools.[2] It was only in the late 1990s that manga emerged as a topic of academic study. In 2002, Douglas McGray identified manga along with other forms of pop culture as part of Japan's "Gross National Cool," changing manga's status from national embarrassment to potential engine of soft power.[3] Not surprisingly, given this history, manga has only emerged recently as a topic of academic study. While manga studies has grown steadily in the past two decades, the field remains small and marginalized. Moreover, manga's sudden change in status from despised to celebrated has led to mythologizing, Orientalizing narratives that have proved stubbornly self-perpetuating. This essay will give an overview of the history of manga, the current state of the field of manga studies, and some reflections on teaching manga as an academic subject.

The Development of Manga

It is a sign of manga's marginal status that a section on the history of manga is necessary, and that terms and definitions must be established before reviewing the state of the field of manga studies. This is not the case for Japanese literature—this volume does not need a chapter on the development of the modern Japanese novel in the Meiji period, nor a definition of what exactly is and is not a novel. This is not the case for film studies or television studies either; although these are newer media, their place in academic discourse is better established, and their histories well known. But with manga, we cannot even begin without defining terms, starting with "manga" and "comics."[4] Because manga in Japan has a distinct history as well as genres and aesthetic conventions that differ from those of the US and Europe, "manga" is often used to indicate publications from Japan, "comics" publications from the US and UK, and "bandes dessinées" or BD publications from France and Belgium.[5] This is admittedly a reductive paradigm that leaves out traditions of *manhwa* or *manhua* from South Korea and China, as well as international hybrid styles. But for the sake of simplicity, in this essay I will use the term manga to indicate publications from Japan specifically.

Manga is a mass medium, relying on modern printing technologies developed in the late nineteenth century for dissemination. The myth that manga has a centuries-old history in Japan has proved as stubbornly persistent as similar invented traditions, such as bushidō, despite repeated debunking.[6] Manga did not develop until after the cinematograph and phonograph, which segmented motion and severed sound from its source, allowing for the division of images into panels and speech into balloons. Eike Exner refers to these as transdiegetic elements, that is, features that exist both within and outside the diegesis.[7] Speech balloons, sound effects, emotive backgrounds, and icons indicating emotional states (such as pain stars or sweat drops) are all transdiegetic as they reflect elements generated within the fictional world, but the characters do not literally see them.[8] Thierry Smolderen traces the development of these techniques, what he calls the audiovisual stage, to American and European newspaper comic strips at the turn of the twentieth century.[9] These techniques were brought to Japan with the translation of the comic strip *Bringing Up Father* in the *Asahi Graph* in 1923, and quickly adopted by Japanese artists.[10]

To be clear, not every combination of text and image is manga. Emaki, ukiyo-e, *Hokusai manga*, none of these are manga in the modern sense. What today is called *Hokusai manga* is a collection of fifteen volumes of sketchbooks by ukiyo-e artist Katsushika Hokusai, published 1814–1879. Although some of the sketches seem satirical, there is no narrative. There has been some debate around Hokusai's use of the term manga; while he did not invent the word, it was not in common usage, and its exact denotation and connotation in the Edo period is unclear. Regardless, the term manga seems to have indicated cartoon or sketch.[11] With the introduction of French- and British-style political cartoons, the term *ponchi-e* became common in the Meiji period, referring to the satirical magazine *Punch*, although these tended to be single-panel images with captions.[12] The term manga was used by Kitazawa Rakuten and others in the Taishō period, where like *ponchi-e* it primarily referred to political cartoons.[13] What is now called "story manga" (*sutorii manga*), meaning serialized, long-form narrative manga, began to appear in boys' and girls' literary magazines in the 1930s such as *Shōnen Club* and *Shōjo Club*.[14] From the 1950s, these magazines increasingly shifted their content from illustrated serialized novels to manga. The division of the industry into magazines for boys and girls determined both target readership and aesthetic style; this is the origin of the two main genres, shōnen and shōjo manga. This focus exclusively on magazine-based story manga to the exclusion of newspaper-based comic strips (*yonkoma*) and political cartoons is a problem in the field of manga studies.[15] Nevertheless, the term manga usually indicates magazine-based story manga.

The postwar "manga boom" of the 1950s was driven by the popularity of Tezuka Osamu's adventure stories for children such as *Astro Boy* (*Tetsuwan Atomu*), although his central place in manga history has been debated in manga studies.[16] By the end of the 1950s, older teen readers longed for more mature content. Tatsumi Yoshihiro and his collaborators coined the term *gekiga* to distinguish stories for older readers, versus manga for children, in an effort to avoid censorship.[17] In the 1960s, gekiga was the main site of narrative and artistic experimentation, mainly in rental books (*kashihon*) and in the independent magazine *Garo*, which allowed more freedom than the magazines from major publishers.[18] Many gekiga artists were politically active, and the genre is deeply tied to the student protests of the 1960s.[19] But as manga genres diversified and readers aged, by the 1980s, the term manga no longer implied only stories for children. As the term manga expanded to mean stories for every age and across genres, the term gekiga fell out of usage, and the genre itself merged with *seinen* (manga for adult men).

Given this relatively recent and well-documented history of manga, why is the myth of manga's ancient origins so often repeated? This myth appears in English language popular press books such as the misleadingly titled *One Thousand Years of Manga*, and in Japanese language writing on manga, beginning as far back as 1924 with *Nihon mangashi* (A History of Japanese Manga) by Hosokibara Seiki, repeated by more recent writers, such as Shimizu Isao.[20] One reason for the persistence of this myth is the desire to claim for manga the high status of classical art. As Exner writes, "The impulse to bolster the prestige of these oft-diminished forms of expression by tying them to universally respected 'real art' is understandable but counterproductive to evidence-based historiography, since such genealogical claims feed into the myth that manga is metaphysical and ahistorical on the one hand and uniquely and essentially Japanese on the other."[21] In part, this also stems from popular press writing on comics that makes the same rhetorical move, most notably Scott McCloud's *Understanding Comics* which attempts to give comics cultural legitimacy by claiming origins in Egyptian hieroglyphics and William Hogarth's *A Rake's Progress*.[22] In the case of Japan specifically, as Exner notes, appeals to emaki and other classical art also bolsters self-Orientalizing claims of Japanese uniqueness, attempting to explain the current popularity of manga with ahistorical and evidence-free speculation on an unbroken Japanese graphic tradition. This dovetails with Japanese government efforts to promote manga as a form of soft power. Exner describes guidelines issued by the Ministry of Culture and Education in 2000 requiring middle school students be taught that emaki and ukiyo-e are forms of manga and part of Japan's "traditional mode of expression."[23] This ahistorical view obscures manga's actual origins as developing directly from American newspaper comic strips, as well as manga's association with children, with the working class, and with the 1960s counterculture. Ōtsuka Eiji further argues that emphasizing the distant past elides the development of manga in the 1930s and 1940s and connections with fascism.[24] The cultural cachet also works in the reverse, as museums attempt to garner popular interest in exhibits on emaki and ukiyo-e by promoting them as manga.[25]

State of the Field: Manga Studies and Comics Studies

These issues of low status and mythmaking are consistent problems in manga studies as a field, problems which exist in comics studies in English as well. Jospeh Witek characterizes American comics studies as "an argument delivered from a defensive crouch, a discourse addressed not to an audience of informed and sympathetic colleagues but to an imperfectly imagined hangman's jury of deans, intra- and extra-disciplinary experts, the editors and readers of the *Comics Journal*, and the people who write book reviews on Amazon.com, all of these divergent discursive expectations and often contradictory intellectual goals."[26] Bart Beaty, writing in a special issue of *Cinema Journal* on Comics Studies in 2011, notes that "Comics Studies lags about a half century behind the academic study of film."[27] In the years since, the situation has not changed according to the metrics Beaty proposes:

> One of the turning points in the legitimization of Film Studies as a discipline was its ability to develop models of spectatorship that were unique to cinema but also offered useful insights for the study of other art forms. The contributions of scholars like Laura Mulvey and Christian Metz are still taught even outside the confines of Film Studies. Comics Studies, by contrast, has had no such breakthrough, and in fact relies largely on terms borrowed from Film Studies . . . Thus Comics Studies remains peripheral to a broader rubric of media arts . . . For Comics Studies to reach parity with Film Studies, it would have to move beyond the narrowly thematic readings of key works and begin to offer critical insights into comics as a social and aesthetic system that has broader transmedia and intermedia implications.[28]

This is not for lack of trying. Hannah Miodrag's 2013 book *Comics and Language* both tackles the defensiveness and anti-intellectualism she sees in comics studies, and provides examples of various approaches to close reading of comics (both image and text) based in literary studies, linguistics, semiotics, and art history. Miodrag argues that the status anxiety of comics scholars breeds defensive snobbery, as well as mutual hostility between scholars and artists.[29] However, she sees the greatest problem in comics studies as the prominence of McCloud's *Understanding Comics*, which she characterizes as appearing "ex nihilo," or out of nowhere, meaning that McCloud's ideas are not supported by prior scholarship; the ubiquity of citations of his work have foreclosed more rigorous academic inquiry.[30] Regardless of one's opinions of McCloud, her observation about comics studies continually being written about ex nihilo, as if no academic field exists, is unfortunately true, and even more true in manga studies in English. As Jaqueline Berndt writes, "academic theses and papers often give the impression that while manga may serve as a mirror for various social and cultural discourses, neither the media-specific aspects of comics nor the Japanese discourse on comics needs to be taken into account."[31]

The publication that has so far come the closest to Beaty's ideal of appealing to scholars in media studies more broadly is *Unflattening* by Nick Sousanis. Written in comics format, *Unflattening* demonstrates the possibility of graphic approaches to academic discourse, as it engages with comics studies and critical theory to examine why comics have been marginalized and the potential for multimodal discourse. Sousanis discusses the Western cultural suspicion of image and historical primacy of the written word since the Enlightenment, and how this has led to severing text and image as complementary modes of communication.[32] Comics studies has long been defensive about the hybrid nature of comics, in particular avoiding any suggestion that comics are "mere illustration," as if illustration is a degraded or childish medium.[33] However, some genres of comics and manga developed directly from illustration, in particular shōjo manga.[34] Rather than denying this hybrid nature, Sousanis embraces it, making a connection between Deleuze and Guattari's concept of the rhizome and French comics studies scholar Thierry Groensteen's theory of braiding or arthrology in comics.[35] As Sousanis demonstrates visually, comics (and manga) composition not only combines text and image but the image on the page is both segmented into panels and read as a whole. He writes, "Comics hold sequential and simultaneous modes in electric tension. Embedded within the sequential-simultaneous ecosystem that is comics, words and pictures, long kept apart, are allowed to cohabitate."[36]

The question of whether or not manga should be considered literature is another mark of defensiveness in the field. Miodrag writes, "The ongoing anxiety about the supposed hierarchy of words and images means that comics are habitually defended against the benchmark of language and literature. If images—or even the comics form itself—can be argued to work just like verbal language, then comics must be as good as 'proper books.'"[37] The need to constantly insist at the start of any academic study that comics are literature undercuts the claims to academic relevance, yet this stance is still frequently deployed.[38] Miodrag delves deeply into questions of language and semiotics in comics, while also demonstrating that the images cannot be reduced only to signs, but must be analyzed using the tools of art history.[39] As she demonstrates, comics (and manga) are hybrid forms that require hybrid modes of analysis, combining literary close reading with tools of image-based fields such as art history or film studies. In other words, manga has always been literature, in terms of possible analytic approaches. But the question "Is manga literature?" is usually a veiled way of asking if manga are the equal of highbrow literature. Continually posing this question is a form of gatekeeping, not unlike the way that women and minorities have been excluded from literary canons. The fact that the question is repeatedly asked suggests that "no" is a possible answer, or that inclusion remains up for debate.

English-language scholarship on manga began to appear in the 1990s, primarily by scholars trained in either Japanese literature or anthropology, who were taking note of the popularity of manga and anime among their students. Scholars such as Susan Napier, Sandra Buckley, and Anne Allison used the theoretical tools of their training to examine manga and anime, but the primary materials they picked up were "out of nowhere": anime available in English translation, or manga titles plucked at random from the convenience store shelf.[40] The larger context of genre, reception, publication, or fan culture was missing. The journal *Mechademia* was founded in 2006 in part as a counter to this type of scholarship. In an acknowledgment that scholars were often missing history and context of manga and anime, the earliest issues had a peer review board of both scholars and self-identified otaku, although that was later dropped as the journal moved in a more decisively academic direction. However, *Mechademia*'s greater impact has been in making key scholarship in Japanese available in English translation, which has helped to encourage a more systematic and informed approach in manga studies.

Yet there remains a gulf between manga studies in English and Japanese, and the problem is both linguistic and cultural. While the first wave of English language scholarship in manga studies was by academics trained in other fields, the first wave of Japanese language writing on manga was by non-academics who were artists, fans, or editors. This began as early as the 1920s, with artists Kitazawa Rakuten, Okamoto Ippei, and Hosokibara Seiki.[41] In the 1980s and 1990s, the rise of fan culture brought another wave of manga scholarship, for example by Yonezawa Yoshihiro, who co-founded Comic Market, manga artist Natsume Fusanosuke, and editors Fujimoto Yukari, and Otsuka Eiji.[42] This is not a criticism of their work; to the contrary, they are deeply informed and insightful in the history, genre formation, and formal features of manga, and Natsume, Fujimoto, and Ōtsuka later entered academia. But their writing, particularly their earliest books which made them famous, have a chatty, personal tone which clashes with English language scholarly conventions. As Berndt writes,

> Manga Studies in Japan originates mainly from the activities of collectors and critics. Some of them are university professors by now (a fact which . . . is to be related more to recent trends of populism within the Japanese university system than to the allegedly unproblematic status of manga within Japanese society). Yet, decade-long

> research on the institutional offside (*zaiya*) gave rise to two extremes, that is, either over-respecting conventional academism, or conversely, underestimating institutionalized scholarship. Since the 1970s, there has been a strong skepticism against both research in the humanities and intellectual discourse, out of the fear that cultural elites might snatch manga away from its regular readers and misappropriate it for their "foreign" purposes. . . . [This] has gone hand in hand with an increasingly uncritical attitude toward the manga market and industry since the 1990s.
>
> At the same time, the unfamiliarity of manga critics with academia has furthered notions of scholarship which tend to put emphasis on positivist historicism, or structuralist semiotics at the expense of critical theory and political contextualization.[43]

Another problem, as Berndt indicates, is the lack of connection between manga studies and comics studies. The discourse in both fields can be quite insular, as noted above by Witek and Berndt, and this is exacerbated by lack of availability of scholarship in translation. For example, Itō Gō's book *Tezuka is Dead* is the single most important work of scholarship in manga studies of the early 2000s, but it is still untranslated.[44] In 2011, *Mechademia* published a translation of the first chapter, but this does not contain the book's key concepts on systems of representation and on the development of characters. Instead, the translation consists of Itō's criticism of manga studies in Japanese, particularly the fannish adoration of Tezuka and tendency to dismiss manga by more recent artists as "boring."[45] This is a necessary intervention in the field, but as the chapter is squarely situated in a Japanese language context, it is difficult for readers not familiar with the scholars he criticizes to find anything useful. Itō's work is part of a trend in manga studies toward greater academism, including also work by film scholar Yomota Inuhiko.[46] Formalist approaches to manga studies, such as by Natsume, Itō, and Yomota, are a central part of the field in Japanese, that is, studying manga as manga rather than as evidence of sociological or cultural trends.

Another disconnect between manga studies in Japanese and in English is the attention afforded to the two major genres, shōnen and shōjo manga. In Japanese-language scholarship, shōnen manga is the primary subject, to a problematic extent, as shōnen is usually the unmarked case indicated by the word "manga," without critical reflection on that bias.[47] Scholarship on shōjo manga in Japanese is often relegated in anthologies to a single chapter. While there are significant book-length studies of shōjo manga, as Takahashi Mizuki notes, until recently, these tended to be written in a personal memoir style.[48] Conversely, English language scholarship on manga has neglected shōnen and seinen manga almost entirely. Although I have written a book tracing the narrative and aesthetic genealogy of shōjo manga, no equivalent book in English exists for the development of shōnen manga.[49] This is due to the scholarly preference for primary texts that can be more easily labeled subversive of gender norms. For example, in *Manga Cultures and the Female Gaze*, Kathryn Hemmann analyzes how shōjo manga employs "a female gaze to subvert gendered character tropes and thus provides a viable means of female empowerment while queering the gendered nature of manga genres."[50] This despite the fact that the selected primary texts are not so clearly received as subversive in Japan. Numerous books and articles in English analyze boys' love (BL) manga, discussing male-male romance through a queer theory lens.[51] However, in Japan since the mid-1990s, BL has been criticized by queer men for appropriating and misrepresenting their culture, and for promoting homophobia and heteronormativity, as these are narratives written by and for heterosexual women.[52] Ishida Hitoshi reignited this so-called *yaoi ronsō* (yaoi debate) in 2007 by accusing BL artists and fans of defensiveness in insisting that their fantasies have no relation to the lived reality of gay men.[53] Wherever one falls on the *yaoi ronsō*, however, when two marginalized groups are pitted against each other in public debate, both sides lose. Furthermore, greater engagement with similar genres outside Japan, namely m-m slash fiction and m-m romance novels by heterosexual female authors would provide context for how these genres sometimes reproduce internalized misogyny and homophobia.[54]

Pedagogical Approaches to Manga in the University Classroom

Despite the fact that manga studies scholars have been present in Japanese literature departments for more than two decades, and that teaching manga, anime and other forms of popular culture is an outgrowth of film studies, media studies and other related fields, manga is still viewed with suspicion and hostility by some Japanese literature scholars. In other essays in this volume, manga is the stand-in for larger problems in academia: the erosion of academic rigor, the slide toward entertainment rather than education, the sense that serious subjects like highbrow literature are losing out to popular media. However, there is more at stake than merely anxiety over slipping standards. The larger, unstated fear is of loss of authority in the classroom, fear that if literature professors bow to pressure to include manga in the syllabus, they will be faced with students who know more than they do. But rather

Figure 1: Manga adaptation of Natsume Sōseki's *Kokoro*, by Arisu Sari. Bunkyosha, 2021.

than researching the field, some instructors pressured to include manga fall back on what they already know. A senior professor once told me gleefully that he put "manga" in the title of his class, but the only manga he assigned was an adaptation of *The Tale of Genji*, which he used as a trojan horse, as the true focus of the course was on the original text of *Genji*, not manga.

To those literature instructors considering including manga under duress, I say: don't. Don't pluck individual titles at random, don't create bait-and-switch titles for your classes, and don't drop primary texts into the syllabus without a plan for engaging seriously with the field. Teaching the manga *Tale of Genji* "out of nowhere" only demonstrates to students that the manga is not as good as the original. There are some excellent manga adaptations of classic Japanese literature, such as an adaptation of *Kokoro* illustrated by Arisu Sari using the visual conventions of BL manga, which highlight the homoerotic subtext of the novel (Figure 1).[55] But any use of manga adaptations in teaching should treat them as the adaptations and remediations that they are, not a usurper of the original novel.

Relying only on adaptations of classic literature also ignores the fact that manga has its own canon and classics, which are now increasingly available in English translation. It is a misconception that students are only interested in pop culture topics. To the contrary, when manga or other pop culture texts are included in the syllabus, if it is approached with any kind of intellectual rigor, it ceases to be entertainment and becomes schoolwork. Any topic, even *bundan* novels, can spark student interest if taught in an engaging, relevant way. Students tend to arrive in a literature class primed for discussion of serious topics, while students often resist academic approaches to manga, anime, and film because they mistakenly think the class will not be intellectually demanding. The use of manga in the classroom must be aligned with the pedagogical goals of the class as a whole, and not merely a cynical attempt to boost enrolment numbers. In a volume I co-edited, *Teaching Japanese Popular Culture*, we discuss two major approaches to using manga and other pop culture texts in the classroom: teaching *about* pop culture and teaching *with* pop culture.[56] In the former approach, teaching about manga, for example, the goals of the class are to learn the history, genres, visual and narrative features of analyzing manga. In the latter approach, manga are primary texts in, for example, a language or history course. Both approaches are useful, depending on the goals of the course. But if the former approach is taken, even if manga is only part of the syllabus, the instructor should be familiar with manga studies as a field, even if secondary sources are not assigned. For those instructors and students seeking to engage seriously with manga, the ideal place to start is *Manga: A Critical Guide*, which provides an overview of the medium and field in a brief, accessible format, and *The Cambridge Companion to Manga and Anime.*[57]

In terms of teaching manga alongside Japanese literature, there are some classic titles that lend themselves more readily to close reading, which are more literary, and which are available in translation. These titles are also major classics in manga history. Tezuka Osamu's entire oeuvre has been translated, and of these, *Phoenix* and *Buddha* are examples of his more mature work.[58] Mizuki Shigeru, best known for his supernatural series for children, *Gegege no Kitaro*, also produced a tremendous body of serious work for adults, including two autobiographical volumes, *NonNonba* and *Onwards Towards Our Noble Deaths.*[59] The short stories by gekiga pioneer Tatsumi Yoshihiro published in the volumes *The Push Man* and *Abandon the Old in Tokyo* reflect those left behind in Japan's high-growth era of the 1970s.[60] Publisher Drawn & Quarterly has been releasing the complete translation of short stories by avant-garde auteur Tsuge Yoshiharu, with extensive notes by art historian Ryan Holmberg. Of these, the most notable are "Red Flowers" (which was in part inspired by a short story by Dazai Osamu) and surrealist masterpiece "Nejishiki" (Screw-style), which was instrumental in proving that manga could be art and not merely entertainment.[61] Drawn & Quarterly has also begun publishing Shirato Sanpei's *The Legend of Kamui*, a magisterial examination of class struggle in the Edo period, and a major influence on the student protestors of the 1960s. In the genre of shōjo manga, two major classics are *The Rose of Versailles* by Ikeda Riyoko and *The Heart of Thomas* by Hagio Moto, a bildungsroman in the style of Hermann Hesse.[62] While it is somewhat problematic to promote only "classics" of manga and those titles which are more literary and not necessarily representative of most genres, there is utility in seeing the development and history of manga, and selecting those titles that fit most easily into a literature classroom.

Works Cited

Allison, Anne. *Permitted and Prohibited Desires: Mothers, Comics, and Censorship in Japan.* University of California Press, 2000.

Bauer, Carola K. *Naughty Girls and Gay Male Romance/Porn: Slash Fiction, Boys' Love Manga, and Other Works by Female "Cross-Voyeurs" in the U.S. Academic Discourses.* Anchor Academic Publishing, 2013.

Beaty, Bart. "IN FOCUS: Comics Studies Fifty Years After Film Studies: Introduction." *Cinema Journal* 50, no. 3 (2011): 106–10.

Berndt, Jaqueline, ed. *Comics Worlds and the World of Comics: Towards Scholarship on a Global Scale.* 1st ed. Global Manga Studies 1. International Manga Research Center, Kyoto Seika University, 2010.

Berndt, Jaqueline. "Considering Manga Discourse: Location, Ambiguity, Historicity." In *Japanese Visual Culture*, edited by Mark MacWilliams, 295–310. M. E. Sharpe, 2008.

Berndt, Jaqueline. "The Intercultural Challenge of the 'Mangaesque': Reorienting Manga Studies after 3/11." In *Manga's Cultural Crossroads*, edited by Jaqueline Berndt and Bettina Kümmerling-Meibaur, 65–84. Routledge, 2014.

Berndt, Jaqueline, ed. *The Cambridge Companion to Manga and Anime*. Cambridge University Press, 2024.

Buckley, Sandra. "'Penguin in Bondage': A Graphic Tale of Japanese Comic Books." In *Technoculture*, edited by Constance Penley and Andrew Ross, 163–96. University of Minnesota Press, 1991.

Chute, Hillary. *Why Comics?: From Underground to Everywhere*. HarperCollins, 2017.

Exner, Eike. *Comics and the Origins of Manga: A Revisionist History*. Rutgers University Press, 2021.

Fujimoto Yukari. *Watashi no ibasho wa doko ni aru no? Shōjo manga ga utsusu kokoro no katachi*. Gakuyō Shobō, 1998.

Hagio, Moto. *The Heart of Thomas*. Translated by Rachel Thorn. Fantagraphics Books, 2012.

Hatfield, Charles. *Alternative Comics: An Emerging Literature*. University Press of Mississippi, 2005.

Hemmann, Kathryn. *Manga Cultures and the Female Gaze*. Springer International Publishing, 2020.

Holmberg, Ryan. "The Manga of Garo, 1964–1973." *Orientations* 41, no. 4 (2010): 1–6.

Ikeda, Riyoko. *The Rose of Versailles*. Translated by Jocelyne Allen. 5 vols. Udon Entertainment, 2019.

Ishida, Hitoshi. "Representational Appropriation and the Autonomy of Desire in *Yaoi*/BL," translated by Katsuhiko Suganuma. In *Boys Love Manga and Beyond: History, Culture, and Community in Japan*, edited by Mark McClelland, James Welker, Kazumi Nagaike, and Katsuhiko Suganuma, 210–33. University Press of Mississippi, 2015.

Itō, Gō. "Tezuka Is Dead: Manga in Transformation and Its Dysfunctional Discourse." Translated by Miri Nakamura. *Mechademia* 6 (2011): 69–82.

Itō Gō. *Tezuka izu deddo: Hirakareta manga hyōgenron e*. NTT Shuppan, 2005.

Iwashita Hōsei. *Shōjo manga no hyōgen kikō: hirakareta manga hyōgenshi to "Tezuka Osamu."* NTT Shuppan, 2013.

Koyama-Richard, Brigitte. *One Thousand Years of Manga*. Rizzoli, 2008.

Lent, John, ed. *Pulp Demons: International Dimensions of the Postwar Anti-Comics Campaign*. Farleigh Dickinson University Press, 1999.

Levi, Antonia, Mark McHarry, and Dru Pagliassotti, eds. *Boys' Love Manga: Essays on the Sexual Ambiguity and Cross-Cultural Fandom of the Genre*. McFarland & Co., 2008.

Lewis, Mia Elise. "Visions of Possible Girls: Intersectional Feminist Narratives in Contemporary Japanese Boys' Comics." PhD diss., Stanford University, 2022.

McCloud, Scott. *Understanding Comics: The Invisible Art*. Harper Paperbacks, 1994.

McGray, Douglas. "Japan's Gross National Cool." *Foreign Policy*, no. 130 (June 2002): 44–54.

McLelland, Mark, Kazumi Nagaike, James Welker, and Katsuhiko Suganuma, eds. *Boys Love Manga and Beyond: History, Culture, and Community in Japan*. University Press of Mississippi, 2015.

Miodrag, Hannah. *Comics and Language: Reimagining Critical Discourse on the Form*. University Press of Mississippi, 2013.

Mizuki, Shigeru. *NonNonBa*. Translated by Jocelyne Allen. Drawn & Quarterly, 2020.

Mizuki, Shigeru. *Onward Towards Our Noble Deaths*. Translated by Jocelyne Allen. Drawn & Quarterly, 2022.

Munson, Todd. *The Periodical Press in Treaty-Port Japan: Conflicting Reports from Yokohama, 1861–1870*. Global Oriental, 2013.

Nagaike, Kazumi. "Queer Readings of BL: Are Women 'Plunderers' of Gay Men?" In *International Perspectives on Shojo and Shojo Manga: The Influence of Girl Culture*, edited by Masami Toku, 64–73. Routledge, 2015.

Napier, Susan. *Anime from Akira to Princess Mononoke: Experiencing Contemporary Japanese Animation*. Springer, 2001.

Natsume Fusanosuke. *Manga no yomikata*. Takarajima, 1995.

Natsume Sōseki, and Arisu Sari. *Kokoro*. Bunkyosha, 2021.

Oshiyama Michiko. *Shōjo manga jendaa hyōshōron: "dansō shōjo" no sōkei to aidenteitei*. Sairyūsha, 2007.

Ōtsuka, Eiji. "An Unholy Alliance of Eisenstein and Disney: The Fascist Origins of Otaku Culture." Translated by Thomas Lamarre. *Mechademia*, no. 8 (2013): 251–77.

Ōtsuka Eiji. *Sengo manga no hyōgen kūkan: kigōteki shintai no jubaku*. Shohan. Hozokan, 1994.

Rosenbaum, Roman. "The Gekiga Tradition: Towards a Graphic Rendition of History." In *Graphic History: Essays on Graphic Novels And/As History*, edited by Richard Iadonisi, 260–83. Cambridge Scholars Publishing, 2012.

Rosenbaum, Roman. "Towards a Graphical Representation of Japanese Society in the Taishō Period: *Jiji* Manga in *Shinseinen*," 2021, 22.

Shamoon, Deborah. *Passionate Friendship: The Aesthetics of Girls' Culture in Japan*. University of Hawai'i Press, 2012.

Shamoon, Deborah, and Chris McMorran, eds. *Teaching Japanese Popular Culture*. Asia Past & Present: New Research from AAS. Association for Asian Studies, 2016.

Shimizu Isao. *Manga no rekishi*. Iwanami Shoten, 1991.

Shirato Sanpei. *The Legend of Kamui*. Translated by Richard Rubinger and Noriko Rubinger. Drawn & Quarterly, 2025.

Smolderen, Thierry. *The Origins of Comics: From William Hogarth to Winsor McCay*. Translated by Bart Beaty and Nick Nguyen. University Press of Mississippi, 2014.

Sousanis, Nick. *Unflattening*. Harvard University Press, 2015.

Stewart, Ronald. "Manga as Schism: Kitazawa Rakuten's Resistance to 'Old-Fashioned' Japan." In *Manga's Cultural Crossroads*, edited by Jaqueline Berndt and Bettina Kümmerling-Meibauer, 27–49. Routledge, 2013.

Suter, Rebecca. "Reassessing Manga History, Resituating Manga in History." In *Rewriting History in Manga: Stories for the Nation*, edited by Nissim Otmazgin and Rebecca Suter, 175–83. East Asian Popular Culture. Palgrave Macmillan, 2016.

Suzuki, Shige (CJ). "Tatsumi Yoshihiro's *Gekiga* and the Global Sixties: Aspiring for an Alternative." In *Manga's Cultural Crossroads*, edited by Jaqueline Berndt and Bettina Kümmerling-Meibauer, 50–64. Routledge, 2013.

Suzuki, Shige (CJ), and Ronald Stewart. *Manga: A Critical Guide*. Bloomsbury Publishing, 2022.

Takahashi, Mizuki. "Opening the Closed World of Shōjo Manga." In *Japanese Visual Culture*, edited by Mark MacWilliams, 114–36. M. E. Sharpe, 2003.

Tatsumi, Yoshihiro. *Abandon the Old in Tokyo*. Translated by Yuji Oniki. Drawn & Quarterly, 2006.

Tatsumi, Yoshihiro. *The Push Man and Other Stories*. Translated by Yuji Oniki. Drawn & Quarterly, 2012.

Tezuka, Osamu. *Buddha*. Translated by Yuji Oniki and Maya Rosewood. Vertical, 2003.

Tezuka, Osamu. *Phoenix*. Translated by Caleb D. Cook. 4 vols. UDON Entertainment, 2023.

Tsuge, Yoshiharu. *Nejishiki*. Translated by Ryan Holmberg. Vol. 3. The Complete Mature Works of Yoshiharu Tsuge. Drawn & Quarterly, 2023.

Tsuge, Yoshiharu. *Red Flowers*. Translated by Ryan Holmberg. Vol. 2. The Complete Mature Works of Yoshiharu Tsuge. Drawn & Quarterly, 2021.

Witek, Joseph. "American Comics Criticism and the Problem of Dual Address." *International Journal of Comic Art* 10, no. 1 (2008): 218–25.

Yomota Inuhiko. *Manga genron*. Chikuma Shobō, 1994.

Yonezawa Yoshihiro. *Sengo shōjo mangashi*. Shinpyōsha, 1980.

Notes

1. Todd Munson, *The Periodical Press in Treaty-Port Japan: Conflicting Reports from Yokohama, 1861–1870* (Global Oriental, 2013), 93.

2. John Lent, ed., *Pulp Demons: International Dimensions of the Postwar Anti-Comics Campaign* (Farleigh Dickinson University Press, 1999).

3. Douglas McGray, "Japan's Gross National Cool," *Foreign Policy*, no. 130 (June 2002): 44–54.

4. Shige (CJ) Suzuki and Ronald Stewart, *Manga: A Critical Guide* (Bloomsbury Publishing, 2022), 3–5.

5. Jaqueline Berndt, "The Intercultural Challenge of the 'Mangaesque': Reorienting Manga Studies after 3/11," in *Manga's Cultural Crossroads* (Routledge, 2014), 65–84.

6. Jaqueline Berndt, "Considering Manga Discourse: Location, Ambiguity, Historicity," in *Japanese Visual Culture*, ed. Mark MacWilliams (M. E. Sharpe, 2008), 295–310.

7. Eike Exner, *Comics and the Origins of Manga: A Revisionist History* (Rutgers University Press, 2021), 26.

8. Exner, *Comics and the Origins of Manga*, 37.

9. Thierry Smolderen, *The Origins of Comics: From William Hogarth to Winsor McCay*, trans. Bart Beaty and Nick Nguyen (University Press of Mississippi, 2014), 137.

10. Exner, *Comics and the Origins of Manga*, 94.

11. Evgeny Steiner, "Endlessly Variegated Pictures: A Pictorial Encyclopedia of Old Japanese Life (An Introduction to Hokusai Manga's Full Edition with Commentaries)," *Higher School of Economics Research Paper* WP BRP 49 (2014): 14; Suzuki and Stewart, *Manga*, 17.

12. Munson, *The Periodical Press in Treaty-Port Japan*, 98.

13. Roman Rosenbaum, "Towards a Graphical Representation of Japanese Society in the Taishō Period: Jiji Manga in Shinseinen," 2021, 22; Ronald Stewart, "Manga as Schism: Kitazawa Rakuten's Resistance to 'Old-Fashioned' Japan," in *Manga's Cultural Crossroads*, ed. Jaqueline Berndt and Bettina Kümmerling-Meibauer (Routledge, 2013), 27–49.

14. Suzuki and Stewart, *Manga*, 44.

15. Rebecca Suter, "Reassessing Manga History, Resituating Manga in History," in *Rewriting History in Manga: Stories for the Nation*, ed. Nissim Otmazgin and Rebecca Suter, East Asian Popular Culture (Palgrave Macmillan, 2016), 180.

16. Suzuki and Stewart, *Manga*, 60–61.

17. Shige (CJ) Suzuki, "Tatsumi Yoshihiro's *Gekiga* and the Global Sixties: Aspiring for an Alternative," in *Manga's Cultural Crossroads*, ed. Jaqueline Berndt and Bettina Kümmerling-Meibauer (Routledge, 2013), 50–64.

18. Ryan Holmberg, "The Manga of Garo, 1964–1973," *Orientations* 41, no. 4 (2010): 1–6.

19. Suzuki, "Tatsumi Yoshihiro's *Gekiga* and the Global Sixties: Aspiring for an Alternative"; Roman Rosenbaum, "The Gekiga Tradition: Towards a Graphic Rendition of History," in *Graphic History: Essays on Graphic Novels And/As History*, ed. Richard Iadonisi (Cambridge Scholars Publishing, 2012), 260–83.

20. Brigitte Koyama-Richard, *One Thousand Years of Manga* (Rizzoli, 2008); Isao Shimizu, *Manga no rekishi*, Iwanami shinsho (Iwanami Shoten, 1991); Exner, *Comics and the Origins of Manga*, 181.

21. Exner, *Comics and the Origins of Manga*, 190.

22. Scott McCloud, *Understanding Comics: The Invisible Art* (Harper Paperbacks, 1994).

23. Exner, *Comics and the Origins of Manga*, 189.

24. Eiji Ōtsuka, "An Unholy Alliance of Eisenstein and Disney: The Fascist Origins of Otaku Culture," trans. Thomas Lamarre, *Mechademia*, no. 8 (2013): 251–77.

25. Exner, *Comics and the Origins of Manga*, 186–87.

26. Joseph Witek, "American Comics Criticism and the Problem of Dual Address," *International Journal of Comic Art* 10, no. 1 (2008): 219.

27. Bart Beaty, "IN FOCUS: Comics Studies Fifty Years After Film Studies: Introduction," *Cinema Journal* 50, no. 3 (2011): 106.

28. Beaty, "IN FOCUS," 108.

29. Hannah Miodrag, *Comics and Language: Reimagining Critical Discourse on the Form* (University Press of Mississippi, 2013), 5.

30. Miodrag, *Comics and Language*, 6.

31. Berndt, "Considering Manga Discourse: Location, Ambiguity, Historicity," 295.

32. Nick Sousanis, *Unflattening* (Harvard University Press, 2015), 35–38.

33. Miodrag, *Comics and Language*, 87.

34. Deborah Shamoon, *Passionate Friendship: The Aesthetics of Girls' Culture in Japan* (University of Hawai'i Press, 2012).

35. Sousanis, *Unflattening*, 62.

36. Sousanis, *Unflattening*, 63–64.

37. Miodrag, *Comics and Language*, 10.

38. Hillary Chute, *Why Comics?: From Underground to Everywhere* (HarperCollins, 2017), 3; Charles Hatfield, *Alternative Comics: An Emerging Literature* (University Press of Mississippi, 2005), 33.

39. Miodrag, *Comics and Language*, 13.

40. Susan Napier, *Anime from Akira to Princess Mononoke: Experiencing Contemporary Japanese Animation* (Springer, 2001); Sandra Buckley, "'Penguin in Bondage': A Graphic Tale of Japanese Comic Books," in *Technoculture*, ed. Constance Penley and Andrew Ross (University of Minnesota Press, 1991), 163–96; Anne Allison, *Permitted and Prohibited Desires: Mothers, Comics and Censorship in Japan* (University of California Press, 2000).

41. Suzuki and Stewart, *Manga*, 4.

42. Yonezawa Yoshihiro, *Sengo Shōjo Mangashi* (Shinpyōsha, 1980); Fusanosuke Natsume, *Manga No Yomikata* (Takarajima, 1995); Fujimoto Yukari, *Watashi No Ibasho Wa Doko Ni Aru No? Shōjo manga ga utsusu kokoro no katachi* (Gakuyō Shobō, 1998); Ōtsuka Eiji, *Sengo manga no hyōgen kūkan: kigōteki shintai no jubaku*, Shohan (Hozokan, 1994).

43. Jaqueline Berndt, ed., *Comics Worlds and the World of Comics: Towards Scholarship on a Global Scale*, 1st ed., Global Manga Studies 1 (International Manga Research Center, Kyoto Seika University, 2010), 12.

44. Itō Gō, *Tezuka Izu Deddo: Hirakareta Manga Hyōgenron e* (NTT Shuppan, 2005).

45. Itō Gō, "Tezuka Is Dead: Manga in Transformation and Its Dysfunctional Discourse," trans. Miri Nakamura, *Mechademia* 6 (2011): 81.

46. Yomota Inuhiko, *Manga Genron* (Chikuma Shobō, 1994).

47. Mia Elise Lewis, "Visions of Possible Girls: Intersectional Feminist Narratives in Contemporary Japanese Boys' Comics" (PhD diss., Stanford University, 2022), 8.

48. Mizuki Takahashi, "Opening the Closed World of Shōjo Manga," in *Japanese Visual Culture*, ed. Mark MacWilliams (M. E. Sharpe, 2003), 114–36. Examples of significant book-length studies on shōjo manga are Oshiyama Michiko, *Shōjo Manga Jendaa Hyōshōron: "Dansō Shōjo" No Sōkei to Aidenteitei* (Sairyūsha, 2007); Iwashita Hōsei, *Shōjo manga no hyōgen kikō: hirakareta manga hyōgenshi to "Tezuka Osamu"* (NTT Shuppan, 2013).

49. Shamoon, *Passionate Friendship: The Aesthetics of Girls' Culture in Japan*.

50. Kathryn Hemmann, *Manga Cultures and the Female Gaze* (Springer International Publishing, 2020), 13.

51. Antonia Levi, Mark McHarry, and Dru Pagliassotti, eds., *Boys' Love Manga: Essays on the Sexual Ambiguity and Cross-Cultural Fandom of the Genre* (McFarland & Co., 2008); Mark McLelland et al., eds., *Boys Love Manga and Beyond: History, Culture, and Community in Japan* (University Press of Mississippi, 2015).

52. Kazumi Nagaike, "Queer Readings of BL: Are Women 'Plunderers' of Gay

Men?" in *International Perspectives on Shojo and Shojo Manga: The Influence of Girl Culture*, ed. Masami Toku (Routledge, 2015), 64–73.

53. Hitoshi Ishida, "Representational Appropriation and the Autonomy of Desire in *Yaoi*/BL," in *Boys Love Manga and Beyond: History, Culture and Community in Japan*, 210–33.

54. Carola K. Bauer, *Naughty Girls and Gay Male Romance/Porn: Slash Fiction, Boys' Love Manga, and Other Works by Female "Cross-Voyeurs" in the U.S. Academic Discourses* (Anchor Academic Publishing, 2013), 89.

55. Natsume Sōseki and Arisu Sari, *Kokoro* (Bunkyosha, 2021).

56. Deborah Shamoon and Chris McMorran, eds., *Teaching Japanese Popular Culture* (Association for Asian Studies, 2016).

57. Suzuki and Stewart, *Manga*. Berndt, Jaqueline, *The Cambridge Companion to Manga and Anime* (Cambridge University Press, 2024).

58. Osamu Tezuka, *Phoenix, Vol. 1: Dawn* (VIZ Media, 2014); Osamu Tezuka, *Buddha 1: Kapilavastu* (Kodansha USA, 2006).

59. Mizuki Shigeru, *NonNonBa* (Drawn & Quarterly, 2020); *Onward Towards Our Noble Deaths* (Drawn & Quarterly, 2022).

60. Tatsumi Yoshihiro, *The Push Man and Other Stories* (Drawn & Quarterly, 2012); *Abandon the Old in Tokyo*, trans. Yuji Oniki (Drawn & Quarterly, 2006).

61. Yoshiharu Tsuge, *Red Flowers*, vol. 2, The Complete Mature Works of Yoshiharu Tsuge (Drawn & Quarterly, 2021); *Nejishiki*, trans. Ryan Holmberg, vol. 3, The Complete Mature Works of Yoshiharu Tsuge (Drawn & Quarterly, 2023).

62. Ikeda Riyoko, *The Rose of Versailles*, trans. Jocelyne Allen, 5 vols. (Udon Entertainment, 2019); Hagio Moto, *The Heart of Thomas*, trans. Rachel Thorn (Fantagraphics Books, 2012).

PART II

The Question of Language

CHAPTER 7

World Literature and Japanese-Language Literature

Hideto Tsuboi

1. International or Global?

In recent years, the following words have often been used as keywords in international conferences around the world, including in Japan: international, interdisciplinary, border-crossing, borderless, transregional, transnational, and global. I have been the organizer of such conferences and, in turn, have been invited as a speaker on numerous occasions. But to be honest, I've grown quite critical of using these keywords in our scholarship. This is because there are quite a few cases in which the contents of the discussions are not necessarily consistent with "international" or "transnational" topics in the first place. However, considering the differences between the terms "international" and "global," it would be meaningful for those who are involved in Japan Studies and the humanities proper to correctly distinguish their meanings.

Although "international" and "global" may appear similar and are often used interchangeably, they are, in fact, discrete terms in their own right. While the term "international" has been widely used since the 1980s, re-popularization of the term "global" is of more recent vintage, dating to around the turn of the twenty-first century. Needless to say, this has something to do with the drastic changes in world capitalism and the system of nation-states over the past three to four decades. The term "international" literally refers to connections between nations and it is premised on the nation-state system. On the other hand, "global" emerged alongside the descriptor "globalization" to connote a world in which capital, human labor, and goods circulate supernationally in scale.

Let us compare the names of two Japanese organizations. The first is the Kokusai Bunka Kenkyū Sentā, also known as Nichibunken. Its English title is the "International Research Center for Japanese Studies." Curiously enough, the English title does not include the word "culture" as per the Japanese original. This consortium is a recently formed federation of research institutions related to the field of "International Japanese Studies" in Japan. It is already more than thirty-five years since Nichibunken was founded in 1987. Its founding coincided with the rise of the bubble economy in Japan when the words "international" and "internationalization" still had a certain cachet. The second is the Kokusai Nihon Kenkyū Consortium, or in English, the "Consortium for Global Japanese Studies." As its name suggests, in the post-bubble era of the twenty-first century, even in the academic world the term "global" has come to be preferred instead of "international." As in the business world, the reason for this was the spread of political strategies and ambitions in academia to keep pace with the tide of globalization. On the other hand, the term "transnational" is increasingly being used in critical academic fields that oppose globalization. How can we think of the differences between these concepts as an issue in the humanities and for Japan Studies? For example, the conventional system of historical studies was reformed by methodologically adopting a global history approach.

2. What is Global History?

Attempts to deconstruct nationalism and unilateralism in the field of humanities were pioneered at a theoretical level, as Gayatri Chakravorty Spivak used the term "planetary" to avoid the word, "global," which sought to build a critical pillar against the hegemony of globalism. Nevertheless, research and criticism based on the idea of de-nationalization have lagged behind in the practice of humanities. It was the existence of global history in history that played a pioneering role in such a situation. The historian Sebastian Conrad explains global history in his recent book, *What is Global History?* by writing: "Global history is both an object of study and a particular way of looking at history: it is both a process and a perspective, subject matter and methodology. Janus-faced, it resembles other fields/approaches in the discipline, such as social history and gender history."[1] Thus, according to Conrad, global history is characterized by these ambivalent and multifaceted features. Global history tries to capture what has happened in a transnational space that the traditional research of history has not managed to encompass. This will necessarily expand the scope of research. But the impact of the emergence of global history is more than just an extension of the scale of research: new theories are inevitably required in order to understand and describe the broadened space and scope of an emerging discipline.

Consider the stage of history before global history. The discipline of history was originally established as a national history. Anything falling within the national purview would be designated national history; that which fell outside would be relegated to other nation-states—a practice in Japan called "history by country" (*kakkoku-shi*). Japanese education and academic circles have traditionally divided this "history by country" into East and West, and classified them as "Oriental history" (*Tōyō-shi*) and "Western history" (*Seiyō-shi*) or European history. This classification was created after the organization of knowledge exemplified by the university system was imported into Japan from Western Europe and North America after the Meiji period.

Oriental Studies in Western Europe was originally equivalent to Orientology (Orientalistik) referring to research about the Middle East and Western Asia. The establishment of this discipline was integral to cultural domination based on colonial rule by Western powers, and Edward Said later took a critical view of it by challenging the Eurocentric premises of the concept of "Orientalism" itself. It can be said that Japan's Oriental Studies, which continued to develop on the basis of Sinology, has survived to the present day with some fundamental differences from Oriental Studies originating in Western Europe.

There is no precise symmetry between the two "Orients," that is, between the Orient created by the need of the West to be self-identical, by setting it apart as a non-West or Other, and the Orient in Japan, which has been subject to the influence of the Sinosphere. Unlike the Orient in Europe, which was the Other for Western people, the East is not the Other for the Japanese. The East is half-other and half-self for the nation because of the fraught process through which modern Japan finds its identity thrust upon it and self-constructed. When we consider the categories of the Orient and Oriental Studies in Japan, we cannot ignore the history of such complicated connotations.

The framework of Oriental History/Western History created a vast lacuna in the image of the world with which Japanese historical research is concerned. In other words, there are areas that do not belong to either the East or the West. These blank spaces can be regarded as distorted representations of the historical image developed in and by Western Europe, where the Orient as a "non-self" or "non-Western Europe" has been so violently forged. In Japan, this distorted historical image also corresponds with the fact that the Sinocentric "Oriental" image of the cultural reach of the Sinosphere has marginalized the diverse regions of India, South Asia, and Southeast Asia.

In Japanese history education from elementary school to high school, the subject matter has been consistently bifurcated into Japanese history and World history, but world history is overwhelmingly focused on Western history, whereas Chinese history is given a certain amount of coverage, but all other regions of the world, including Asia, receive only a few pages at best. Here, the "world" is very close to representing "Western Europe," and not much else.

The paradigm for this way of thinking, which Naoki Sakai, after Stuart Hall, has called "The West and the Rest" is spread and shared not only in Japan, but also throughout the world. Nor is it limited to the field of history. Irmela Hijiya-Kirschnereit, a German scholar of modern Japanese literature, has pointed out that in Japan the term "foreign literature" is used exclusively in reference to "Western literature," and that non-Western regions are not included in the category of "foreign literature," except for China.

Literary studies are a typical disciplinary formation that has developed under the framework of "The West and the Rest." It is true that "foreign literature" has sometimes been called "world literature" in contemporary Japanese academia. From the perspective within Japanese society, there is a prevailing notion that "foreign countries" are equivalent to the "West," and the "West" has occupied the entirety of the "world." Yet again, the equation that the World equals the West holds firm.

However, even if we remove such Japanese bias, how does the category of world history differ from the level of national history previously mentioned? And to what extent does it meet or exceed the definition of national history? Unfortunately, world history is not nearly as significant in the Japanese academy as we might expect. World history, after all, is nothing more than an aggregate of "history by country" or simply put, a collection of national histories. World history embraces this erasure of the world's undocumented regions and their inhabitants. In this context, the border of the nation-state is regarded as inviolable and is only described externally in historical descriptions of conflicts and wars.

Global history can be evaluated as an attempt to exceed the limits of world history as an aggregate of national histories by transcending borders and the framework of nation-states. To give a specific example, historian Hirakawa Arata attempted to place the foreign strategy of the daimyo from the Warring States period in the context of the world history from the Age of Discovery in a popular Japanese-language publication.[2] While being in the position of studying Japanese history, he tried to connect Toyotomi Hideyoshi's invasion of Korea, the state policy toward Christianity, and Tokugawa Ieyasu and Date Masamune's viewpoints on overseas trade in the context of the Western history during the same period. As such Hirakawa's research can be regarded as one of the achievements of global history in the field of Japanese history. However, as Hirakawa writes, these stratagems by Japan's early modern unifiers were based on the ambition and necessity to defend and expand the borders of the kingdoms against the European empires (despite the fact that the nation-state had not yet been constructed as such).

When global history attempts to overcome world history, military and economic movements such as aggression and trade play a critical role. In the early modern period in particular, the issue of colonization also appears as a consequence. It should be noted that today's globalism is far from the kind of optimism that celebrates the prosperity of what Marshall McLuhan called "the global village." Instead, it has a strong negative aspect of creating unequal societies and stages of development at the same time around the world, and that global history is also deeply implicated in the construction of this negative history of the world.

3. World Literature and Japanese-Language Literature

How, then, can we think about the issue of global in the field of literature? In literature, it is national literature or "literature by country" (***kakkoku bungaku***) that corresponds to national history in the field of history. In the Meiji period of Japan, "national people's literature" (***kokumin bungaku***) was used relatively widely along with "national literature" (***kokubungaku***), although both terms can be translated to the same "national literature" in English.

It goes without saying that this national literature was established by the rise of nationalism and maintained as an influential device of the nation-state along similar lines to national history. Just as Japan has its national literature, so, too, does Korea. In Korea, the term national literature or ***kokumunhaku*** (which corresponds with the Japanese ***kokuminbungaku***) is still used today as the name of a discipline in academic fields in the university system.

It is an irony that this name, which is full of nationalism, is still used in Korea, but its usage has a historical background. It derives from the contrast between Japan and Korea in the historical assessment of nationalism. In recent years in Japan, both ***kokubungaku*** (national literature) and ***kokugogaku*** (national language studies) disappeared from the names of departments in universities and academic societies and switched to *Nihonbungaku* (Japanese literature) and *Nihongogaku* (Japanese linguistics). On the other hand, in Korea, the use of Japanese as the national language (*kokugo*) was forced during the period of Japanese colonial rule, and Japanese literature, not Korean literature, was taught as the national literature (*kokubungaku*) in curriculums at Keijō Imperial University (*Keijō Teikoku Daigaku*) established by Japan. After liberation from Japanese colonial rule, Korean people acquired "their own" national literature and linguistics as a modern discipline for the first time. In the middle of the twentieth-century, Japan's immediate challenge was to break away from nationalism, while in Korea nationalism was positioned as something to be acquired.

In Japan today, the terms that mean national literature, national language, and national history have been replaced with globalized terms such as *Nihonbungaku*, *Nihongo*, and *Nihonshi* (Japanese literature, Japanese language, and Japanese history, respectively). This change merely relativizes national literature in regard to literature by country, in much the same way that national history is relativized as history by country.

To return to the point about "foreign literature" above, Asian literature has not been included in the category of foreign literature for a long time in Japan. In other words, in Japan "foreign literature" is nearly synonymous with Western literature, that is, something that is non-Asian, non-Islamic, and non-African. Modern Japanese literature is a child born out of Western literature as an "Other" and has naturalized being subject to Western Europe as representing the entire world, without being acknowledged by Western literature as a parent and also while erasing the secret of its own birth.

It is the conceit of world literature that it has the potential to render fluid the boundary between Japanese literature and foreign literature. At the same time, it is the area of Japanese-language literature that should overlap and be differentiated from this premise. The establishment of the category of world literature is similar to global history in that it focuses on spatial migration and transnational boundary crossing, and in its attempts to introduce new methodologies corresponding with the changes of its discursive objects, particularly in the sense of exceeding the articulations of nation-states. However, it can be said that world literature, no less than global history, aims toward this worldliness because it is deeply rooted in the fluctuation of boundaries in translation and distribution, beyond the dimension in which national literature has been self-sufficient under the constraints of linguistic disconnection.

One of the studies that attempts to conceptualize world literature in literary theory is Franco Moretti's *Distant Reading* (2013). Moretti tries to explain why only a few authors and literary works, such as Conan Doyle's *Sherlock Holmes*, have been canonized and distributed widely in the literary market. He applies a literal global network and analyzes the works statistically while excluding the method of close reading. In other words, for Moretti, world literature is literature that has become popular around the world. So, in his sense, world literature can be called "marketed world literature."

But Moretti's elitist, ex-post facto, post-market-success vision of world literature achieved through the inductive method does not seem to bring about the methodological change of consciousness or the discovery of new possibilities in literary text that global history does. In other words, such an image of world literature can only serve to fix the hierarchy of literature or identify new inequalities. In this sense, Moretti's vision of world literature is undoubtedly consonant with the unquestioned virtues of globalism.

World literature has created a gap between canonized literary works and countless works that will otherwise be forgotten. Murakami Haruki is probably the most symbolic name for such world literature in Japan today. Murakami, along with mystery and crime fiction writers Higashino Keigo and Miyabe Miyuki, is a writer whose works have now been translated into many languages around the world. Although I can't quantify it like Moretti does, if you compare the number of people who read Murakami's original novels in Japanese to those who read it in Chinese, Korean, English, or any other language's translations, the latter number should surpass the former. David Damrosch defines world literature as a production of enrichment through translation, and in that sense, Murakami's works have made them into the world literature category.

Kawamura Minato, a literary critic, described Murakami's position as follows, in what I considered to be an accurate assessment:

> Looking back at the past winners of the Nobel Prize in Literature award, Kawabata Yasunari's winning of the award showed, "There is literature in Japan, too." And Ōe Kenzaburō's winning of the award told the world that "There is also modern literature in Japan." If Murakami wins the award, his work will be evaluated as saying, in effect: "There is world literature in Japan, too."[3]

For better or worse, in any case, Murakami Haruki has yet to win the Nobel Prize for Literature.

Once situated outside of the Japanese market, Murakami no longer has the image of a "Japanese writer who writes in Japanese." Murakami's recognition as a writer of world literature coincides with the current Japanese national policy of providing cultural and subcultural content such as animation and manga to the world. The problem, at the very least, is that Murakami seems to be the only one who is being tasked with world literature. Insofar as it betrays Moretti's methodology, it is quite ironic that only Murakami is considered the object of "close reading," not of "distant reading." In this situation, "the West and the Rest" has devolved into "Murakami and the Rest."

Of course, this is only a mention of one "phenomenon." There may be some writers who are now writing in Japanese who have gained access to world literature. For example, Tawada Yōko has created works in two languages, German and Japanese, and by attempting to translate her own works, she has continued to relativize Japanese from both external and internal perspectives. On the other hand, some writers are absorbed from the outside to the inside of the Japanese language. These writers tend to return to so-called "Japanese nationalism." Mizumura Minae, for example, falls into this category. However, whether one is outside or inside Japan has nothing to do with one's qualification in world literature. This is a characteristic of the Global Age.

Such legitimate critiques about the limitations of world literature will not only open the way for new humanities and literary studies, it will also close them. I would like to refer to Korean critic Cho Yŏng-il's book entitled *The Structure of World Literature* (2016) as another reprisal of this same concept of "world literature." This book analyzes the historical structure according to which modern literature was not available in prewar Korea, while modern literature as world literature was available in Japan during its period of colonial rule. However, this vision of world literature from an East Asian perspective definitely emerges in Cho's invectives against modern Korean literature.

Cho's criticism of native literature and nationalism itself in this book is extremely ironic when compared to modern Japanese literature. Because he argues that for the first time in a nation-state that has gone to war and colonized other countries in modern times, it will be possible to gain access to modern literature and world literature. What we should keep in mind, however, is that the wars and colonial rule there have a historical character peculiar to East Asia, and that they are assumed to be based on Japan. The structure of the "West and the Rest" is operating doubly through the medium of Japan. Or it could be said that Cho ironically showed the historical negativity of world literature.

Just as global history has expanded its potential by visualizing negative history after the Age of Discovery, reversing the world literature from East

Asia leads to the existence of "Japanese-language literature" discovered from the negative legacy of Japanese colonialism. Although historical research has been shifting from world history to global history, literature has not yet produced the next phase of world literature, that is to say a global literature.

Why doesn't global literature work? There are many possible answers to this question. The most important of these is the language barrier. Historical studies always run into linguistic barriers, too, but the language barrier has a decisive influence on literature, which places linguistic expression at its core. Nevertheless, "Japanese-language literature," which is one of the very small genres created by the spread of languages across national borders, is in a different phase from the idea of world literature, which is to move across languages through translation and distribution. For now, I would like to continue to think about the reason that Japanese literature, in its different phase, has opened up a world completely different from that of post-Meiji era national literature. From this point of view, it would be significant to evaluate the works of Ainu literature written by Chiri Yukie and others, and Japanese works written by Korean writers during the colonial period.

Modern Japanese linguistics started with the comparative study of neighboring languages such as Ainu, Ryukyu, and Korean. Modern Japanese literature, on the other hand, introduced Western literature and translated it into Japanese, shaping itself while marginalizing or ignoring literature from Korea, Taiwan, the Ainu, and so on. The Asian Pacific War, on the other hand, destroyed Japanese colonial rule, and at the same time, displaced a large number of Japanese people, sending them to camps in Siberia and factories in the former Manchuria. Concurrently in the United States during the war, 120,000 Japanese Americans were detained in various incarceration centers. The literary expression of people placed between these countries is very local and minor, but in fact, I think it is possible to arrive at the possibility of new "world literature" from the literary expression of people placed in-between such boundaries.

Notes

1. Sebastian Conrad, *What Is Global History?* (Princeton University Press, 2016), 11.

2. Hirakawa Arata, *Sengoku Nihon to daikōkai jidai: Hideyoshi Ieyasu Masamune no gaikō senryaku*, chūō kōron shinsha, 2018.

3. Kawamura, Minato, 2017.

Works Cited

Cho, Yŏng-il. *Sekai bungaku no kōzō: Kankoku kara mita Nihon bungaku no kigen* (The structure of world literature: the origins of modern Japanese literature as seen from Korea). Translated into Japanese by Takai Osamu. Iwanami Shoten, 2016.

Conrad, Sebastian. *What is Global History?* Princeton University Press, 2016.

Hirakawa, Arata. *Sengoku Nihon to daikokai jidai: Hideyoshi Ieyasu Masamune no gaikō senryaku* (Sengoku Japan and the age of discovery: diplomatic strategies of Hideyoshi, Ieyasu, and Masamune). Chuōkōronsha, 2018.

Kawamura, Minato. "Is Haruki Murakami world literature? We ask Minato Kawamura." *Nikkei* electronic version, February 24, 2017. Accessed Jan. 21, 2025. https://style.nikkei.com/article/DGXMZO13259490T20C17A2000000/

Moretti, Franco. *Distant Reading*. Verso, 2013.

Sakai, Naoki. *Translation and Subjectivity: On "Japan" and Cultural Nationalism*. University of Minnesota Press, 1997.

CHAPTER 8

The History and Present of Japanophone Literature

Migration, Border Crossing, and Materiality

Hibi Yoshitaka

1. What Is Japanophone literature?

Modern Japanese literature has not been written only by Japanese people born within the Japanese archipelago. Modern and contemporary literature written in the Japanese language has been, and continues to be, produced by people living in various places, nationalities, ethnic groups and who possess their own native languages. In Japan today, the term "Japanophone literature" emphasizes the diversity of such writers and their backgrounds. In this chapter, while touching on the research related to representative writers and poets, I have organized the historical trends related to Japanophone literature in modern and contemporary times, and at the same time, attempt to clarify the corresponding subjects of research and viewpoints of analysis. In particular, the following three points are emphasized: (1) to rethink Japanophone literature in the history of the negotiations between Japan and the world in the modern age, especially East Asia, and the migration of people; (2) to consider research on Japanophone literature as a starting point for border crossing of a variety of academic fields; and (3) to focus on the material infrastructure and networks that supported people's activities of cultural productions and the relationships with the various agents who worked within them.

First, let me briefly define what kind of literature belongs to "Japanophone literature." Broadly speaking, "Japanophone literature" can refer to all literary works written in Japanese. However, I use it here in a narrower sense: Japanophone literature is literary works written in the Japanese language, but it should be used in such cases as when the writer was/is a non-native speaker of Japanese; where the writer's ethnicity was/is not Japanese (although how "Japaneseness" is defined can itself be problematic); or when the writer lives or lived outside Japan. This is done to emphasize the distance from Japanese literature produced within the homeland.

In keeping with this definition, we can refer to the concept of the "exophone" by Tawada Yōko and the "xenophone" by Ray Chow as adjacent to Japanophone literature. Tawada says, "I have often heard words like 'immigrant literature' and 'Creole literature,' but in a broader sense, 'exophony' refers to the general state outside of the mother tongue. Immigrants aren't the only ones who write in foreign languages, and their language isn't necessarily Creole" (Tawada 2003, 3). According to Chow, meanwhile, "xenophone" language is anarchic, rebellious, and a fluid mixture of various accents and tones (Chow 2014).

I emphasize that the concept of Japanophone literature should be used to resist an enclosing, domestic, and territorial thinking. Japanophone literature challenges the idea that Japanese literature is orthodox and canonical when it is or was written in a unitary Japanese language by Japanese people born and living in Japan. Therefore, there is no need to dissect the scope of Japanophone literature. The national boundaries between Japan as a nation-state and as a country have fundamentally changed (Oguma 1998). Embedded in these changes are the Ainu and Okinawan peoples, who were forcibly marginalized in space, ethnicity, and language.[1] Their literature thus rigorously re-interrogates the boundaries of "Japan" and "Japanese."

To put it another way, thinking about Japanophone literature means thinking about the expression of the *contact zone* and the experience within there. As I will discuss later, the space of creating and receiving Japanophone literature was also the space of negotiation where many ethnic groups encounter one another. At the same time, there was the space where the imperialistic logic of colonial rule was carried out and where all forms of literary expression were placed in a series of tensions such as dominator and dominated, oppression and resistance, hatred and fraternity, and exclusion and tolerance. Japanophone literature was born, circulated, and consumed in such a multi-layered and dynamic environment.

2. Japan, Japanese Language, and Japanophone Literature in Migration: Opening Meiji Japan and Increased Mobility

If Japanophne literature is characterized by differences in nationality, ethnicity, place of residence, language, and fluidity, then it is only natural that its prosperity occurs in an era when people are actively moving internationally.[2] Japanophone literature was born after the ban on travel by the Tokugawa Shogunate was lifted, and people living in Japan went abroad, or foreigners came to live in Japan. It is important to consider the problem of Japanophone literature in the context of continuously changing global geopolitics and its history.

Japan, which was opened to the world at the end of the Edo period, was incorporated into the international shipping routes of European and American steamship companies, and at the same time, entered a variety of interests such as national politics, diplomacy, journalism, and academic fields. Diplomats, soldiers, interpreters, journalists, teachers, researchers, and their families came to Japan from the West. Lafcadio Hearn, also known in Japan as Koizumi Yakumo, is probably the most brilliant figure in the field of Japanophone literature in its earliest stage.

Of course, Westerners were not the only ones who came to modern Japan. Rather, the overwhelming majority were students from East Asia (Nagai et al., 1973). Japan, which quickly established higher educational institutions with the leading imperial universities in Tokyo and Kyoto, became a foothold for acquiring Western knowledge, with the added advantage of closeness in terms of geographical distance and cultural similarities. Students from Korea came to Japan as early as around 1880 during the Joseon Dynasty and studied at various schools such as the Military Academy and Keio University. Yi Kwang-su, who wrote a short story, "Ai ka?" in Japanese in 1909, was the first foreign student to leave his mark in Japan as a literary figure. In 1919, Kim Dong-in co-founded *Creation*, a Korean-language literary magazine, in Japan.

The period of study abroad from Qing Dynasty China started in the 1890s, and had its peak in 1905 and 1906, with about 10,000 students coming to Japan every year. Among them were Sun Yat-sen, Zhou Enlai, and Chiang Kai-shek, who became politicians; Lu Xun, Guo Moruo, Tian Han, and Ikudayu Da-fu, who became literary figures; and Qiu Jin, who was a female revolutionary poet. Lu Xun studied in Tokyo and Sendai since 1902, and after completing his medical studies, he permanently turned to literature.

Taiwanese students came around 1901 when the Japanese colonial rule of Taiwan had already started (Kawahara 1997). Shimomura Sakujirō (2003) has pointed out that during the initial stage of the New Literature Movement in Taiwan, there were attempts to create novels in vernacular Chinese and Japanese language, both of which were influenced by the New Literature Movement of China. In the 1930s, Chang Wenquan, Wu Kunhuang, and Wu Yung-fu, all of whom were Taiwanese students studying in Japan, established the Taiwan Art Society and published the first issue of the magazine *Formosa* (Nakajima et al. 2014).

It is also necessary to consider the reverse flow, that is, the migration of people leaving Japan. From the end of the Edo to the Meiji period, Japanese envoys, inspection teams, and students began to cross the oceans. Among them are many eminent figures such as Fukuzawa Yukichi and Tsuda Umeko who greatly influenced the formation of modern Japanese culture; and Mori Ōgai, Natsume Sōseki, Arishima Takeo, and Nagai Kafū, who were renowned experts in modern literature of Japan. Yet the Japanese who went overseas were not only government delegates and elite civilians. In the Meiji period, many people went abroad to work as migrants and sojourners. The beginnings of Japanophone literature abroad stems from the outflow of people from such a wide range of classes.

3. What Made Japanophone Literature Possible: Materiality, Networking, and Agents

Literature does not consist solely of writers and readers. A literary work is produced with a variety of media, such as books, magazines, and newspapers, and with agents and cultural environments, such as the people and companies that provide, distribute, and sell it. The development of Japanophone literature across borders and languages also needs to be viewed in the context of the emergence and persistence of the cultural environment; in particular, the spread of the material infrastructure, various agents of literature and print culture, and other such components that formed a network.

First, let us consider the case of Japanese immigrant literature in North America. Newspapers played an important role in the development of Japanophone literature in the area, where the publication of books and magazines in Japanese language did not develop so much. They published short stories on their own, serialized novels and accepted contributions from local poets and novelists.[3]

It should be noted that literary works that Japanese immigrants in North

America read were not limited to the works that were published in the immigrant dailies. As I will discuss in a moment, a lot of bookstores took their business to Honolulu, San Francisco, Los Angeles, Seattle, and Vancouver, and frequently imported books and magazines from Japan. The vigorous literary productions by immigrants were supported by the influx of vernacular information from Japan.

There were also networks connecting immigrants who loved literature. For example, at the Los Angeles Olympics in 1932, haiku coteries on the West Coast of North America held a haiku gathering, and compiled it into a haiku collection, *Kyoka* (炬火) (Hibi, 2015). This included not only haiku poets who were Japanese immigrants, but also haiku poets in Hawaii and Japan. This kind of cooperation also continued in concentration camps of Japanese Americans during World War II. There were coterie magazines which were mailed to other camps so they could read one another's works.

For the flourishing of literary activities to occur, it was necessary for there to be a network that extends beyond a single literary person or community. The network consisted of people, information, and materials, and widespread in locales both sparse and dense, being influenced by laws, customs, interests, and power relationships in each area. Let us explore this in detail by focusing on the material basis of books and their distribution.

When considering Japanophone literature as a transnational literature, it is important to consider the agents responsible for importing and exporting books, for example overseas distributors and retailers in foreign cities. Maruzen was the most famous trader who transported books from Europe and America to Japan. Founded in 1869, Maruzen imported and sold Western books and magazines, as well as stationery and clothing, which greatly affected the production of knowledge in modern Japan.

On the other hand, one of the representative wholesalers who transported books from Japan to overseas, specifically in East Asia, was Ōsakayagō Shoten, run by Hamai Matsunosuke. The company expanded its business not only in Manchuria and the Kwantung Leased Territory, but also in the Korean Peninsula with its base in Keijō (Seoul), and established a wholesale agency in Taiwan in partnership with Japanese booksellers in big cities in Taiwan. Ōsakayagō Shoten grew to become the largest overseas wholesaler covering a wide area of Japanese territory in East Asia. In addition, there were big distributors beside Ōsakayagō Shoten, such as Tōkyōdō and Hokuryūkan, medium-size distributors in Tokyo such as Sanseidō, distributors in the Kansai region such as Yanagihara Shoten and Shinshindō, distributors in the Kyushu region such as Kikutake Kinbundō and Ōtsubo Junshindō. We should not forget Yokohama Shoji, later, Japan Publications

Trading Co., Ltd., an exporter that transported books to North and South America (Hibi 2016). The owner was Mochizuki Seiji who used to work at the Yorozu Shōten in Sacramento, USA.

Now let us turn to look at retail bookstores. The main roles of retail bookstores are to sell products at stores, deliver special orders, including periodicals, to customers in town, and commission orders to publishers. Each local city had one or a few core bookstores. The owners of such regional big bookstores were key agents of the book distribution network. They became important intellectual nodes in each region by serving as leaders of local unions and managing local bookstores, serving as wholesalers for the sale of national textbooks for elementary and junior high schools, serving as intermediaries for the transfer of central publications to smaller bookstores, and supplying books to local and school libraries.

These regional core bookstores were not only born in various parts of modern Japan, but also in big cities in overseas expansion areas. There used to be Niitakadō Shoten in Taipei; Tanabe Shoten in Taichung; Keijō Branch of Ōsakayago Shoten and Nikkan Shobō in Keijō; Hakubundō in Pusan; branches of Ōsakayago Shoten in Manchuria; Ōmidō in Toyohara, Sakhalin; Goshadō in San Francisco; Satō Shoten in Los Angeles; Mitsuwadō in Seattle; Endō Shoten in São Paulo; and more.[4]

The intellectual space provided by bookstores should also be noted. Bookstores selling Japanese books that spread overseas had sometimes become important places for cultural activities. The most famous example is Uchiyama Shoten, a bookstore in Shanghai run by Uchiyama Kanzō.[5] Uchiyama Shoten was not only a bookstore where books were sold, but also a sort of salon where both Japanese and Chinese intellectuals gathered. Similarly, Mitsuwadō in Seattle, attracted literary-minded immigrants and became one of the cradles of Japanese literary circles in Seattle (Takeuchi 1929, 589).[6] Overseas bookstores, where new information in Japanese was gathered, served as a contact zone where Japanese writers and intellectuals gathered, and where Japanese and local people met through books.

4. The Birth of Japanophone Literature: The Case of North America and South America

When Japanese people went abroad, Japanophone literature went with them. At the end of the nineteenth century, Japanese vernacular newspapers began to be published first in Pusan, Taipei, Honolulu, San Francisco, etc., and the first Japanophone literature abroad in modern times emerged in dailies or magazines compiled in those places.[7] Japanese literati from the prewar period in America include Okina Kyūin, who wrote many fictional works; Yamazaki Isshin, who compiled an anthology of Japanese immigrant literature; and the poet Togawa Akira. Amateur writers appeared in the literary sections of Japanese newspapers such as Hawaii's *Nippon Jiji*, Vancouver's *Tairiku Nippō*, San Francisco's *Shinsekai* and *Nichibei*, and Los Angeles's *Rafu Shinpō*. Literary magazines such as *Shūkaku* were likewise created in the 1920s and 1930s. When Nisei educated in the United States began to be active in communities, literary creation in English language also began. Toshio Mori, Hisaye Yamamoto, and John Okada were pioneers of this Nisei literature. The second generation also published a general magazine such as *Current Life* that carried literary works.

Mexico is the earliest recipient of Japanese immigrants to Americas except for the United States and Canada, and it appears in the Migration Survey of Japan since 1892 (Ishikawa 2018). Brazil, which went on to possess the largest population of immigrants, had a record of only 799 persons in 1908.[8] As for Japanophone literature, Brazil is still the most actively Japanophone country in Latin America (Nishi 2018). Hosokawa Shūhei has pointed out that in the very first type-printed edition, not the earlier mimeographed edition, of a Japanese-language newspaper in São Paulo, *Seishu Shinpō*, there was an article by Koyama Rokurō, the proprietor of the newspaper, that called for "Engaging in creation of Japanese immigrant literature" (Hosokawa 2013, 14). Beginning in the mid-1910s, Japanese newspapers such as *Nanbei* and the *Nippaku Shinbun* began to publish poems, short stories, and commentaries in the literary sections, forming the cradle of Brazilian Japanophone literature. Hosokawa calls the period after 1925, the start of the national policy immigration, the "establishment period (period of colonial literature)" and regards the period up to 1940 as the "period of prosperity" (Hosokawa 2012, 33). From 1941, under the new dictatorship of President Vargas, schools for foreigners were closed, publishing in foreign languages was banned, and Japanophone literature was prohibited. Japanophone literatures in other Latin American regions are still poorly known, but the research has made gradual progress. In terms of reprints, a collection of works by Masuyama Akira, a Japanophone literature writer of Argentine immigrants, *The Story of the Guarani Forest*, was published in Japan.

5. Literature of Japanese Expatriates and Native Speakers of Japanese: East Asia, South Asia, and Northeast Asia

The history of Japan cannot be written separated from the colonial expansion of the Empire of Japan and its development of cultural rule toward neighboring regions. The history of Japanophone literature has also developed in tandem with this history of modern Japanese empire. Japanophone literature written by Japanese expatriates can be divided into the following categories based on the writer's background: (1) the literature of travelers; (2) literature of immigrants; and (3) Nisei, or second generation, literature. However, this division exists largely for the sake of convenience. In reality, the boundary between these divisions is flexible. For example, there are more than a few novelists such as Abe Kōbō and Nishikawa Mitsuru who were born in a foreign country or spent their childhood there, and there are also novelists such as Nagai Kafū and Okina Kyūin who wrote stories both in the country they immigrated to, and in Japan after they returned (see Hibi 2014, chapter 8).

Understanding these challenges of classification, I will characterize each as follows. In the first group, there are many examples of literary figures who visited Shanghai, such as Tanizaki Jun'chirō and Akutagawa Ryūnosuke. Natsume Sōseki's visits to Manchuria and Korea, and Satō Haruo's visit to Taiwan, are also often noted by literary scholars. Hayashi Fumiko and Kobayashi Hideo, who visited the battlefield as war writers, Takami Jun, Ibuse Masuji, and Abe Tomoji, who was drafted by the army to write about Southeast Asia, as well as Hino Ashihei, who served as a soldier, might be added to the first group. There are also many writers who visited Europe, such as Shimazaki Tōson, Yosano Hiroshi and Akiko, Yokomitsu Riichi and Kaneko Mitsuharu and Mori Michiyo.

In the second group, it is difficult to distinguish clearly between immigrants who settle down and migrant workers who eventually go back home (so-called *dekasegi* or sojourners). For the time being, those who are willing to live permanently may be classified as immigrants, while those who are not may be classified as migrant workers, but many move or stay without knowing the future. With regard to the writers in this second group, it is possible to subdivide them further into those who are full-time writers, those who are semi-full-time writers, those who have other jobs, and those who are amateur writers. However, there were few full-time writers in foreign countries, where the number of readers was limited and there were not many newspapers or magazines in which to publish. On the other hand, there were relatively numerous writers who created literary works while working as newspaper and magazine reporters. There are examples in various places: Tamura Toshiko, a reporter in Vancouver and Shanghai; Nishikawa Mitsuru, a reporter at the *Taiwan Nichinichi Shinpō*; Yamada Seizaburō, a reporter of the *Manchurian Newspaper*; Okina Kyūin, a reporter for the *Nichibei* in San Francisco; Nakanishi Inosuke, a reporter for the *Keijō Nippō* in Seoul; and Katō Asadori, an editor-in-chief for the *Jawa Nippō* in Java. On the other hand, there were those who wrote literature while working as company employees and government officials. Among them, including those who became writers after leaving their job, we find Tanaka Hidemitsu in Seoul; Kiyama Shōhei, Nitta Jirō, Kitamura Kenjirō, and Aoki Minoru in Manchuria; Nakajima Atsushi in Palau, and Tani Jōji in the United States.

In the third group are writers born in foreign countries. As depicted in the early works of Abe Kōbō, these people often felt a sense of belonging to their birthplace, and cultural distance from Japan and Japanese people. This feeling contributed to the background of their literary works in adulthood. Furthermore, most of them had the experience of *hikiage*, or repatriation, after the collapse of the Japanese empire. The literature of this second generation living in *gaichi*, or colonial, regions became part of *gaichi* literature, and at the same time, became part of literature representing the *hikiage* experience.

The following are Japanese writers who were born in the Korean Peninsula: Kajiyama Toshiyuki in Seoul; Furuyama Komao in Sinuiju; Morisaki Kazue in Daegu; Gotō Meisei in Yongheung County; Muramatsu Takeshi in Seoul; Kobayashi Masaru in Jinju, South Gyeongsang Province; Hashida Sugako in Seoul. Literary writers born in Taiwan include Haniya Yutaka in Taipei and Ozaki Hotsuki in Hsinchu. Those born in Manchuria include Gomigawa Junpei and Kiyo'oka Takayuki in Dalian, Betsuyaku Minoru in Shinkyō, and Nakanishi Rei in Mudan River. Ikushima Jirō was born in Shanghai, and Nakajima Naoto was born in Hawaii. Another notable literati was the *zainichi*, or Korean resident in Japan, Ri Kaisei/Lee Hoesung, who was born in Sakhalin and became the first novelist of Korean ancestry in Japan to receive the Akutagawa Prize.

Some writers spent their childhood or adolescence in foreign countries. Yuasa Katsue and Nakajima Atsushi were born in Japan but raised on the Korean Peninsula. They were classmates at Keijo Junior High School. Mori Atsushi, Hino Keizo, Ōyabu Haruhiko, and Itsuki Hiroyuki were also brought up in the Korean Peninsula. Writers born and raised in Manchuria in Japan include Abe Kōbō, Sawachi Hisae, Miki Takashi, Amazawa Taijirō, Miyao Tomiko, and Uno Kōichirō. There also were Hayashi Kyōko in China, Nishikawa Mitsuru and Hamada Hayao in Taiwan, and Yuzurihara Masako and Miyauchi Kanya in Sakhalin. Ariyoshi Sawako also spent her elementary school days in the Dutch East Indies.[9]

For the sake of convenience, explanations have been made for each ethnic group so far, but it should be noted that this is not sufficient when considering the historical reality of immigration and colonial culture. Japanese literary spaces in Seoul, Taipei, Dalian, and Xinjiang were multiethnic.

There were Japanese residents as migrants and local residents, and on both sides, there were people in various positions. The space of Japanese language in foreign countries is a contact zone where people, language, and information engaged in various negotiations and conflicts. The literature produced there imbues in its texts the voices of oppression, affection, self-preservation, resistance, and incongruity echoed or whispered in the contact zone.

6. From the End of World War II to the Present: Repatriation, Memory, Decolonization

Japan's defeat in the Pacific War brought about a major change in Japanophone literature. It is said that about one-tenth of the total Japanese population at that time, including military personnel, civilian personnel, and civilian employees, were living abroad, and most of them returned to Japan within a few years after the war. This is the so-called *hikiage* phenomenon. From the point of view of Japanophone literature, *hikiage* was the process of dismantling and rearranging the literary world of the Japanese empire which consisted of multiple ethnic groups. The colonial literary circles that were composed of Japanese authors from overseas and local ethnic groups broke up after the war, and writers in each region began to create works in their own vernacular language. Japanophone literatures in colonial cities were either lost or undermined. The pluralistic state of the individual creator, however, cannot easily disappear. In this sense, the postwar history of Japanophone literature in the former colonized regions were efforts to describe each postwar period by switching between multiple languages or containing Japanese language. It is also necessary to pay attention to the fact that there were people who did not, or could not, return to their homeland in the immediate postwar period; for instance, Japanese soldiers were detained in Siberia, Japanese specialists were kept and forced to work there, Japanese "war orphans" were left to local Chinese people in the confusion of *hikiage*, and Koreans in Sakhalin were not permitted to return to the Korean peninsula.

Japanophone literature will provide important suggestions for people to review and reconsider the history of themselves and others. In this section I will provide a brief overview of postwar Japanophone literature in terms of (1) *hikiage*; (2) Korean and Taiwanese writers; and (3) the literature of postwar Okinawa, North and South America. In the first group, the literature of Japanese returnees overlaps with the literature of the aforementioned overseas Japanese residents, especially those of the second generation. Abe Kōbō used *hikiage* as a theme in his early novels *To the Signpost of the End* and *Beasts Head for Home*. In addition, many writers and poets had various experiences of *hikiage* from Manchuria, Korea, Taiwan, Sakhalin, Shanghai, and other former Japanese overseas territories, such as Gōtō Meisei, Kiyo'oka Takayuki, Hayashi Kyoko, Nishikawa Mitsuru, Ri Kaisei/Lee Hoesung, and Fujiwara Tei. When we include critics and researchers with *hikiage* backgrounds, there are also Haniya Yutaka and Ozaki Hotsuki, as well as the drama writer Betsuyaku Minoru. Among cartoonists, there are also many *hikiage* people such as Akatsuka Fujio, Yamaguchi Taichi, and Chiba Tetsuya.

In the second group, the literary activities of Korean residents in Japan and Taiwanese of the Japanese-language fluent generation are also important. After the war, we have Kin Darusu /Kim Tal-su, who wrote *Genkainada* (1954) and *Taihaku Sanmyaku* (1969); Kyo Nanki/Ho Nam-gi, who also wrote poems in Korean languages and published a collection of poems *Hinawaju no uta* (Japanese, 1951); and Kin Jisho/Kim Shi-jong, who were active in a Korean poet coterie magazine in Osaka and published the collection of poems *Niigata* (1970). Literature of second-generation Korean writers has also begun to flourish: Kin Sekihan/Kim Sok-pom, who wrote "Kazanto" (1983–97); Ri Kaisei/Lee Hoesung, who won the Akutagawa Prize for *Kinuta wo Utsu On'na* (1972); and I Yanji/Lee Yang-ji, who also won the Akutagawa Prize for *Yuhi* (1989). As modern novelists, there are Yū Miri, who won the Kishida Prize for Drama for *Sakana no Matsuri* (1993), the Akutagawa Prize for *Kazoku Shinema* (1997) and the National Book Award for Translated Literature in the United States for *Tokyo Ueno Station* (2020). There are also writers such as Sagisawa Megumu, Gen Getsu, Yan Sogiru/Yang Sok-il, Kang Nobuko, Kaneshiro Kazuki, Che Shiru/Che Sil, and I Yondoku. The history of Korean women's literature in Japan has been neglected, but in recent years, Son Hee-won (2014) has begun to excavate this history.

After World War II, Taiwan also had Japanophone literature represented by authors and works such as Kyū Eikan /Chiu Yonghan's *Dakusuikei* (1954), Wu Chuo-liu's *Asia no Koji* (1956), and Chang Wenquan's *Ti ni Hau Mono* (1975). Contemporary novelists such as On Yūjū, Higashiyama Akira, and Ri Kotomi should be mentioned here as well.

Japanophone literature, which tackled the problem of postcolonialism, has spread to other regions. For the third group, I would like to mention briefly the postwar Japanophone literature of Okinawa, North America, and South America. At the end of the Pacific War in Asia, Okinawa experienced fierce ground battles and suffered great casualties. After the defeat, Okinawa came under the rule of the United States. The military government was replaced by the United States Civil Administration of the Ryukyu Islands, which served as a logistics base for the Vietnam War in the Cold War geopolitical structure. Okinawa was transformed into an island of US bases. As the island-wide struggle over land for military use began and movements to return administrative control to the island mounted, poetry magazines appeared one after another such as *Coral Reef* and *Atoll*; the literary magazine by Ryūkyū University called *Ryūkyū Bungaku*; newspapers with literary pages such as *Uruma Shinpō* and the *Okinawa Times*; and a literary magazine, *New Okinawa Literature*. The Akutagawa Prize was awarded to Ōshiro Tatsuhiro in 1967 and to Higashi Mineo in 1971.

In 1972, Okinawa was returned to Japan and became Okinawa Prefecture. However, the incorporation of Okinawa into Japan during the period of its active economic growth transformed Okinawan society. At the same time, a number of issues, including those concerning US military bases, were carried over from 1972 onward. Chinen Seishin's play *Jinruikan* (1976) and Yoshida Sueko *Kamaara Shinjū* (1984) were published, and in 1996, Matayoshi Eiki won the Akutagawa Prize for *Buta no mukui* (1996). After the war, Okinawa's postwar literature has become one of the focal points that cast a sharp critical view on the world of literature in Japan, due to various issues and contradictions such as the harsh war experience, the succession of memories, the subsequent dominance of the American military, the disparity and discrimination with Yamato, or mainland Japan, the issue of US bases, and fluctuating identity.[10]

Faced with their experiences of internment during World War II, Japanese-American literature in North America carried over a literary network created within internment camps after the war, and some magazines in Japanese continued their long-running activities such as *Nanka Bungei*.

After World War II, Brazil's Nikkei community was divided over whether to believe in Japan's victory or defeat, and they would fight to the bitter end, even to the point of shedding blood. The turmoil, which culminated in the attacks and killings by a fanatical group of the *kachigumi* (victors), the Shindō Renmei, cast a long shadow over the post-war era of the Brazilian Nikkei. Literature was also not immune to the conflict, and, there were more than forty related works (Hosokawa *2012*, 210). In 1953, post-war immigration to Brazil resumed, and the next twenty years were the uplifting period of Brazilian Japanophone literature. There were active coterie and publishing activities such as the publication of the literary magazine *Koronia bungaku* and the creation of the Paulista Literary Award.

What has become of Japanophone literature in the present? As we have already mentioned Korean and Taiwanese writers, let us summarize the other writers. One of the pioneering novelists is Levy Hideo from the United States. He won the National Library Award for translated literature in 1982 for translating the *Manyōshū* into English, and in 1987 won the Gunzō New Writers Award for *Seijōki no Kikoenai Heya*. He has continued to write numerous works up to the present day, winning many awards including the Yomiuri Prize for Literature. Yang Yi, who won the Akutagawa Prize in 2008, is from China, and Li Kotomi who also won the Akutagawa Prize in 2021 and other prizes is from Taiwan.[11] Other writers include David Zoppetti from Switzerland, Shirin Nezammafi from Iran, On Yūjū from Taiwan, and Gregory Khezrnejat from the United States. If we look at poetry, Arthur Binard and Jeffrey Angles were born in the United States, and Den Gen/Tian Yuan was born in China.

There are many Japanese writers and poets living overseas who are active using Japanese language. The leading contemporary writers are probably Murakami Haruki and Tawada Yōko. Iwaki Kei lives in Australia and is writing novels in Japanese. Yokoyama Yūta, who won the 57th Gunzō Prize for New Writers in 2014 when he lived in China and Ishii Yuka, who won the 158th Akutagawa Prize in 2018, lived in India at that time. Novelist Mizumura Minae and poet Hiromi Itō lived in the United States for a long time, although they have now returned to Japan. Apart from famous writers, coterie activities in novels and short poetry are still ongoing in South America.

7. Conclusion: A Study of Japanophone Literature as a Starting Point for Border Crossing

As individual important studies on Japanophone literature have already been introduced in the above descriptions and footnotes, I would like to give an overall summary here and conclude this chapter. Studies of Japanophone literature can be roughly divided into the following: the study of *gaichi* literature centered on the former colonies in East Asia; the study of Korean literature in Japan; the study of the experiences of Japanese writers who were born in Japan and migrated abroad; the study of immigrant literature in North and South America (including Hawaii), which developed while maintaining a relationship with the study of Asian literature in North America; and the study of Japanophone writers and poets active in recent Japan. These research areas tend to be studied independently of each other.

But this situation of Japanophone literary studies is clearly problematic. First, migration in modern times often occurs multi-regionally. For example, those who returned from Manchuria to Japan sometimes went out and resettled again in Brazil. In addition, the people, materials and information that connected the homeland and *gaichi* spread widely as a network with multiple layers. The book circulation introduced in this chapter would be a good example. In other words, literary and cultural research, which tends to be conducted on the basis of region and ethnicity, has many drawbacks in order to grasp the actual situation of Japanese immigrants and their experiences.

The study of Japanophone literature, therefore, needs to be conceived as a cross-border study across multiple regions, or as an intersection of researches that brings together studies of multiple regions and ethnic groups. In doing so, it is necessary to pass on to the next generation the results that have been uncovered in the past concerning individual ethnic groups, regions, and writers. Only after cross-border is combined with an awareness of differences according to historical contexts can the value of a panoramic vision of border crossing be realized. The study of Japanophone literature should be understood within the context of a multidimensional structure of networks based on these historical changes.

Finally, I would like to add that thinking about Japanophone literature is directly related to considering the problems of a multiethnic society in the present. Researchers on Japanophone literature should be urged to consider ethnic conflicts in Japanese society in the past and present through literature, and to intervene in these problems by engaging in literary activities including literary criticism, translation, and academic research. Even today, the illusion of a racially homogeneousness strongly pervades Japanese society. The idea of "Japan owned by the pure Japanese" is widespread, from conservative ideologues to ordinary people's consciousness. At present, Japan is rapidly and steadily shifting its course toward accepting labor migrants. The persistence of this illusion will undoubtedly lead to problems in the multiethnic symbiosis of Japanese society. It is an important agenda to get the vision and sensitivity of Japanophone literature to constructively intervene in this fantasy of racially homogeneous thinking.

Notes

1. For literature of the Ainu, see Sakata; Okawada; Suda. For Okinawan literature, see Bhowmik's chapter in this volume.

2. It is possible to think of Japanophone literature from a more backward perspective. For example, Levy Hideo dates back its period to Manyōshū considering the theory that Yamanoue no Okura was a foreigner (Levy 62).

3. See Tamura and Shiramizu; Tamura; Hibi, *Japanīzu*, especially chapter 3.

4. For São Paulo bookstores, see Mack (2022).

5. See Koizumi; Ōta; Uchiyama.

6. For Japanese literature in Seattle, see also Mack (2007).

7. About the history of Japanophone literature in North America and the survey of research in Japan concerning this field, see Ajiakei Amerika Bungaku Kenkyūkai; Mizuno; Hibi (2014). As for the survey of research in the US, see Vassil; Kobayashi.

8. See Takumu-shō Takumu-kyoku, ed. 19. There were 781 Japanese contracted immigrants and more than a dozen free immigrants, the number varies according to the documents, on board the Kasado Maru, the first immigrant ship to Brazil. See Nihon Imin 80 nenshi Hensan Iinkai 36.

9. The study of Japanophone literature in Japanese Overseas territories has been progressing in recent years. For example, a research group at Korea University has published *Zaichō Nihonjin to Shokuminchi Chōsen no Bunka* 1, 2 and *Zaichō Nihonjin Nihongo Bungaku Josetsu*. As for Japanese people in Shanghai and the concession culture, see Ōhashi et al., eds.; Takatsuna et al., eds.

10. As for Modern literature in Okinawa, see Okamoto; Nakahodo; Shinjō; Okamoto et al., eds.

11. For Yang Yi, see Ko's chapter in this volume.

Works Cited

Ajiakei Amerika Bungaku Kenkyūkai, eds. *Ajiakei Amerika bungaku: kioku to sōzō* (Asian American literature: education and imagination). Ōsaka kyōiku Tosho, 2001.

Chow, Rey. *Not Like a Native Speaker: On Languaging as a Postcolonial Experience.* Columbia University Press, 2014.

Hibi Yoshitaka. *Japanīzu Amerika: imin bungaku, shuppan bunka to shūyōjo* (Japanese America: immigrant literature, print culture and incarceration). Shinyōsha, 2014.

Hibi Yoshitaka. "Shi ga supōtsu o ttau Toki: 1932-nen no Rosanzerusu Orinpikku no ba'ai (When poetry sings for sports: the case of the 1932 Los Angeles Olympics). *Kokyō Nihongo bungaku kenkyū* 2 (2015): 111–24.

Hibi Yoshitaka. "Senzen gaichi no shomotsu toritsugi: Ōsakayagō Shoten, Tokyodō, Kansai-kei, Kyūshū-kei nado" (Book sellers in the pre-war colonies: Ōsakayagō Shoten, Tokyodō, Kansai-kei, and Kyūshū-kei). *Intelligence* 16 (2016): 134–48.

Hosokawa Shūhei. *Nikkei Burajiru imin bungaku 1: Nihongo no nagai tabi, rekishi* (Nikkei Brazilian immigrant literature vol 1: the long voyage of Japanese; history). Misuzu Shobō, 2012.

Hosokawa Shūhei. *Nikkei Burajiru imin bungaku 2: Nihongo no nagai tabi, hyoron* (Nikkei Brazilian immigrant literature vol 2: the long voyage of Japanese; criticism). Misuzu Shobō, 2013.

Ishikawa Tomonori. "Chunanbei e no imin" (Immigration to Central and South America). In *Nihonjin to kaigai iju: imin no rekishi, genjo, tenbo, edited by* Nihon Imin Gakkai. Akashi Shoten, 2018.

Izumi Tsukasa. *Nihon tōchiki Taiwan to teikoku no "bundan": "bungaku kenshō ga tsukuru "Nihongo bungaku"* (Taiwan under Japanese rule and the imperial "literary establishment": Japanese-language literature forged by literary examination). Hitsuji Shobō, 2012.

Kaku Nanen, ed. *Bairingaruna Nihongo: Tagengo tabunka no aida* (Bilingual Japanese: Between multilingualism and multiculturalism). Sangensha, 2013.

Koizumi Yuzuru. *Ro Jin to Uchiyama Kanzō* (Lu Xun and Uchiyama Kanzō). Kōdansha, 1979.

Kwon, Nayoung Aimee. "Japanophone Literature? A Transpacific Query on Absence." *MFS Modern Fiction Studies* 64, no. 3 (2018): 537–58.

Levy Hideo. "*Manyōshū* no Jidai" (The age of the Manyōshū). In *Wareteki Nihongo: The World in Japanese*. Chikuma Shobō, 2010.

Mack, Edward. *Acquired Alterity: Migration, Identity, and Literary Nationalism*. University of California Press, 2022.

Mack, Edward. "Seattle's Little Tokyo: Bundan Fiction and the Japanese Diaspora." In *Reading Material: The Production of Narratives, Genres and Literary Identities, edited by* Dennis Washburn and James Dorsey, 7–16. Proceedings of the Association for Japanese Literary Studies, vol. 7 (2007).

Muroi Mitsuhiro. *Tawada Yōko noto* (Tawada Yōko notes). Hutago no Raiondō, 2020.

Nakahodo Masanori. *Kindai Okinawa bungaku no tenkai* (The development of modern Okinawan literature). San'ichi Shobō, 1981.

Nakajima Toshio, Kawahara Isao, Shimomura Sakujiro, eds. *Taiwan kingendai bungakushi* (Modern to contemporary Tawainese literary history). Kenbun Shuppan, 2014.

Nakane Takayuki. *"Chōsen" hyōshō no bunkashi: kindai Nihon to tasha o meguru Chi no Shokuminchika* (Representation and literary history of Korea: Modern Japan and the colonialization of territory of the Other). Shinyōsha, 2004.

Ōhashi Takehiko et al., *Shinbun de miru senji Shanhai no bunka shōran: "Tairiku Shinpō" bungei bunka kiji saimoku* (Overview of wartime Shanghai culture in newspapers: Mainichi Shimpō literary and cultural articles in detail). Yumani Shobō, 2012.

Okamoto Keitoku. *Gendai Okinawa no bungaku to shisō* (Contemporary Okinawan literature and thought). Okinawa Taimususha, 1981.

Okamoto Keitoku et al., eds., *Shinsōban Okinawa bungakusen: Nihon bungaku no ejji kara no toi* (New edition Okinawa literature selection: questions from the edge of Japanese literature). Bensei Shuppan, 2015.

Okawada Akira. *Mukai Toyoaki no tōsō: ishu konkosei no sekai bungaku* (The Struggle of Toyoaki Mukai: the hybridity of world literature). Miraisha, 2014.

Ōta Naoki. *Densetsu no Nitchū bunka saron: Shanhai Uchiyama Shoten* (The legendary Sino-Japanese cultural salon: Uchiyama Bookstore in Shanghai). Heibonsha, 2008.

Sakata Minako. *Ainu kōshō bungei no ninshikiron: rekishi no hōhō to shite no Ainu sanbun setsuwa.* (Epistemology of Ainu oral literature: Ainu prose tales as a method of history). Ochanomizu Shobo, 2011.

Shinjō Ikuo. *Tōrai suru Okinawa: Okinawa hyōshō hihanron* (Okinawa rising: Okinawan cultural criticism). Inpakuto Shuppankai, 2007.

Suda Shigeru. *Kingendai Ainu bungakushiron: Ainu minzoku ni yoru Nihongo bungaku no kiseki.* (History of modern Ainu literature). Jurōsha, 2018.

Takanezawa Noriko ed. *Gendai josei sakka dokuhon 7: Tawada Yōko* (Contemporary women authors' reader, vol. 7: Tawada Yōko). Kanae Shobō, 2006.

Takatsuna Hirohumi et al., eds. *Senji Shanhai no media: bunkateki porityikusu no shiza kara* (Wartime Shanghai media: from the perspective of cultural politics). Kenbun Shuppan, 2016.

Takeuchi Kōjiro. *Beikoku Seihokubu Nihon iminshi* (Japanese immigrant history of the American northwest). Taihoku Nipposha, 1929.

Tamura Norio, and Shiramizu Shigehiko, eds. *Beikoku shoki no Nihongo shinbun* (Early US Japanese newspapers). Keisō Shobō, 1986.

Tamura Norio. *Amerika no Nihongo Shinbun* (Japanese-language newspapers in the US). Shinchōsha, 1991.

Uchiyama Kanzō. *Kashinroku: Nitchū Yukō no Kakehashi*. Heibonsha, 2011.

Zaichō Nihonjin Nihongo Bungaku Josetsu (An introduction to Japanese-language literature by the Japanese in colonial Korea). Youkrack, 2017.

Zaichō Nihonjin to Shokuminchi Chosen no Bunka 1. (The Japanese and culture of colonial Korea, vol. 1). Youkrack, 2014.

Zaichō Nihonjin to Shokuminchi Chosen no Bunka 2 (The Japanese and culture of colonial Korea, vol. 2). Youkrack, 2015.

CHAPTER 9

Modern Japanese Literature and Sinitic Literary Traditions

Matthew Fraleigh

The sort of texts now seen as belonging to the category of "Japanese literature" and thus what is thought germane or essential to its academic study is now very differently configured than it was just a generation ago. It is not at all unusual anymore to think of modern and contemporary "Japanese literature" as including Japanese-language literature written by individuals who are not Japanese, for example, or incorporating Japanese-language literature published outside the boundaries of present-day Japan (whether by Japanese émigrés or colonial subjects). Yet one of the most thoroughgoing changes to the field in its full chronological sweep has been the expansion of the category of "Japanese literature" to include a vast body of works that was produced by Japanese individuals and widely enjoyed in Japan over the centuries but was not written in Japanese. The last two decades have brought a growing recognition that across all periods of Japanese literary practice from antiquity through the modern period, Sinitic modes of expression (poetry and prose composed in literary Sinitic, the shared written language of the Sinographosphere) had a centrality and significance that have been overlooked (or explicitly rejected) by dominant narratives of national literary history. When modern Japan's academic departments of "national literature" were launched in the early 1890s, they defined themselves through their exclusive attention to works written in Japanese, which had recently been re-conceptualized as Japan's "national language." As Michael Brownstein has shown, the literary canons of Japanese national literature produced in the early decades of the Meiji era were likewise premised upon, indeed defined by, the exclusion of literary Sinitic texts (441–45). Even the name by which Sinitic genres are commonly known in Japan today (*kanshibun*, Sinitic poetry and prose) is a modern neologism that grew out of these tremendous epistemic shifts of the late nineteenth century.[1]

One well-worn narrative arc of Meiji Japan's development imagines an abrupt turn away from fusty Chinese texts and traditions as the country embraced Western models of literature, cultural practices, and social forms. Yet scholars have increasingly come to wrestle with the fact that the Meiji period in fact saw a remarkable expansion and unprecedented flourishing of Sinitic poetic composition in Japan, including the founding of numerous societies devoted to the practice, the establishment of literary magazines showcasing Sinitic genres (half a dozen just in the late 1870s), and the pioneering of new forms of readership, literary collaboration, and public engagement in the Sinitic poetry sections of several daily newspapers. Far from being a curious premodern holdover, Sinitic forms were in many ways at the vanguard of cultural life in early Meiji. Sinitic quatrains were the preferred poetic genre through which hundreds of Meiji-era travelers to the West wrote about their experiences. Sinitic literature was particularly well suited to taking full advantage of new cultural realities, such as the presence of Qing diplomats and other Sinospheric intellectuals who could serve as new readers and potential interlocutors of Japanese literary production; and far from being antithetical to Western cultural and literary forms, Sinitic was rather an important medium through which they entered Japanese discourse. While previous scholars might have taken passing notice of what seemed a curious "boomlet" in the proliferation of Sinitic poetry and prose works in early Meiji, these works are no longer regarded as a strange epiphenomenon but rather as an essential part of the literary context in which modern Japanese literature took shape and to which many of the most celebrated modern Japanese writers also contributed. This essay explores some of the ways in which the field has been reshaped by the inclusion of Sinitic texts in the last two decades and discusses some of the reasons for these changes before introducing a few important issues that remain areas of lively debate and discussion among specialists in Japanese *kanshibun* today.

One of the most basic shifts evident in research on Japanese *kanshibun* over the last few decades is who is doing work on this subject: a matter that relates directly to a larger categorical question: what, ultimately, *is* Japan's Sinitic poetry and prose? Many of the studies published in English from the 1970s through the 1990s were works written by eminent Sinologists as a kind of side-line. For example, Burton Watson's *Japanese Literature in Chinese*, a two-volume set featuring a well-chosen sample of translations of Sinitic poetry and prose from antiquity to the modern day, was of monumental importance in introducing this rich body of literature to an Anglophone readership, including even many specialists in Japanese literature, who were no doubt aware of Japanese Sinitic traditions but may never have engaged substantially with them. A decade later, Judith Rabinovitch's translation and analysis of the tenth century military chronicle *Shōmonki*, Sonja Arntzen's study and translation of the Sinitic poetry of Ikkyū (1394–1481), and Robert Borgen's examination of the early Heian academy through the figure of celebrated (and later deified) poet Sugawara no Michizane (845–903) were all published in 1986. In spite of these important interventions, it remained the case through the 1990s that much of the work being done on Japan's Sinitic traditions still came from individuals originally trained as Sinologists, such as David Pollack's *The Fracture of Meaning*, also published in 1986. Another early pioneer of the emerging sub-field of Japanese Sinitic literary expression was the distinguished scholar and translator of Chinese poetry Jonathan Chaves, who contributed to a book-length multi-media consideration of the early Edo-period Sinitic poet Ishikawa Jōzan's Shisendō, the "Hall of the Poetry Immortals" that Jōzan created on the outskirts of Kyoto in commemoration of his thirty-six favorite Chinese poets (see Rimer, Addiss, Suzuki, and Chaves). The dominant disciplinary division of labor was again evident a few years later, when Chaves collaborated with the scholar of Japanese literature and comparatist J. Thomas Rimer to translate the tremendously influential mid-Heian bilingual anthology of verse, *Japanese and Chinese Poems to Sing* (The Wakan rōei shū), with Rimer translating the Japanese poems and Chaves translating the Chinese-language poetry by both Japanese and Chinese poets. One additional Sinological scholar who has been particularly active in the field of Japanese Sinitic literary studies is Timothy Bradstock; his numerous publications produced in collaboration with Judith Rabinovitch have provided foundational translations for Japan's Sinitic poetic tradition from earliest times through the late Edo period. As the works I have mentioned here suggest, Anglophone scholarship concerning Japan's Sinitic traditions through the end of the twentieth century was largely confined to pre-Meiji texts. I call attention to the substantial role that Sinologists played in producing the foundational Anglophone scholarship on Japan's Sinitic traditions not to propose some kind of narrow parochialism or to diminish in any way the contributions of these scholars, but simply to point out that even through the last years of the twentieth century, the mainstream of Japanese literary scholarship had yet to enthusiastically embrace Japan's Sinitic traditions as a central concern of its own scholarly enterprise.

In an important essay from 1998, Jonathan Timothy Wixted (himself a scholar whose academic work up until that point had largely focused on Chinese poetry and literary theory) called out the lack of attention that Japanese literary scholars had thus far given to Japan's Sinitic traditions. Wixted's article was an urgent appeal to scholars to address this lacuna and remedy a situation he soberly assessed as follows in the article's opening lines:

> In terms of its size, often its quality, and certainly its importance both at the time it was written and cumulatively in the cultural tradition, *kanbun* 漢文 is arguably the biggest and most important area of Japanese literary study that has been ignored in recent times, and the one least properly represented as part of the canon. (23)

But the field has started to look very different today. For example, the greater profile that Japan's Sinitic traditions have recently acquired is obvious if one simply compares the contents of massive multi-volume authoritative editions of the Japanese literary canon published by one prestigious academic publisher in successive generations. Iwanami Shoten's influential compendium of annotated editions of the classical literary canon, the 100-volume *Nihon koten bungaku taikei* (1957–67), contained just three volumes featuring Sinitic poetry by Japanese poets, but the 100-volume collection it published a generation later, *Shin Nihon koten bungaku taikei* (1989–2005), more than tripled this number. For the modern period as well, Iwanami's thirty-volume companion set of annotated editions of Meiji period texts (*Shin Nihon koten bungaku taikei: Meiji-hen*, 2001–13) contains several volumes devoted to Sinitic poetry and prose, a marked increase in comparison to the major multi-volume sets of modern canonical works issued a few decades earlier by various other publishers, which ignored Sinitic expression entirely or perhaps limited its appearance to a single volume. These new publication efforts demonstrate the scholarly community's reassessment of and commitment to serious examination of Sinitic traditions from Japan's modern era, but they also show the reading public's burgeoning interest in this area. For example, the earliest substantial monographic examination of Meiji period Sinitic literature, Kinoshita Hyō's *Meiji shiwa* (1943), had already been out of print for half a century before Iwanami re-published the work in 2015 as part of its *Iwanami bunko* collection of convenient and inexpensive paperbacks.

The shifting contours of the field are also evident in recent comprehensive literary histories. The inner jacket flap of *The Cambridge History of Japanese Literature* (edited by Haruo Shirane and Tomi Suzuki with David Lurie and published in 2016), for example, highlights its greater attention to Sinitic texts as a distinguishing feature of the volume's coverage: "The book also places

Japanese literature in a wider East Asian tradition of Sinitic writing . . ."[2] In addition to clarifying regional connections and facilitating comparison with Chinese and Korean literary history, the greater attention to Japan's Sinitic texts permitted a new understanding of the content of the Japanese literary tradition itself. As editor Haruo Shirane wrote in the introduction to the work, "it is only in recent decades, as popular genres and the enormous tradition of Literary Sinitic or Sino-Japanese (*kanbun*) writings have received renewed attention alongside better-studied materials, that the full complexity and variety of the Japanese literary heritage has come into view" (1).

Or consider the way that academic libraries have categorized books pertaining to Sinitic literary traditions practiced outside of China. When the Library of Congress set up its classification system (which almost all academic libraries in North America use), the paradigm of monolingual national literatures was dominant, which meant that "Japanese literature" was somewhat uncritically taken to mean literature written in the Japanese language. Literature written by Japanese authors in Literary Sinitic obviously did not fit this framework, but it was typically categorized at the Library of Congress as "Chinese literature" in one of two ways. In one common approach, works by and about Sinitic poets from early modern Japan, for example, would be grouped alongside those by and about their Chinese contemporaries. According to this schema, books by and about the Japanese Sinitic poet Kan Chazan (1748–1827) would be found alongside books by and about the late Qing literatus and statesman Kang Youwei (1858–1927) and the late Chosŏn period literatus Kang Sehwang (1713–1791): all three being literary figures who wrote Sinitic poetry and prose during China's Qing dynasty and whose Romanized family names begin with "K." In addition to this approach configured in terms of the sequential temporal units of Chinese literary history's periodization, a second approach was formulated spatially. It placed Japan among other overseas sites at the very end of a series of call numbers allotted to Chinese literature tied to specific regions: following works on the literature of various domestic Chinese cities and regions came literature in Chinese from overseas Chinese communities. Literature in Chinese produced by Japanese authors was sometimes categorized here as well. In situating Japan as one of several extraterritorial sites on the periphery of Chinese civilization, this second framework bears some similarities to the rubric of *yuwai hanji* (overseas Sinographic texts) that has begun to attract attention in the past two decades in China. Whether conceived in terms of its contemporaneity with literature in China or as a spatial extension thereof, Sinitic literature from Japan was clearly not part of the category "Japanese literature."

But all of this changed in July 2000, when the Library of Congress adopted a new policy for classifying Sinitic texts from outside China, determining that henceforth "Japanese and Chinese literature . . . written solely in Chinese characters by Japanese and Korean authors will no longer class with Chinese literature, but with Japanese and Korean literature." The Library also authorized the creation of new subject headings such as "Kanbun (Japanese prose literature)," "Kanshi (Japanese poetry)," and "Hanmunhak (Korean literature)." The result of this change in cataloging policy means that works pertaining to Kan Chazan that the library subsequently acquired have been categorized alongside those concerning his Japanese contemporaries, whether they composed mainly in Japanese, such as Kamo no Suetaka (1754–1841), or mainly in Sinitic, such as Kashiwagi Jotei (1763–1819). In creating new subject headings to reflect the terms by which these texts are designated in local languages, the Library of Congress recognized that Sinitic texts were an inextricable part of the literary traditions of both Japan and Korea.

As these shifts in the placement of Sinitic literature within the Library of Congress's classification scheme reveal, such texts do not fit readily into nineteenth-century models of "national literature," premised as they were in Japan and elsewhere upon assumptions of phonocentricism and the unitary linguistic coherence of a national literary canon.[3] Moreover, in the case of Sinitic literature, an unexamined assumption about the monolingualism of a given text has proven additionally problematic. Looking through large-scale union catalogs such as WorldCat, it is not unusual to find disagreements in the bibliographic metadata over what language a given Sinitic text is written in; one library might categorize a certain Sinitic text published in Japan as written in the Chinese language while another might categorize the same text as being written in the Japanese language.[4] In a sense both libraries are correct, for while the written form of the text might give it broad regional intelligibility as Literary Sinitic, it is also the case that such texts were often approached in Japan through the *kundoku* methodology of "vernacular reading." In this reading practice, the Literary Sinitic text is transformed into a distinct (and usually highly Sinified) register of Japanese: a sort of "translationese" that preserves as closely as possible the diction and structure of the written text while construing it in accord with Japanese syntax and with the necessary grammatical particles and inflections. The question of how we should understand *kundoku* is an area of tremendous interest and active research in the field today. Some scholars view the work of *kundoku* as "indubitably a translation," albeit a special form of "bound translation" (Kornicki, 166) while others have argued that *kundoku* "is not translation in any conventional sense" (Denecke, 210).[5] This phenomenon of "vernacular reading" was not unique to Japan; scholars such as Kin Bunkyō, Peter Kornicki, and Zev Handel who have broadly examined related phenomena across the Sinosphere are providing important new perspectives on the various ways in which Chinese texts were read and produced and how the Chinese script was adapted in Korea, Vietnam, Japan, and other areas on the periphery of Chinese traditional civilization.[6] As Handel notes in his book, "for approximately two millennia the Literary Sinitic written language was the vehicle for the transmission of cultural knowledge throughout East Asia and adjacent areas, knitting the region together in a common intellectual enterprise encompassing art, religion, philosophy, historiography, political theory, and cosmology" (2), but that this narrative of regional commonality is not the one he examines in the book, which instead focuses on the ways in which the Chinese script was transformed and adapted locally.

The changes in terminology evident in the Library of Congress's classification scheme (from "Chinese poetry—Japan" to "Kanshi (Japanese poetry)," for example) also foreground shifts in how these texts have been conceptualized and which of their features are being emphasized: their portability across an entire region and extremely high degree of mutual intelligibility on the one hand, or the local cultural context in which they arose and the practices of reception in which they were embedded on the other. The topic of how such forms of Sinitic literature are designated in English may seem a trivial matter or even a distraction. After all, it is in some ways an issue that arises as an artifact of translating into English the name of a particular mode or genre. Wouldn't using Japanese terms bypass the problem? This seems like a straightforward solution; indeed, when it created new subject headings for types of Sinitic literature in 2000, the Library of Congress avoided having to choose a single English term from among the various alternatives by strategically employing vernacular terms. But it is also important to be cognizant of the fact that "kanshi" as used by Anglophone academics usually means something different from what "kanshi" means in Japanese. Specifically, the Japanese term "kanshi" includes all Sinitic poetry, regardless of authorial nationality; in Japanese usage, Du Fu and Natsume Sōseki both wrote *kanshi*. But Anglophone usage of *kanshi* specifically designates Sinitic poetry composed by Japanese poets. Similarly, in Japanese usage "kanbun" refers to literary Sinitic texts, regardless of authorship and provenance, whereas it is sometimes used in English to refer to *kundoku* reading practices.

If scholarship is going to be cumulative and cooperative, as it should be, clearly it is important for scholars to be able to understand precisely what other scholars are discussing. Yet it is equally clear that terminology is not neutral. The terms that one scholar selects to discuss a cultural or literary phenomenon naturally reflect how that scholar envisions the materials, what that scholar sees as the most interesting or noteworthy aspects of the topic, and what that scholar wishes to highlight. Even today, as Sinitic texts from Japan have attracted new attention, scholars still make use of a wide variety of terms to designate them in English. There are good arguments to be made for each of the alternatives that have been proposed.

To briefly sketch the stakes involved in the naming issue, consider *kanshi* (Sinitic poetry) as an example. Almost all of the early Anglophone scholars to take up these texts simply called them "Chinese poems." This term recognizes the fact that Japanese Sinitic poetry, like Sinitic poetry composed anywhere else in the Sinosphere, is written in accord with the grammar of classical Chinese, shares formal and rhetorical features with Chinese models, and for many of the most prevalent genres, conforms to rules of rhyme and even complex patterns of tonal prosody (the alternation of level and oblique tones) established by Chinese precedent. The term also arguably reflects how many Sinitic poets in Japan conceptualized the practice; consider Natsume Sōseki's musings on his own Sinitic poetic composition in 1910:

> Suppose someone were to ask me: "Why does a man like you, who doesn't really have a firm grasp on the distinction between level and oblique tones, whose knowledge of rhyme categories are just vague memories, go to such trouble laboring over ingenious literary designs that have their effect only on a Chinese person?" In truth, even I wouldn't know how to answer. However, leaving the matter of level and oblique tones and rhyme characters aside, the charm of Sinitic poetry has become Japanized through a long process of transmitted learning that extends from the Heian period down to the present. It is no easy task to wrest it from the minds of Japanese of my generation.[7]

Sōseki's remarks reveal his sense that even though his own modes of reception might not be able to fully appreciate the auditory effects of the poems he labored to create, nevertheless scrupulous attention to such features was an essential part of composing in the form. At the same time, to call such works "Chinese poems" might fail to do justice to Sōseki's observation that the enjoyment of Sinitic poetry had long become domesticated as an inextricable part of Japanese literary sensibility. An approach that labeled *kanshi* "Chinese poems" might run the risk of re-affirming the texts' historical exclusion from the modern category of Japanese literature by re-inscribing them within the territory of "Chinese literature." For this reason, some Anglophone scholars looked for a term that did not so directly invoke the modern nation state of China. Wixted was an early champion of the term "Sino-Japanese," which he argued would unmistakably foreground the texts' importance to Japanese literary history and would also take account of the fact that for much of Japanese literary history, Sinitic texts were approached through the *kundoku* methodology, by which a Japanese reader construed the Sinitic text into a form of Japanese. It would also acknowledge the occasional departures from normative Sinitic that can be found in some Japanese works. Yet, to follow Wixted's proposal to use the term "Sino-Japanese" for compositions by Japanese individuals while reserving "Chinese" for compositions by Chinese individuals introduces a distinction that does not exist in Japanese, where works in literary Sinitic are known by the same term regardless of authorial nationality. Furthermore, inasmuch as the term "Sino-Japanese" implies that the language of Sinitic works composed in Japan is a Sinified variant of Japanese, other scholars have proposed using "Japano-Chinese" to reflect better the reality that Sinitic produced by Japanese writers is fundamentally a form of Chinese even as it may show local idiosyncrasies. Another term that some have proposed to use for Japanese *kanshi* is "Chinese-style poems," which identifies the origins of the poems' form in China while not also relegating the poems themselves to a location outside the province of Japanese literature. Moreover, "Chinese-style" addresses the possibility of *kundoku* reception by agnostically deferring a definitive statement about the texts' linguistic status, recognizing that "although many texts consisting of Chinese characters arranged according to the rules of literary Chinese syntax no doubt were composed as Chinese, it is not always possible to be certain that the language which the writer of such a text intended to represent was Chinese as opposed to Japanese" (Seeley, 25). At the same time, authors who use this term generally reserve "Chinese-style poems" for compositions by Japanese individuals while using "Chinese poems" for those by Chinese individuals; thus, like Wixted's proposal for "Sino-Japanese," it introduces a distinction in English terminology that is not present in the Japanese.

My own approach on the contentious matter of terminology has been to try first to understand how a key term such as *kanshi* (and its pre-1880s equivalent, *shi*) was used and understood within Japanese and then try to find the best way to express that range of meaning in English. Struck by how Victor Mair's use of "literary Sinitic" to talk about "classical Chinese" facilitated discussion of such texts beyond the borders of China, I ultimately settled on "Sinitic poetry." While the term Sinitic has become noticeably more common in recent years, the matter is far from settled: for example, Brendan Morley discusses the naming issue at length in a recent article, noting that while "literary Sinitic" may be a useful term to describe orthodox or "pure" *kanbun*, it is also inadequate if applied to works on the other end of the spectrum: those written in so-called *hentai kanbun*, a "variant" form that incorporates a great deal of Japanese vocabulary and constructions. On the other hand, Morley also argues that "we should be open to the possibility that, at least in some cases, the English phrase 'in Chinese' might come closest to conveying how premodern Japanese writers using Literary Sinitic actually conceived of their own enterprise" (342). In an article published in 2020 about Mori Ōgai's *kanshi*, a few of which playfully flaunt their use of Japanese vernacular vocabulary, Wixted reiterated his longstanding advocacy for "Sino-Japanese" while also suggesting two novel alternatives: "In sum, it would seem preferable to say that Ōgai's *kanshi* are written in 'Sino-Japanese,' in 'Japanese-Sinitic,' or in 'E.A.-criture'—not that they are 'in Chinese'" (285). The neologism "E.A.-criture," Wixted explains "(derived from "East Asian-criture") would encompass sinographic writing in Japan, Korea, and Vietnam, and include China as well" (n. 41). Perhaps rather than hoping that a single definitive term could neatly cover the entire body of *kanshibun* broadly conceived, it is best to understand the variety of terms that have been proposed as indicating both the internal heterogeneity of the category and the range of perspectives that may be fruitfully employed in approaching these texts and highlighting certain of their aspects. As Haruo Shirane observed in a preliminary note on conventions in *The Cambridge History of Japanese Literature*: "Because the variety of approaches to rendering such Japanese words in English reflects debates within the field, we have avoided imposing an artificial unity on translations of titles and terms" (xviii).

The relatively new term "Sinographic" presents an exciting opportunity to bring scholars working principally on particular Asian literary traditions into dialogue with one another on shared issues. But, by "Sinographic texts" do we mean simply works that were written solely in Sinographs? Such a capacious definition would include all the poems in the *Man'yōshū*, for example, even those where Sinographs are used exclusively for their phonetic value. Or, since Japanese *kana* are derived from Sinographs, any text written in Japanese is arguably a Sinographic text, too. One may wonder if such a capacious definition would essentially be no definition at all. If one seeks to understand the various ways in which the Chinese script was used throughout the region, then such a broad framework for "Sinographic" might make sense, but even if the term "Sinographic" is understood to include both literary Sinitic texts and vernacular texts written in Sinographs, there are important differences between the two. My sense is that many scholars use the term "Sinographic texts" to mean works that had some substantial degree of portability within the Sinosphere. In any case, it is important for us to think through the definition and be clear about how we are using the term.

Handel posits a clear conceptual distinction in the mind of the writer between composing in one's own vernacular and composing in the "cosmopolitan writing" of Sinitic.[8] Central to the issues of terminology, categorization, and conceptualization that I have discussed above is the related question of the extent to which the language of Sinitic texts was considered "foreign" by Sinospheric practitioners. It is common to read assertions by modern Anglophone scholars, including some champions of greater attention to these materials, stating that texts written in literary Sinitic were not considered foreign to non-Chinese Sinospheric practitioners until very late; some assert even into the twentieth century (Denecke, 211; Wixted, "*Kanbun*," 23). It is easy to understand the motivation to make that claim, for it seeks to counteract one major reason that Sinographic texts have historically been overlooked by those studying the national literary traditions of non-Chinese East Asian cultures. In the Japanese case, as the field of "national literature" took shape in the 1890s, the concept's phonocentric and monolingual underpinnings meant that Sinitic texts were jettisoned from the canons of Japanese literature precisely because they were deemed "foreign" and therefore inauthentic, peripheral, or somehow lesser.

But we must be very careful in specifying what we mean by "foreign." I agree that many premodern and modern producers of Sinographic texts in Japan did not regard such materials as "foreign" in the sense of "unfamiliar"—indeed they were central to the learning of many. Yet as the aforementioned reflections of Natsume Sōseki on his own Sinitic poetry composition suggest, it is problematic to imagine that he and other traditionally educated Japanese lacked a fundamental awareness of literary Sinitic texts as being written in a foreign language (that is, a language originating outside of Japan that was governed by a syntax and grammar completely distinct from those of the local language and with an evolving lexicon intimately tied to its Chinese sources). Our zeal to counteract the historical rejection of these texts and reclaim them within local national literary traditions may lead us to make assertions that are demonstrably incompatible with the understandings of historical practitioners of *kanshibun*.

In a 1986 collection of essays by prominent postwar scholars of Sinitic poetry from early modern Japan, the eminent authority on Japanese literature of the period, Nakamura Yukihiko observed that *kanshi* was Japan's only widespread poetic form in which Japanese write in a foreign language and form "as is" (2). He even compared this phenomenon to Russians of a certain era writing in French. Nakamura's statement clearly reveals his understanding of Sinitic as a foreign language. Is this conceptualization unique to present-day scholars? Consider remarks made in 1951 by Suzuki Torao (1878–1963), educated in Meiji, who was a leading scholar of Chinese literature and lifelong Sinitic poet. It was wrong to discard something like Sinitic poetry just because it was foreign, he wrote, before going on to argue that "it is useful to put oneself in the position of writing from another country's vantage point" (*Gayū* 2, 26).

Suzuki Torao's appeal to the "nation" in this essay may make us wonder if his understanding is solely the byproduct of the modern framework of nation-states. What about Japanese who came of age in the late Edo period? The scholar, poet, and journalist Narushima Ryūhoku (1837–1884), who lived through the transition from Edo to Meiji, more than once spoke of the composition of *kanshi* and *kanbun* as analogous to writing in a foreign language. In an 1879 essay he compared the low level of scholarship in Western languages with the high level of Japanese Sinology, writing "How many Japanese are there who can write Western prose with precision and elegance, or produce their poems with delicate skill? . . . Certainly it is true that the Japanese who can freely wield a brush in this way, as a Japanese Sinological scholar writes the poetry and prose of China, are few indeed" (*Dekinei sōdan* 7, April 17, 1879, 2a).

So is this all just a post-Meiji phenomenon that we can chalk up to the rise of nationalist consciousness? In *Katsugen shiwa*, published in 1787, the Tendai Buddhist priest Rikunyo (1734–1801) takes up well over eight hundred terms from Sinitic poetry and writes about their meaning.[9] It is impossible to read his remarks without concluding that he fundamentally conceives of Sinitic as a foreign language (one that he had devoted his life to studying). Even the preface to the volume, written by another priest named Daiten Kenjō (1719–1801), makes this point: "investigating and elucidating the meaning of words constitutes the beginning of study. How much more is this true in the case of a Japanese who studies Chinese?"

We might imagine that this conception of the foreignness of literary Sinitic came only in the wake of Ogyū Sorai's (1666–1728) famous insistence in the late seventeenth and early eighteenth century that Japanese scholars directly confront the foreignness of literary Sinitic texts. In *Yakubun sentei* (1715), for example, he argues that the ubiquitous practice of *kanbun kundoku* vernacular reading is nothing more than interlingual translation, cautioning that Japanese learners so accustomed to employing it might fail to fully appreciate that "our land has its own language and China has its own language."[10] But even before Sorai, and even among those who did not share his disdain for *kundoku* approaches, one does not have to look far to find statements by Japanese intellectuals that clearly situate literary Sinitic as a foreign language. In *Bunkun*, the neo-Confucian scholar Kaibara Ekiken (1630–1714) attributes the difficulties Japanese readers face in reading canonical literary Sinitic texts to the fact that the language is foreign: "The letters and the words of the teachings in the four books and the five classics are unfamiliar to the eyes and ears of our Japanese people." By contrast, "Japanese songs are in the language of our land and thus the words are easy to read and the meaning easy to apprehend" (3, 326–27). In the same text, Ekiken also adduces the foreignness of the Chinese language in his dismissal of Japanese efforts to compose Sinitic poetry. Even enthusiastic composers of Sinitic poetry such as Arai Hakuseki (1657–1725) clearly understood literary Sinitic as a foreign language.

These examples suggest strongly that Japanese producers of Sinitic texts perceived them to be written in a language distinct from Japanese. If that is the case, then perhaps the long tradition of writing *kanshibun* in Japan should be understood as a case of exophony. The term "exophony" refers to literary activity that is undertaken in a language other than the writer's native language. In perhaps the first essay to apply the concept of exophonic literature to the case of Japanese Sinitic poetry, Fukushima Riko quotes bilingual author Tawada Yōko's reflections on the value of her unique "accent."[11] Rather than seeing her Japanese-accented German as something to be ashamed of or a fault that ideally would be removed from her speech or writing in German, Tawada instead argues that it is fundamental to her compositional process and that it permits her to discover aspects of German that native speakers might not notice. Tawada quotes the linguist Tanaka Katsuhiko who observes that not only the pronunciation of exophonic writers but their very conceptual process is also accented. Indeed, Tanaka goes one step further in saying that unless an exophonic writer's writing and thinking is accented in some way then there is no point for them to write in a foreign language (Tanaka, 77; qtd. in Fukushima, 68).

We can see in this line of thinking a potential rationalization or justification for Japanese Sinitic literature; namely, a Japanese Sinitic poet's work has value and is interesting to the degree that it is distinctly accented: that is, to the degree that it departs from broader (perhaps dominant or hegemonic) norms. Following such an argument to its logical conclusion, the most noteworthy or significant examples of Sinitic poetry from Japan would seem to be those that are most idiosyncratically Japanese. It is perhaps no coincidence that one of the best-known studies of Japanese Sinitic poetry to be published in English, and the only one that has ever been published in the flagship *Journal of Asian Studies*, is David Pollack's 1979 article on the popular genre of *kyōshi* or "wild poetry," which flourished from the late eighteenth century into Meiji. These comic works, with their jarring disjunction between form and content and their flagrant flouting of propriety, are certainly one important part of Sinitic literature in Japan. But I think we risk grossly misunderstanding the nature of Sinitic expression in Japan if we imagine that such playful departures are the mainstream. Their humorous effect depends precisely on the audience appreciating how the poet willfully deviates from the accepted norm. A literary history giving disproportionate weight to *kyōshi* and other highly local varieties of Sinitic might shed light on important disjunctions between the languages and cultural contexts but it would also yield a picture all but unrecognizable to practitioners of Sinitic poetry from the period in question.

One of the key themes inherent to the discussion of Sinitic poetry and prose in a larger regional context is the tension between universality and particularity. It is worthwhile to consider, for example, what might be distinctive or unique about Japanese Sinitic poetry, what sets it apart from other traditions of Sinitic poetry. Many comparatist scholars have proposed answers to this question, noting for example the relative commonness of particular genres, the popularity of particular models, or the different ways in which certain themes and natural phenomena are depicted. The prominent Sinologist Ishikawa Tadahisa, for example, has written about the sharply contrasting ways the ocean tends to be invoked by Japanese and Chinese Sinitic poets, noting that it constitutes a major theme for (especially later) Japanese Sinitic poets but not for Tang poets, many of whom may never have seen the ocean (1–12). Yet if attention to local idiosyncrasies becomes too extreme, it can also cause us to lose sight of the participation of Japanese Sinitic forms in larger regional traditions.

An excessive attention to what is atypical or distinctive about a particular Sinitic tradition can end up re-inscribing the very nationalism that excluded Sinitic texts from "national literature" in the first place. I think it is important for us as scholars and communicators with nonspecialists and with the general public to be cognizant of a widespread tendency to focus on what is distinctive or unique about Sinographic texts in a particular locality. Certainly this attention to local specificity is important, but I think it must be balanced with awareness of commonality. We might suspect that early modern Japanese Sinitic poets secretly yearned to break free of the confines of the form, to throw off the yoke of Chinese orthodoxy, to thumb their noses at tradition. This is a tempting narrative. It makes a good story; we can easily imagine a triumphant scene of self-confident rejection. Yet using Sinitic poetry to express distinctive forms of local culture and particular elements of the poet's lived world was not necessarily incompatible with the genre's cosmopolitan orientation. From the eighteenth century onward, Japan's early modern Sinitic poets became increasingly interested in depicting distinctive flora and fauna, specific places, and unique cultural phenomena. Yet even as they turned to newfound subject matter, they also devised ways to render the local while preserving some degree of global (or regional) intelligibility.

Alongside a recent surge in interest in Sinitic texts within Japanese and Korean literary studies, it is exciting to see interest in this burgeoning field from within Chinese studies as well. Within the last few years, there have been articles in prominent Chinese literary studies journals such as *Journal of Chinese Literature and Culture* as well as in *Frontiers of Literary Studies in China* focused on Sinitic literary traditions outside China, such as Richard Lynn's discussion of late Qing diplomat Huang Zunxian's engagements with Japan's Sinitic literary tradition and the Meiji cultural milieu and Xiaohui Zhang's consideration of Sōseki's *kanshi*. Similarly, Oxford University Press has recently published two substantial reference works on Chinese Literature, *The Oxford Handbook of Classical Chinese Literature: 1000 BCE–900 CE* (2017) and *The Oxford Handbook of Modern Chinese Literatures* (2016), both of which include essays on Sinitic writing in Japan and other Sinospheric sites beyond China. In China itself, Zhang Bowei was an early pioneer of research into what he termed "overseas Sinographic texts," publishing prolifically on the topic and founding an academic journal devoted to it in 2005, *Yuwai hanji yanjiu jikan*.

The "border-crossing" category that the Association for Asian Studies instituted for its annual conference more than twenty years ago once seemed cutting edge. But such border-crossing is now increasingly mainstream. It is no longer rare at all for graduate students to develop advanced competence in two or more Asian languages. Indeed, many enter with native proficiency already in one. While the job market remains largely configured in terms of national literary traditions, the shifting profile of our graduate programs presents a wonderful opportunity for a more regional, explicitly comparative approach to Japanese literature and East Asian studies more generally.

Notes

1. See Fraleigh, *Plucking*, 4–7; and Fraleigh, "Taking Stock," 236–43.

2. The same text appears on the Cambridge University Press website's "Information" concerning the volume; see the "book description" at https://doi.org/10.1017/CHO9781139245869

3. See, for example, Shirane and Suzuki, 4–5, 71–77.

4. Nor is this a problem unique to North American cataloging practice; similar discrepancies can be found in how a given Japanese Sinitic text is categorized by multiple libraries in Japanese union catalogs such as CiNii.

5. For a discussion of this issue, see Fraleigh, "Rearranging."

6. John Whitman has also pointed out parallels to vernacular reading practices outside Sinographic East Asia.

7. *Omoidasu koto nado*, section 5.

8. Handel, 16.

9. See Fraleigh, "Approaching Classical Chinese Poetry."

10. For a complete translation of *Yakubun sentei* and extensive discussion of it, see Pastreich. The relevant passage I translate here appears in Pastreich's translation on p. 147.

11. Tawada and other scholars, such as Robert Stockhammer, have developed the term "exophonic literature" in distinction from related terms such as "immigrants' literature" or "foreigners' literature," and also from such literary phenomena as creole or pidgin literature. Tawada uses the term "exophony" to refer broadly to creative acts in which the author steps outside the bounds of his or her native language (6–7). In English, Keaveney's recent article applies the concept of exophony to Natsume Sōseki's exchanges with Masaoka Shiki in Sinitic.

Works Cited

Arntzen, Sonja. *Ikkyū and* The Crazy Cloud Anthology*: A Zen Poet of Medieval Japan.* University of Tokyo Press, 1986.

Borgen, Robert. *Sugawara no Michizane and the Early Heian Court.* Council on East Asian Studies, Harvard University, 1986.

Brownstein, Michael. "From *Kokugaku* to *Kokubungaku*: Canon-Formation in The Meiji Period." *Harvard Journal of Asiatic Studies* 47, no. 2 (1987): 435–60.

Fraleigh, Matthew. "Approaching Classical Chinese Poetry in Early Modern Japan: Intralingual and Interlingual Translation Strategies in Rikunyo's 'Remarks on Poetry.'" *Sungkyun Journal of East Asian Studies* 23, no. 2 (Fall 2023): 137–62.

Fraleigh, Matthew. *Plucking Chrysanthemums: Narushima Ryūhoku and Sinitic Literary Traditions in Modern Japan.* Harvard University Asia Center, 2016.

Fraleigh, Matthew. "Rearranging the figures on the tapestry: what Japanese direct translation of European texts can tell us about *kanbun kundoku.*" *Japan Forum* 31, no. 1 (2019): 4–32.

Fraleigh, Matthew. "Taking Stock of a Tradition: Early Efforts to Write the History of Sinitic Poetry Expression in Japan." In *Rethinking the Sinosphere: Poetics, Aesthetics, and Identity Formation*, edited by Qian Nanxiu, Richard J. Smith, and Zhang Bowei, 235–68. Cambria Press, 2020.

Fukushima Riko 福島理子. "Gohō kara miru kinsei shijintachi no kosei: 'ekusofonii' toshite no kanshi toiu shiten kara" 語法から見る近世詩人たちの個性：“エクソフォニー”としての漢詩という視点から. Takigawa, Nakamoto, Fukushima, and Gōyama, 60–68.

Handel, Zev. *Sinography: The Borrowing and Adaptation of the Chinese Script.* Brill, 2019.

Ishikawa Tadahisa 石川忠久. *Nihonjin no kanshi: fūga no kako e* 日本人の漢詩：風雅の過去へ. Taishūkan Shoten 大修館書店, 2003.

Kaibara Ekiken. *Ekiken zenshū*. 8 vols. Ekiken Zenshū Kankōbu, 1911.

Keaveney, Christopher. "Swapping odes in a sacred language: the *Kanshi* exchange of Natsume Sōseki and Masaoka Shiki and its meaning." *International Journal of Asian Studies* 20 (2023): 611–30.

Kin Bunkyō. *Literary Sinitic and East Asia: A cultural sphere of vernacular reading*. Edited by Ross King. Brill, 2021.

Kornicki, Peter Francis. *Languages, Scripts, and Chinese Texts in East Asia*. Oxford University Press, 2018.

Lynn, Richard John. "Pursuit of the Modern While Preserving Tradition: The Japan Poems of Huang Zunxian." *Frontiers of Literary Studies in China* 12, no. 2 (2018): 182–216.

Mair, Victor. "Buddhism and the Rise of the Written Vernacular in East Asia: The Making of National Languages." *Journal of Asian Studies* 53, no. 3 (1994): 707–51.

Morley, Brendan. "*Kanbun*, *Kundoku*, and the Language of Literary Sinitic: Terminological Issues in the Study of Sinography in Japan." *Japanese Language and Literature* 56, no. 2 (October 2022): 329–54.

Nakamura Yukihiko 中村幸彦, ed. *Kinsei no kanshi* 近世の漢詩. Kyūko shoin 汲古書院, 1986.

Pastreich, Emanuel. "Grappling with Chinese Writing as a Material Language: Ogyū Sorai's *Yakubunsentei*." *Harvard Journal of Asiatic Studies* 61, no. 1 (2001): 119–70.

Pollack, David. "*Kyōshi*: Japanese 'Wild Poetry.'" *Journal of Asian Studies* 38, no. 3 (May 1979): 499–517.

Pollack, David. *The Fracture of Meaning: Japan's Synthesis of China from the Eighth through the Eighteenth Centuries*. Princeton University Press, 1986.

Qian Nanxiu, Richard J. Smith, and Zhang Bowei, eds. *Rethinking the Sinosphere: Poetics, Aesthetics, and Identity Formation*. Cambria Press, 2020.

Rabinovitch, Judith. *Shōmonki: The Story of Masakado's Rebellion*. Monumenta Nipponica, 1986.

Rabinovitch, Judith, and Timothy Bradstock, eds. and trans. *An Anthology of* Kanshi *(Chinese Verse) by Japanese Poets of the Edo Period (1603–1868): Translations of Selected Poems with an Introduction and Commentaries*. Edwin Mellen Press, 1997.

Rabinovitch, Judith, and Timothy Bradstock, eds. and trans. *The* Kanshi *Poems of the Ozasa* Tanzaku *Collection: Late Edo Life through the Eyes of Kyoto Townsmen*. International Research Center for Japanese Studies, 2002.

Rabinovitch, Judith, and Timothy Bradstock, eds. and trans. *Dance of the Butterflies: Chinese Poetry from the Japanese Court Tradition*. Cornell University East Asia Series, 2005.

Rabinovitch, Judith, and Timothy Bradstock, eds. and trans. *No Moonlight in My Cup: Sinitic Poetry* (Kanshi) *from the Japanese Court, Eighth to the Twelfth Centuries*. Brill, 2019.

Rimer, J. Thomas, and Jonathan Chaves, eds. and trans. *Japanese and Chinese Poems to Sing: The* Wakan rōei shū. Columbia University Press, 1997.

Rimer, J. Thomas, Stephen Addiss, Hiroyuki Suzuki, and Jonathan Chaves. *Shisendo: Hall of the Poetry Immortals*. Weatherhill, 1991.

Seeley, Christopher. *A History of Writing in Japan*. Brill, 1991.
Shirane, Haruo, and Tomi Suzuki, eds. Inventing the Classics: Modernity, National Identity, and Japanese Literature. Stanford University Press, 2001.
Shirane, Haruo, and Tomi Suzuki with David Lurie, eds. *The Cambridge History of Japanese Literature*. Cambridge University Press, 2016.
Takigawa Kōji 滝川幸司, Nakamoto Dai 中本大, Fukushima Riko 福島理子, Gōyama Rintarō 合山林太郎. *Bunka sōchi toshite no Nihon kanbungaku* 文化装置としての日本漢文学. Bensei Shuppan 勉誠出版, 2019.
Tawada Yōko 多和田葉子. *Ekusofonii: bogo no soto e deru tabi* エクソフォニー: 母語の外へ出る旅. Iwanami shoten 岩波書店, 2003.
Watson, Burton, ed. and trans. *Japanese Literature in Chinese*. 2 vols. Columbia University Press, 1975–76.
Whitman, John. "The Ubiquity of the Gloss." *Scripta* 3 (2011): 95–121.
Wixted, John Timothy. "*Kanbun*, Histories of Japanese Literature, and Japanologists." *Sino-Japanese Studies* 10, no. 2 (1998): 23–31.
Wixted, John Timothy. "*Kanshi* as 'Chinese Language.'" In Rethinking the Sinosphere: Poetics, Aesthetics, and Identity Formation, edited by Qian Nanxiu, Richard J. Smith, and Zhang Bowei, 269–96. Cambria Press, 2020.
Zhang, Xiaohui. "The Pursuit of the Dao: Natsume Sōseki and His *Kanshi* of 1916." *Journal of Chinese Literature and Culture* 5, no. 1 (2018): 148–78.

CHAPTER 10

Literature and the Cultural Politics of Immigration

Between Lee Hoesung and Yang Yi in "The Era of the Immigrant"

YoungRan Kō

Translated by Seth Jacobowitz

1. The Discourse of Immigration and Yang Yi's Debut

Since April 2019 when the Immigration Control Act amendment went into effect, the word "immigration" (*imin*) has been relentlessly bandied about in the mass media. Considering that until recently one might be forgiven for thinking that immigration scarcely held any value in Japan, there is clearly a dramatic sea change underway. In fact, until now, whenever a labor shortage was identified in medical care, social welfare, or construction, it was technical trainees and foreign students who shouldered the burden.[1] To the extent that this is premised on such persons not entering the regular workforce, it has strengthened the persistence of low-wage labor and substandard working environments. The current amendment establishes two stages of "special trainee" residency status. In the case of "special no. 2," one of the requirements for obtaining permanent residency is to complete a "five year working period" (a period not accepted by all occupations). The target is to reach about 340,000 people.[2] This system is integrated with the "introduction of point-based preferential immigration treatment for highly-skilled foreign professionals" framework introduced on May 5, 2012. As will be discussed in detail at the end of this paper, the hierarchical arrangement that appears between the two systems includes a hierarchy operative in all aspects of Japan's politics, culture, economy, society, and so on. Moreover, such "immigrant" discourses are structured so as to turn a blind eye toward resident Koreans and Taiwanese who are "living witnesses" to colonial rule. It should be noted that this trend is not unrelated to the environment surrounding literature and culture.

The August 10, 2008 issue of the *Asahi shinbun* morning edition carried an advertisement for the journal *Bungei shunju*. It is remarkable for its unusual size, filling up the entire fourth page and a third of the fifth page. Advertisements double the usual size also appeared in the *Mainichi shinbun*, *Yomiuri shinbun*, and *Nihon keizai shinbun*, as well as major daily papers. *Bungei shunju* regularly advertises on the tenth of every month, mostly in the dailies (morning edition) and using advertisements in the center aisles of public transit train cars. On this day, however, the four corners of the full-page ad on page four in the *Asahi* were filled with the photograph of a novelist. What was even more astonishing was that it announced the unabridged publication of her Akutagawa Award–winning work.

On July 15 of the same year, it was announced that Yang Yi had won the Akutagawa Award. Rather than comment about her award-winning novel *Toki ga nijimu asa* (A morning when time blurs), which was published in the June 2008 issue of *Bungakkai*, attention was focused on her place of origin. Headlines such as "For the first time in the history of the Akutagawa Award, a foreigner has won whose native language isn't Japanese" appeared in the article "Reflecting on the selection process" in the July 17, 2008 evening edition of the *Mainichi shinbun*; "it's also the first time a Chinese has won" appeared in an article in the July 16, 2008 morning edition of the *Asahi*, and so on. Similar articles appeared in the Chinese and Korean mass media. For instance, there was a quote from the *Mainichi* in South Korea's *The Kyunghyang Shinmun* (July 16) that "a new door had opened for Japanese literature," and the article reflected on the fact that for the first time since 1972, when resident Korean author Lee Hoesung won the Akutagawa Award, there was a "foreign" (*gaikokujin*) award-winner who was considered a "resident" (*zainichi*) as well. *Rengō nyūsu* (July 16), meanwhile, saw Yang's victory as symbolic of a "national opening up of Japanese literature," in contrast to the awkward expression used in an editorial in the *Asahi* (July 17) that saw her as merely having a different identity as "a foreigner who since infancy was raised in a Japanese-speaking environment." In other words, Yang Yi was championed as representing something other than a familiar resident identity.

The *Asahi* editorial, which described Ian Hideo Levy as "a pioneer of border-crossing authors" for winning the 1988 Noma Literary Award for New Writers with his novel *Seijōki no kikoenai heya* (A room where the *Star-Spangled Banner* can't be heard), placed Yang Yi amid the "sudden surge" of foreigners that came with global mobility. However, this trend is not seen as having a connection to the genealogy of resident Korean literature. When comparing what the *Asahi* called the sudden surge in foreigners after Hideo Levy's debut—Shirin Nezammafi, Hideo Levy, David Zoppetti, etc.—with "indigenous" authors who were "foreigners raised in a Japanese-speaking environment" came down to the criterion of whether or not Japanese was their mother tongue. Moreover, in contrast to the resident Koreans who are "living witnesses" to colonial rule by the Japanese empire, the word "foreigner" that was mobilized every time Yang Yi was mentioned now took on the meaning of newcomers to Japan who entered with a visa from another foreign country.

Still, I want to call attention to the significance of the fact that Lee Hoesung in 1972, akin to Yang Yi in 2008, had also been considered the first foreign award-winner. The distance between Lee Hoesung being marked a foreigner and Yang Yi is that of a living witness to colonial rule vs. newcomer to Japan: a temporal distance based on different historical contexts. It can also be represented schematically as "Japanese as mother tongue vs. Japanese as acquired language" (July 7, 2008 *Mainichi*), or as memory of the past in the perfect tense vs. representing the future in the present continuous tense.

By raising the question in this way, the commonalities both authors share are revealed. This is not simply to say they are both "foreigners," but that they belong to a larger frame of reference. What matters here is that the term "foreigner" has a parallel relationship to the question of *jus sanguinis* for determining nationality. Accordingly when the term "multi-ethnic state" (*taminzoku kokka*) is used in Japanese, it avoids confronting *jus sanguinis* as the legal basis for nationality, bypassing the involvement of existing legal terminology. In this chapter, I wish to interrogate once more the term "nationality," specifically how bodies, published works, and languages are mobilized according to the 1965 normalization of Japan-Korea relations and 1972 normalization of Japan-China relations. In so doing, I wish to explore what role the discourse of "foreigners" in literature and culture plays in structuring the imaginary of Japan as a nation-state. This has important ramifications for suturing the here-and-now to past events.

2. The Allegory of Nationality

Yang Yi has reminisced that since her teens, "a deep longing for Japan called out to her." ("People" column in the July 16, 2008 issue of the *Asahi*.) Of course, a world of difference lies between Yang Yi's longed-for Japan, which the Japanese media happily reported, and a resident Korean writer, who cannot fail to talk without mentioning colonial rule. Still, her "longed-for Japan" (May 29, 2012 issue of the *Mainichi*) in actuality is the one that regulates immigration and movement to other countries; attention is not directed toward what a "stateless person" might have brought to the table, including in Yang Yi's own family.

> My uncle ran a Chinese restaurant in Yokohama. As a member of the Guomindang, he fled first to Taiwan, and later made a life for himself in Japan. I was finally about to get in touch with him when he was already in his late seventies. The color photos he sent were really eye opening. Especially how my cousins looked. They wore colorful Western clothes, sophisticated makeup, and even had permed hair. It was night and day from our lives. When I saw them, I was so jealous I could almost die. ("Running Through Time: Yang Yi 6 Life in the Japan She Longed For," *Mainichi*, May 29, 2012).

One of the cousins mentioned in this recollection is Chen Tien-shi, the author of *Stateless* (*Mukokuseki*).[3] At the immigration counter in airports in both Taiwan and Japan, she was refused entry and told to return where she came from. This appears in an anecdote she relates from 1992.[4]

In the first case, the (imposed) choice to remain stateless made by Yang Yi's aunt and uncle came about as a result of the normalization of Japan-China relations in September 1972. This severed official relations between Japan and Taiwan. Needless to say, when the nationality selection problem arose, the overseas Chinese (*Huaqiao*) recognized by the 1951 Treaty of Peace with Japan's stateless persons provisions and the overseas Chinese who moved to Japan switched places. Yang Yi's aunt and uncle only received a "loss of nationality certificate" from the Taiwanese government, and then, because they did not change their nationality to another country, they chose to live as stateless permanent residents in Japan.

Although this form of life is different from the letter of the law, such statelessness cannot be disentangled from the concept of "Korean domicile" (*Chōsen-seki*) that came out of the negotiations to normalize relations between Japan and Korea in 1965. In the same way that Yang Yi's uncle's family became stateless, in January 1972 "Korean domicile" appeared in Japan's alien registration system. According to the interpretation of the Japanese Ministry of Justice, the "stateless" Lee Hoesung won the Akutagawa Prize for *Kinuta o utsu onna* (The cloth fuller), and in June of the same year visited South Korea, using "Korean domicile" for his nationality.

Here we must pay attention to the difference between Korean domicile and South Korean citizenship (*Kankoku-seki*). To say that he changed from one to the other means that he legally changed his nationality. This is because Japan's alien registration law draws a line between Korean domicile and South Korean citizenship. In other words, Korean domicile neither differentiates between the partitioned north and south halves of the Korean peninsula, nor does it take a political stance on rule by the Democratic People's Republic of Korea versus the Republic of Korea. As Kim Thae-sik astutely observes, the lived realities of resident Koreans "cannot be neatly divided into North and South."[5] From a legal perspective, the nationality of resident Koreans depends on the fact that South Korea, North Korea, and Japan do not recognize dual citizenship, as all three determine nationality based on *jus sanguinis*. As a result, it is not the Japanese alien registry law, but the laws on nationality determined by the two governments in the divided Korean peninsula that regulate it.

As regards the problem of Korean domicile and South Korean citizenship, there is also the complicated picture following normalization of relations between Japan and South Korea. The Japanese government officially recognized only the government of South Korea, but did not do so with North Korea, with which it has still not normalized relations. Based on the "Treaty on Basic Relation Between Japan and the Republic of Korea," the "Legal Status Agreement for Resident Koreans" stipulates that only resident Koreans holding South Korean citizenship will be granted the right of permanent residency. Lee Hoesung's first two trips to South Korea as "Korean domicile" made evident the seeming incompatibility of Korean domicile and South Korean citizenship during this period of fierce battles.

3. The Symbolism of "Resident Koreans" in South Korea and Lee Hoesung's Emigration

Until May 1998, when Lee Hoesung announced in Seoul that he had taken South Korean citizenship, he was able to make five trips to the country. To recap the previous occasions,

1st time: he received the Gunzō New Writer Award in June 1969 for *Mata futatabi no michi*, visited South Korea in October 1970
2nd time: he received the Akutagawa Award in January 1972 for *Kinuta o utsu onna*, and he visited South Korea in June 1972
3rd time: he traveled in November 1995
4th time: he traveled in October 1996

It goes without saying that it was extremely unusual that he was able to enter the country five times in this way while retaining Korean domicile. In order for resident Koreans who have Korean domicile to enter South Korea, they have to be issued a provisional passport as their travel certificate. This is tantamount to temporarily becoming South Korean, and on this basis of this set-up, they are allowed to enter the country. Of course Japanese Immigration Control handles this passport as well. Based on his own experience, writer Kim Sok-pom noted, "There is an unregulated internal rule that resident Koreans who hold Korean domicile may only enter the country twice until they are required to switch their citizenship to South Korea (this is a "principle" for which there are many exceptions)."[6]

Since the Kim Dae-jung administration's June 15th North-South Joint Declaration (2000), the South Korean government has softened its stance on the problem of Korean domicile holders entering the country. For example, it is now possible "to visit South Korea in the name of Sōren (the General Association of Korean Residents)" and "in 2002 to attend the Pusan Asian Games under the General Association Brethren Support Group." What this shift makes clear is that "rejection of resident Koreans into South Korea is subordinate to developments in the North-South relationship."[7] However, even in the transition period in February 2003 from Kim Dae Jung to Roh Moo-hyun that is considered to have had the most moderating effects, there were cases like that of Cho Kyunghee, who decided it would not be appropriate to attend the "The Postcolonial Situation of Resident Koreans" conference in Seoul due to the Korean domicile issue.[8] According to Cho, who has been at the forefront of this issue, "Most Korean domicile cases start with an inquiry by phone where you are instructed to either give up entering South Korea or applying for the required change in nationality." The customary practice of calling for a change in nationality, which "borders on harassment," has been criticized as "a customary practice that is severely and inconsistently applied since it is decided by each consulate or supervisor's subjective judgments instead of arising from a sound legal foundation." In recent years due to the coercive approach, which the consulates have adopted during interviews when pressing for the change in nationality, the National Human Rights Commission had determined that it constitutes a human rights violation, resulting in an increase in the number of lawsuits. On the other hand, during the Lee Myung-bak administration, the issuing of temporary transit documents for those with Korean domicile was almost entirely abandoned. Moreover, even if one does not make the switchover to Korean citizenship, "there are instances where even with Korean citizenship, one is refused the issuance of the travel certificate."[9] It cannot be denied that these developments are related to the worsening of relations with North Korea and Japan during the Lee Myung-bak administration. In other words, the question of allowing Zainichi Koreans to travel to South Korea is an indicator not only of North-South relations, but Japan-South Korea relations as well. Beginning with the North Korean kidnappings and continuing into the latest nuclear testing controversies, the deterioration of relations to the North and acts of relation have likewise framed the Japanese government's official posture in its tightening restrictions on Zainichi Koreans' ethnic schools.

Lee Hoesung divided his own entry into South Korea into three periods.[10]

1. The two trips he made during the Park Chung-hee administration
2. The entry ban during the Chun Doo-hwan and Roh Tae-woo administrations
3. The entry ban followed by three visits during the Kim Young-sam administration

However, when we consider the era of Lee Hoesung's entry into South Korea from the historical and cultural context of Japan's relationship to South Korea, the first and third periods involved his issuance of temporary transit documents, which in South Korea overlapped with the period of highest regard for Zainichi Koreans. Let's consider the first period. From the outset of taking office, Park Chung-hee declared "To make up for the shortfall in foreign currency, we encourage Zainichi Koreans to invest in our country."[11] According to Kwon Heok-tae's *Chōsen Nippō* (Korea Report; 1994–2006), what emerges from a detailed study of the media archives of the time are the stereotypes of Zainichi Koreans such as "*han-chokubari*" (those who abandoned their language and ethnicity) vs. heroes (success stories like the pro wrester Rikidōzan); "reds" (Zainichi Korean exchange student spy cases, etc.) vs. anti-Communist fighters (the Zainichi student volunteers who fought in the Korean War); the nouveau riche and investors who contributed to South Korean development. Around the 1970s,[12] the same signifying constellation was expansively reproduced not only through print matter, but also film and audio-visual media.[13] As Kwon Heok-tae rightly points out, "it has an inseparable relationship with its psychological enemy, Japan."[14]

Just prior to Lee Hoesung's first trip to South Korea, Kim Chi-ha's arrest (June 1970) also came as a great shock to Japan, while the Sŏ Sŭng foreign exchange student spy case (April 1971) occurred before his second visit. These events led to Park Chung-hee's desire for long-term dominance, linked by the stringent controls of the October 15, 1970 Garrison Decree and the December 6 emergency powers bill rammed through the National Assembly.

The itinerary of Lee Hoesung's visit and his schedule while in South Korea are mentioned in his "acquisition record" published in the late nineties, which said only, "someday if the opportunity presents itself, I hope to talk about it. I do not have the slightest sense of shame troubling my thoughts or conscience about it," but without going into further detail.[15] Nevertheless, in regard to his 1972 visit, he not only expressed the sentiment "North or South, it is still my ancestral land" in a travelogue, but also gave lectures in his "mother tongue" of Japanese at Seoul University and Ewha Womans University. These were commissioned as articles such as "A Turning Point in the History of Partition" for the *Tōa Nippō* (East Asia Report) and "Impressions of South Korea" for the *Kankoku Nippō* (South Korea Report), which were collected and republished as *North or South, It is Still My Ancestral Land* (Kawade Shobōsha, 1974). The difference between his first visit, and the second, which came less than two years later, arose due to Lee Hoesung's "decision to acquire South Korean citizenship," and pivoted around the controversy that came to be known as the "nationality vs. statelessness" debates with fellow Zainichi novelist Kim Sok-pom.

One issue that the two visits have in common is the fact that South Korean officials handled them both. On the first visit, Lee notes, "even if one didn't change nationality, the South Korean officials encouraged Chongryon (General Association of Korean Residents in Japan) members and sympathizers to come to South Korea" (from the aforementioned *North or South, It is Still My Ancestral Land*).[16] Nevertheless, none of the South Korean media reported on his first visit. By contrast, when he came as the Akutagawa Prize–winning novelist on his second trip, he "was surrounded by a gaggle of reporters at the airport," and after giving interviews there, he set off for the hotel in a press car provided by the Korean Report Company. A member of the National Intelligence Service (KCIA) rode in the car with him, to which Lee objected. Thereafter the man wasn't seen again, but reporters for the Korea Report surveilled his every movement. In any case, this time the Korean media massively reported on Lee's entry into South Korea, with no fewer than twenty-six articles about it in the *Far East Report* and *The Kyunghyang Shinmun* daily newspaper. Lee admitted, "To the younger me, who was simply a Zainichi Korean author, the exaggerated interviews at the airport and heartfelt reception seemed entirely due to the fact that I'd won the Akutagawa Prize."

Interestingly, what emerges from a survey of the Korean language newspaper coverage of Lee is that the Korean media took it as a sign of his cutting ties with Chongryon and North Korea, as indicated by the article, "Zainichi overseas author Lee Hoesung has declared that he renounces North Korean nationality. Having finally found your ancestral land, please do not vacillate," which appeared in the October 10, 1973 *Far East Report*. It is well known that Lee began to write novels in Japanese after January 1, 1967, when he quit the Chōsen Shinpōsha and broke with Chongryon. Nevertheless, in the Korean language articles six years later, the fact of terminating his association with Chongryon was represented as abandoning his nationality, and written up as though it were a recent event. If this problem can be combined with the problem of the representation of Zainichi Koreans noted above, then what lay behind the question of Lee's "Korean domicile" was the way his name was used to signify against a "*han-chokubari*" identity, and instead was elevated to that of a "hero" who made full use of his "mother tongue," that is, as an Akutagawa Prize winner. Instead of his being "red" by virtue of relinquishing North Korean citizenship and being a critic of Chongryon, there was now an attempt to establish his name as another anti-Communist byword.

On the other hand, the third and fourth times, and of course his fifth visit when he made the declaration of taking South Korean citizenship, are intimately bound up with the question of globalization. Lee has said he seriously began to contemplate changing nationality between November 3 and 15, 1995, after his third visit to South Korea. However, regardless of when Lee himself made the decision, we must also consider how this act signifies in a larger context. On May 28, 1998 he went to Seoul and gave an exclusive interview the next day to the *East Asia Report* where he made the declaration of taking South Korean citizenship. Around the same period, he prepared his "Record of Taking South Korean Citizenship" to be made public and left the country. Despite the fact this event involved the same person, it did not have the same significance in a Japanese-language discursive space as it did in a Korean one.

Let's begin with the latter. In the May 30th issue of the *East Asia Report*, articles on Lee Hoesung's acquisition of South Korean citizenship, including the interview, were given ample coverage on the first and third pages. What draws our attention in particular is the effect from the front-page layout.

Under the headline "Japan's Akutagawa Prize Winner, Zainichi Author Lee Hoesung Sweeps Away 'Resented Statelessness' and Heads to South Korea" (photograph) are the two smaller headlines: "Abandoning 'Chōsen' Citizenship to Take 'South Korean' Citizenship" and "IMF Spreads the Pain." The articles accompanying the headlines are structured in such way as to include smaller, follow-up headlines like "IMF $18 Billion: Additional Support for South Korea Approved." Since the currency crisis in that era, a discourse has arisen in the Korean-language speaking world over "heightened interest in overseas brethren as human resources," along with the concept of "overseas brethren" itself. This discourse has been critiqued from the contexts of "Korean business network theory" and "the national interest."[17] The period in which this kind of critique emerged was one in which "diaspora" emerged as a key research concept, and especially "Korean diaspora" became a source of great interest. Kim Woo-Ja has explained it as giving rise to this signifying constellation that, "reveals a sudden interest in it since the onset of the Korean financial crisis in the mid-1990s as a place of convergence for several opposing interests."[18]

At the Korean governmental level, Kim Woo-Ja not only points out that until this period "there was no interest in Koreans who left the country," but also that the "Act on Immigration and Legal Status of Overseas Koreans" was passed by the Korean parliament on August 12, 1999 and came into force from December of that year as "a process for the limited inclusion of exiles" was found during the currency crisis.[19] The law on overseas "brethren"[20] was designed to grant virtually the same legal basis for immigration and residency, entailing the same rights as those enjoyed by citizens of South Korea, but "the biggest challenge lay in determining who qualified as 'overseas brethren.'"[21] The conclusion at this time was "limited to those who currently have South Korean citizenship (overseas citizens), or who have or possessed in the past a direct lineage (brethren with foreign citizenship)."[22] As a result, this excluded all "brethren" who left the country prior to the founding of the South Korean republic, but this would be revised again in 2004 to include them as well. However, Korean domicile is still not included in the category of "brethren."

Nevertheless, when Lee Hoesung made his declaration of taking South Korean citizenship, it cannot be denied that from the perspective of the government's "South Korean economic development and survival strategy in a global society," this was taken as a positive sign from someone popularly regarded as an "overseas brethren." It was not the literary value of works by this Akutagawa Prize–winning resident-Korean author that mattered, but rather that he was perceived as a "successful person," "a South Korean to be proud of" that made all the difference.[23] We can further see in December 1999 that his "Journal on Taking South Korean Citizenship" was included in its entirety in the Overseas Policy Materials (Research Institute on the Question of Overseas Brethren). As I mentioned in the introduction of this chapter beginning with Yang Yi, a foreign writer for whom Japanese is not a "mother tongue," this issue has become structurally paired with the context of the Japanese language. I will pursue this further in the next section.

4. Heading Toward the Basis for a New Controversy

How should we think about the intersection of national identity and personal identification? As Chen Tien-shi points out, when we think of nationality and passports, it is not only the "top-down control" of a nation's people by bureaucracy, but also the individual's ability to secure their rights for freedom of movement, including the "bottom-up control" based on the individual's free will to secure or change their nationality or passport. The matters of statelessness and holding multiple citizenships cannot be excluded from this problematic.

Let us, then, return to the case of Yang Yi and the editorial in the *Asahi Shinbun* on her receiving the Akutagawa Prize:

> The population of foreigners living in Japan has risen sharply to 215,000. Chinese make up more than 60,000 of this number. Many are highly educated people who come to Japan to continue their studies. It is to be expected that someone representative of this trend such as Ms. Yang should emerge. (*Asahi*, July 17, 2008).

When we look to the figures on the foreign population in Japan, the number stood at 782,910 in 1980, but reached 1,362,371 in 1995. It goes without saying the number has continued to escalate rapidly since the 1990s. Yet out of the estimated current 2.15 million foreigners in Japan, 39,000 are "special permanent residents," including some 1,100 that are stateless. "Special permanent residents" thus encompasses statelessness, Korean domicile, South Koreans, and some of the descendants of subjects from former colonial territories. It is impossible to draw a line from the "resident Korean" writer Lee Hoesung to a writer like Yang Yi who uses Japanese even though "it is not her native tongue." Yet since the late 1990s, there have been roughly ten thousand people who gave up Korean domicile or South Korean citizenship to become Japanese citizens, while, as previously noted, "of the 150,000 people who hold Korean domicile, four to five thousand have elected to become South Koreans" such that clearly the trend is toward a reduction in the numbers for Korean domicile.[24]

On July 9, 2012 the alien registration system in Japan was abolished and the new "Residency Management System" was launched to centralize residency management in the country. A residency card is issued instead of the alien registration certificate issued by the municipality. The new system excludes "special permanent residents" from holding residency cards, and issues to them new identification cards. In addition, a "deemed necessary for re-entry" step has been introduced for mid- to long-term residents. For mid-term residents, when leaving Japan they must inform the immigration officer when they will re-enter the country within one year (special permanent residents are within two years). Upon return to Japan, when they present their passport and residency card it is considered a "request for a re-entry permit." However, the Ministry of Justice has explained those foreigners whose residency cards indicate statelessness or Korean domicile for their nationality or region will be denied re-entry because they do not hold a valid passport.

Much as the article I cited in the introduction foregrounds Yang Yi receiving the Akutagawa Prize as a result of the rising number of foreigners in Japan, Kim Sok-pom fears "elimination" as the trend toward the disappearance of resident Korean writers looms in the background. Six months after Yang Yi was awarded the prize, the January 25, 2009 issue of the *Sankei Shinbun* ran an article with the headline "Making the '300,000 International Students' Plan a Reality: Exam Simplification Measures Recommended."

The "300,000 International Students Plan" is a global strategy that aims to increase the international competitiveness of Japan's universities and educational institutions, and to attract the best foreign students "with a target of reaching 300,000 students by 2020." An outline of the plan was finalized in July 2008 by MEXT (Ministry of Education, Culture, Sports, Science and Technology) and six related ministries and agencies.

Based on the same context as the plan to reach 300,000 international students, it was announced that as part of Japan's global strategy a system to simplify residency screening was launched on May 7, 2012 that introduced "preferential treatment based on a point system for advanced human resources." The point system states: "To promote the acceptance of foreigners (equivalent to highly skilled human resources) with advanced abilities and qualities expected to contribute to economic growth and new demand for employment creation, it is a system in which those who reach a certain point total are regarded as 'highly skilled foreigners' and will receive preferential measures for immigration." It seems the foreigner earns points by proving how he or she is an "advanced human resource" who can contribute to the development of this country.

The danger lies in moving from "advanced human resources" to "undesirable foreigners." Even if foreigners wish to become long-term residents, the standard for permitting workers to remain are very strict at present. For example, the following words were prominently displayed (and since removed) on the Ministry of Justice's Immigration Bureau website:

> The Immigration Bureau of the Ministry of Justice connects Japan to the world through immigration administration under the slogan "internationalization in compliance with the rules," while facilitating international exchange between peoples and forcibly deporting foreigners deemed unfavorable to our nation, thereby contributing to the development of a healthy Japanese society.

It is unclear how on what basis this forcible deportation of foreigner unfavorable to the nation would be determined. This question of who is deemed favorable is not unrelated to the discourse of foreign writers. In March 2010, in *Kokusai jinryū* (The immigration newsmagazine), published by the Immigration Services Bureau, there was a special issue on "Japanese literature and foreigners." This is a magazine that relies upon editorial support from the Justice Ministry's Immigration Bureau to publish the latest news about immigrations statistics and revisions to immigration law. "Special Collection One," placed as the first column in the magazine's table of contents, features the writings of Yang Yi and Arthur Binard under the heading "Foreign Writers Active in the Japanese Literary Establishment." The next column, "Special Collection Two," is a compilation related to literary prizes for foreign students. "Special Collection Three," meanwhile, presents foreign students who have begun to write novels in Japanese. This setup, moving from the third category to the first, had as its ultimate target to showcase the work of Yang Yi. This was most likely not done to honor literature as essential to the nation's global strategy, but was directed toward foreigners who seek to attain permanent residency. The positionality of Akutagawa Prize–winning author Yang Yi as a "literary master" (or at least accomplished person) cannot help but stand in stark contrast to fellow Akutagawa Prize–winning author Lee Hoesung, whose declaration of taking South Korean citizenship corresponded to the "South Korean economic development and survival strategy in a global society," which circulated as a declaration on the part of overseas brethren.

A month after the plan to recruit 300,000 foreign students to Japan was made, the most talked about news story was the case of the Filipino family of Arlan Cruz Calderon, his wife Sarah, and their daughter Noriko, who were residents of Warabi City in Saitama Prefecture and had petitioned for a special residency permit following a deportation order for illegal entry into Japan. In response to the Ministry of Justice's decision to only grant the special permit to remain to Japanese-born Noriko, the seventh grader responded at a press conference, "I understand in my mind that my nationality is Filipina, but I cannot help feeling that *I am one hundred percent Japanese*. In fact, asking myself this question made me realize that I am a Japanese person who knows nothing about the Philippines."

When Yang Yi's story of yearning for Japan circulated with the giant advertisement of her head and torso prominently displayed in the journal *Bungei shunju*, one had to wonder at the same time what it concealed. I still do not know how to process Noriko's painful cry that she is "a hundred percent Japanese," much less how to construct the grounds upon which to properly discuss it. Yet, regardless of whether we look to the revised immigration law, which has a plan to begin welcoming some 350,000 workers to Japan, as we can see from an article published in the Dec. 15, 2018 *Asahi Shinbun* that called for "strengthening investigations as foreigners use national health insurance, even if fraudulent cases have not been confirmed," there is a rush to pass bills and crack down on foreigners in Japan. Unlike the "highly skilled human resources," the movement of "workers" is about to start stamping them as a criminal reserve army. There is not much debate over what kind of policies are needed for people entering an unfamiliar environment, and what kind of environment needs to be created. Because of this situation, I would like to continue to think about what kind of pitfalls are associated with the notion of Japan as a multiethnic nation from the perspective of literary studies.

Notes

1. See "Zairyūshi kakubetsu no gaikokujin rōdōsha-sū," in *Shūkan Tōyō keizai*, Jan. 12, 2019.

2. "Kaisei Nyūkanhō ga seiritsu e: 14 shugyō, gaikokujin no shūrō kakudai," in *Nihon keizai shinbun*, December 8, 2018.

3. Chen Tien-shi, *Stateless*, 369–71. Shinchō Bunko, 2011. The quote comes from Yang Yi's afterword.

4. In *Stateless*, Chen Tien-shi recounts a family vacation to Taiwan in 1992. When Chen, who was born and raised in Japan, wanted to visit another country, she had

to obtain a visa in accordance with Taiwan and the third country, and carry with her a Republic of China passport issued by the Taiwanese government. However, as someone born in Japan who holds different citizenship from her parents who lived in Taiwan, she needed a visa to enter Taiwan. For Chen, who always carries a ROC passport when she leaves Japan, it was inconceivable that she would need a visa from the same country that issued her passport. Then, at the immigration counter at Narita Airport, which had granted her permission for her to enter Taiwan, no entry permit was granted when she headed home, either. The re-entry permit had expired.

5. Kim Thae-sik, "Zaigai kokumin kokusei sanseiken to Zainichi Chōsenjin no kokuseki o meguru seiji," Dokkyō daigaku kokusai kyōyōbu, *Mathesis Universalis*, no. 13, vol. 2: March 2012.

6. *Chōetsu to aidentifikeishon*, Shunyōsha, 2012, 382.

7. Yun Gyeongwon (trans. Kim Thae-sik), "Korian daisupora: shokuminchishugi to risan," in Chen Tien-shi et al., eds. *Higashi Asia no diasupora*. Akashi Shoten, 2011, 210.

8. Yun Gyeongwon (trans. Kim Thae-sik), "Korean daisupora: shokuminchishugi to risan," 220.

9. Kim Thae-sik, 99.

10. "Kankoku kokuseki shutoku no ki," *Shinchō* June 1998.

11. Kim Thae-sik, 102.

12. Strictly speaking, this covers the period from the mid-1950s to 1970s. See Kwon Heok-tae's "Zainichi Kankokujin to Kankoku shakai: Kankoku shakai wa Zainichi Chōsenjin o ikani 'hyōshō' shite ita no ka," *Rekishi Hihyō* 76, Spring 2007: 244–45. In Korean.

13. Kim Thae-sik, "Dare ga mediasupora o hitsuyō to suru ka," Seoul daigaku Nihon kenkyuūsho-hen, *Nihon Hihyō*, 4: 2011. In Korean.

14. Kwon Heok-tae, 244–45.

15. Lee Hoesung, "Kankoku kokuseki shutoku no ki," 77–80. *Shinchō*, June 1998.

16. *North or South, It is Still My Ancestral Land*, 43.

17. Kim Thae-sik, "Dare ga daiasupora o hitsuyō to suru no ka," 225.

18. Kim Woo-Ja, "'Dōhō' to iu jiba," *Gendai shishō*, June 2007: 213.

19. *Kim Woo-Ja*, 215.

20. In the prewar era, this term was also used to refer to the overseas brethren of the Japanese empire, whether they resided in Korea or the United States, Brazil or Peru. As such they maintained not only a continued social or cultural identification with the motherland, but also their legal status as subjects of the emperor.—Trans.

21. Kim Woo-Ja, 215.

22. Kim Woo-Ja, 215.

23. See Kwon Heok-tae, 235.

24. Kim Sok-Pom, "Zainichi Chōsenjin no tomo e no tegami," *Asahi Shinbun*, June 10, 1998.

Works Cited

Chen Tien-shi. *Stateless*, 369–71. Shinchō Bunko, 2011.

Chin, Tenji. *Chōetsu to aidentifikeishon* [Overcoming and identification]. Shunyōsha, 2012.

Kim, Sok-Pom. "Zainichi Chōsenjin no tomo e no tegami" [A letter to a resident Korean friend]. *Asahi Shinbun*, June 10, 1998.

Kim, Thae-sik. "Dare ga mediasupora o hitsuyō to suru ka" [For whom is the media-sphere necessary?]. Seoul daigaku Nihon kenkyuūsho-hen, *Nihon Hihyō* 4: 2011.

Kim, Thae-sik. "Zaigai kokumin kokusei sanseiken to Zainichi Chōsenjin no kokuseki o meguru seiji" [Overseas nationals' suffrage and the politics of resident Korean citizenship]. Dokkyō daigaku kokusai kyōyōbu, *Mathesis Universalis*, no. 13, vol. 2: March 2012.

Kim Woo-Ja. "'Dōhō' to iu jiba" [the magnetic field of "brethren"]. *Gendai shishō*, June 2007.

Kwon, Heok-tae. "Zainichi Kankokujin to Kankoku shakai: Kankoku shakai wa Zainichi Chōsenjin o ikani 'hyōshō' shite ita no ka," *Rekishi Hihyō* 76, Spring 2007.

Lee Hoesung. "Kankoku kokuseki shutoku no ki," 77–80. *Shinchō*, June 1998.

CHAPTER 11

Translation and the Crisis of Relevancy in Japanese Literary Studies

Jeffrey Angles

Humanities in the Early Twenty-First Century

In the last decade, a crisis has befallen American higher education. Fiscally conservative politicians supported by a tax-deriding public have aggressively defunded higher education, forcing universities in the public sector to find other ways to make ends meet. State university systems in Michigan, Ohio, Texas, California and elsewhere have seen their level of support drop to such low proportions that it is reasonable to ask if it even makes sense to continue calling them "public" any longer. Capital campaigns, alumni solicitations, and fund-raising activities may alleviate those problems somewhat, but many schools have raised their tuition, making university degrees further out-of-reach of the same people they were meant to help.

As students and their financial guardians turn to loans to pay tuition, students find that after four or more years of study, they likely have crushing debt that will take decades, perhaps even an entire lifetime, to repay. The looming shadow of debt, which alumni must begin repaying soon after graduation, casts a heavy pall over the university experience of many students, who feel pressure to make every credit count. Recognizing that there will be little time before they start paying down their debt, worried undergraduates, often spurred by justifiably concerned parents and family, feel pressure to enter fields and programs that they hear are likely to lead to specific, well-paid careers soon after graduation.

These financial pressures, when combined with the mistaken yet popular belief that the liberal arts will not lead to good, well-paying careers, has led to a perfect storm for the humanities. Since the recession of 2008, students have dropped away from the humanities with astonishing speed, leaving previously well-established programs and courses in fields from anthropology to literary studies under-enrolled and vulnerable to cuts and elimination. There have been numerous studies proving that the assumption that humanities will not lead to successful careers is false.[1] Humanities majors do receive competitive employment and wages—a fact that *The Chronicle of Higher Education* sometimes mentions in its coverage of the subject—and The American Academy of Arts and Sciences has also shown that humanities graduates may start off more slowly than their peers in STEM fields, but over the course of time, they typically close the wage gap and catch up.[2] In fact, *The Washington Post* has reported that Google's human resources department tends, in the hiring process, to value a number of skills, such as communication abilities, critical thinking, and forming connections between disparate ideas—in other words, skills developed in the study of the humanities—far more highly than expertise in STEM fields.[3] In 2014, tycoon David Rubenstein argued at World Economic Forum Davos that American students are losing critical thinking, a skill necessary for success in business. Commenting that career-specific skills can be learned later, he argues the "reasoning skills that come with a well-rounded humanities education actually contribute more over time, both to individual success and to the success of a nation's business culture."[4]

Nonetheless, these real-world pressures have worked in dramatic ways against the humanities and, more importantly for the purpose of this essay, the field of Japanese literary studies. In an age that increasingly believes the purpose of a university education is job training, especially for STEM-related jobs, the study of literature appears more like a non-essential, perhaps even frivolous luxury rather than what it really is—a critical means of examining culture, history, politics, human expression, and the complex conjunctions between the world of the individual and the larger, surrounding society. Equally important, literature fulfills an important social function in developing readers' abilities to empathize with people across perceived differences in age, ethnicity, and social background—critically important traits in our complex, globalized world. Because students and their financial guardians may not necessarily immediately recognize that literature provides an intimate opportunity to study societies, cultures, ideologies, and even the nature of thought and representation itself, students eyeing future debt are more likely than ever before to ask why literature courses are part of an undergraduate Japanese major. Japanese majors who are not humanities specialists may question why their professors might ask them to read literary texts instead of newspaper articles, technical documents, or other non-fictional texts from other fields perceived as more closely linked to financial gain.

The crisis of relevancy destabilizing the humanities is due in large part to socioeconomic trends and cultural shifts, but there are other deep-rooted factors causing the stock of literature to fall within the marketplace of ideas. Perhaps the most important is the fact that non-specialists know relatively little about the field—a fact closely connected to the ambiguous and troubled position of translation within the field of Japanese literary studies itself. Although the situation seems to be changing somewhat within the last decade or so, tenure and promotion committees in many American institutions treat translation as a secondary, derivative activity that contributes less to the field of literary studies than other forms of scholarship, despite the fact that scholars who do translation are often among the most visible leaders of the field, reaching far wider audiences than scholars doing other, less accessible work.

Translation in the Postwar Academy

Since Japan opened its doors to Western culture and commerce in the nineteenth century, translations of Japanese literature into English have come in waves. The first came during the early twentieth century as translators, many of whom were Japanese with high English proficiency, worked to make their classics known to the outside world. After World War II, there was a second and much more significant wave as Westerners who were sympathetic to Japan reshaped and softened the reductive image of Japan that had arisen through its imperial, wartime aggressions. As Japanese literature scholar Edward Fowler noted in "Rendering Words, Traversing Cultures," many of the important American and British translators of Japanese literature in the 1950s and 1960s, such as Donald Keene, Edward Seidensticker, and Ivan Morris, learned Japanese during the war but went to Japan afterward, making Japanese friends and living among the people. Wanting to fashion an image of Japan that would counterbalance the negative impressions held by populations back in their home countries, they translated works of literature by modern, belletristic writers like Kawabata Yasunari, Tanizaki Jun'ichirō, and Mishima Yukio to create an image of Japan as "an exoticized, aestheticized, and quintessentially *foreign* land quite antithetical to its prewar image of a bellicose and immediately threatening power."[5] The translations they produced weren't enormous in number, but they attracted critical attention, putting Japanese writing on the international map of world literature and forging new, softer images that were useful as Japan transitioned from being an enemy of the Allied Powers to a staunch Western ally in the Cold War.

During the era of rapid economic growth during the 1970s and the bubble years of the 1980s, thanks in part to funding from the Japan Foundation, Japanese businesses, and other organizations, studies of Japanese literature grew enormously in the Anglophone world. Numerous scholars working during those years recognized that to study Japanese literature, especially in the Western world where there were relatively few people who speak and read Japanese at a high level, it was essential to have translations of key texts. Without them, students and general readers could never summit the largest literary mountains or peer out over the topography of the field to gain their bearings. As a result, this generation of Japanese literary scholars developed a relatively "translation-friendly" style of scholarship. Keene, for instance, divided his time between producing high-quality translations and guidebooks that survey the terrain of Japanese literature. It is no exaggeration to say that Keene and his contemporaries created the field of Japanese literature in the Anglophone world, mapping it for readers wanting to explore its terrain in more detail. In fact, figures like Keene helped to determine which works of modern Japanese literature would become classics, both in the West and in Japan where publishers and literary critics pay assiduous attention to which Japanese books are being read and discussed abroad.

During this era, most scholarship on Japanese literature tended to focus on individual writers or particular texts, so it was not uncommon to find publications that placed a lengthy scholarly exegesis or biography inside the same volume as a translation, bringing together primary and secondary sources to form a convenient package. Several of these texts have become classics still read by virtually everyone in Japanese literary studies. For instance, Marleigh Ryan's translation of Futabatei Shimei's classic novel *Ukigumo (Floating Clouds)* also contains a long discussion of Futabatei, his era, his interest in Russian literature, and the challenges he faced developing a modern literary voice.[6] Similarly, Robert Danly's *In the Shade of Spring Leaves* couples translations of Higuchi Ichiyō with a biographical introduction that occupies approximately half the thick volume.[7] This style of scholarship, bringing together secondary scholarship with a translation of primary materials, continued through at least the 1990s. For instance, Livia Monnet's translation of Ishimure Michiko's classic of environmental literature, *Paradise in the Sea of Sorrow (Kugai jōdō)*, first published in 1990, also includes a hefty introduction about the activist-author's role in bringing attention to the mercury pollution in Minamata.[8] Similarly, William J. Tyler's 1990 book *The Bodhisattva, or, Samantabhadra* brings together an eloquent introduction to the modernist writer Ishikawa Jun with a translation of his Akutagawa Prize–winning, avant-garde novel *Fugen* from 1936.[9]

During this time, translations were an essential part of the field of Japanese literary studies—not only did they attract broad attention, they also inspired young Japanophiles to read, enter academia, and translate, thus growing the field. Keene and the other scholars of his generation benefited from certain important factors: a growing interest in multiculturalism that encouraged more Anglophone readers to read non-Western literatures, as well as the eagerness of large organizations such as UNESCO and the US National Endowment for the Arts (NEA) to support the translation and publication of world literature. For example, during this period, Keene, Morris, Rimer, Tyler, Seidensticker, and other translators received support from a UNESCO program entitled "Culture and the Future," one of the fourteen major programs UNESCO had in existence at the time. The purpose of the project was "to make available in translation in two international languages, English and French, the masterpieces of world literature" in what was labeled the "UNESCO Collection of Representative Works."[10] Behind this project was a humanistic, idealistic notion:

> The Collection is central to Unesco's [*sic*] action in favour of the strengthening of cultural identity and intercultural relations. For there can be no doubt that the peoples of the world long to reach out beyond the events of their history of yesterday and today and to discover, behind their ways and customs, their traditions, beliefs and values, something that will better confirm their existence in the world and consolidate their place in the universal concert.[11]

Many landmark translations of Japanese authors received UNESCO's financial support and appeared in the collection, including the works of classical authors Murasaki Shikibu, Sei Shōnagon, Kamo no Chōmei, Zeami, and Ihara Saikaku, as well as modern novelists and poets Natsume Sōseki, Mori Ōgai, Nagai Kafū, Tanizaki Jun'ichirō, Abe Kōbō, Kawabata Yasunari, Anzai Hitoshi, Shiraishi Kazuko, and Tanikawa Shuntarō.[12] Through the 1990s, many students and burgeoning scholars grew up on these seminal translations as they explored Japanese literary history.

Translation's Eroding Position in Academia

In the 1990s, as the field of translation studies grew, the common view that translators were working hard to share new ideas, worldviews, and aspects of the human experience with a broader world gave way to a rising awareness that translators, in the act of doing their work, were enacting a form of violence on the texts they were trying to represent. In the provocative 1975 book *After Babel*, George Steiner argues that in the process of taking apart the content, constructs, and even grammar of an original text so that it could be rebuilt from the ground up, translators were engaging in four hermeneutic movements: (1) entrusting themselves to the world of the source text, (2) aggressively reshaping the source to fit the translator's own culture and worldview, (3) incorporating elements of the original into a newly reconstructed, translated world of their own making, and (4) engaging in a form of restitution as they go back and revise, finding a balance between the source text and the newly reconstructed text in the target language.[13] In other words, in the series of back-and-forth movements that happen during translation, translators, whether they like it or not, end up reshaping the source text and source culture into something of their own making.

As translation studies blossomed in Europe and America during the 1980s and 1990s, Steiner's notion of translator-as-violator grew, echoed by translation studies scholars who saw translators as inevitably—although often unintentionally—performing countless subtle acts of domesticization as they attempted to make the language, grammar, structure, and embedded cultural elements comprehensible to a new target audience. The translation studies scholar Lawrence Venuti, for instance, has famously argued:

> A translation always communicates an interpretation, a foreign text that is partial and altered, supplemented with features peculiar to the translating language, no longer inscrutably foreign but made comprehensible in a distinctively domestic style. Translations, in other words, inevitably perform a work of domestication.[14]

Venuti's goal is to make readers aware of the complex negotiations, identifications, and rapprochements involved in translation so that scholars, teachers, students, and general readers can become smarter, more critical consumers of translated work. As he points out, there is a commonly held assumption that translators should be as invisible and unobtrusive as possible, but a translator will never retreat completely into the background—

after all, a translator's fingerprints are on every word, every line, and every page. Venuti, himself a prominent translator of Italian fiction, was making this argument to refocus attention on the work of translators, bring awareness to the complex work they perform.

Ironically, however, at the same time translation studies were advancing our understanding of the complex work that translators perform, academia and the field of Japanese literary studies began to move away from its earlier "translation-friendly" mode of scholarly production to something more "translation-resistant." As John Treat's contribution to this volume notes, during the 1990s, there was a significant shift in the kinds of scholarship that Anglophone academics were doing. Scholars correctly recognized that when earlier generations had focused on the intimate world of a particular text or author, they had often failed to step back and look at the larger, historical picture. Instead of focusing on only a single text or author, English-language dissertations and books on Japanese literature began to use an increasingly comparative perspective to broaden their purview and examine how particular themes manifested themselves across the work of multiple authors, texts, and historical moments. Focus shifted from the world of the author and the text to large themes such as the rise and legacy of empire, the problems of war and its memory, the position of women and minorities within society, and changing representations of sexuality, class, and race. There were enormous benefits to this theory-driven, broad-perspective approach; scholars broke away from writing about established and canonical authors and texts to make forays into new areas—women's studies, LGBTQ+ studies, proletarian studies, media studies, and so on—thus opening new, fruitful avenues of research that were more likely to seem fresh even to colleagues working in Japan. As scholars cast their nets wider, they typically looked at a broader array of texts, meaning it was less feasible to also produce translations of all the texts that would make their scholarship accessible to students and mainstream audiences.

These trends overlapped with the growing crisis in the humanities described at the beginning of this essay to create a perfect storm for translation in the academy. Since the 1990s, pressure has been growing for universities to provide practical educations that would prepare students directly for the workplace instead of humanities-based educations that would teach students to be agile, critical thinkers ready to contribute to a future whose contours are not necessarily already visible. Meanwhile, untenured professors find themselves advocating for the value of their work by pointing to its breadth, historical significance, and social value. In this environment, translation work was increasingly seen as secondary "service to the field" than actual, primary scholarship. In 2010, *The Chronicle of Higher Education* outlined the struggles faced by scholars of non-Anglophone literature in the twenty-first century, stating:

> A long-held standard in the Anglo-American world expects translators of literary works to be seen and heard as little as possible. A translator should get reader and author set up and then fade into the background, like a discreet waiter who keeps the glasses filled while remaining practically unnoticed. That attitude has prevailed in the academic world, too, where translation has often been seen as a sideline or a waste of time, something to do in between stretches of "serious" scholarly work . . . Just as publishers have had an unfortunate tendency not to bother putting translators' names on book jackets—the idea being that translations are harder to sell—so hiring and tenure-and-promotion committees have preferred not to hear about the translation activities of the candidates whose dossiers they review. It's almost as though translation is a bad habit, like gambling, that candidates should conceal rather than advertise.[15]

One well known translator cited in the article comments, "It's not only the deans that need to have their consciousness raised . . . It is something that we're still battling with, not only on the administrative level but also on the level of our own colleagues."[16]

In a bold statement about the critical scholarly value of translation, former president of the Modern Language Association (MLA) Catherine Porter argues that academia tends to see translation through the lends of an "overly simplistic dichotomy: we see scholarship as the creation of new knowledge, teaching as the transmission of knowledge to students." However, this lens blinds people to the real value of translation.

> If we look closely, however, at what has actually counted as scholarship over time, we find that scholars can also be recognized when they create, make accessible, and transmit knowledge by way of textual criticism, scholarly editions, annotated bibliographies, edited anthologies, and so on. Like these later endeavors, translation pulls scholarship in an outward direction, with less emphasis on knowledge creation for its own sake, more emphasis on identifying, interpreting, and conveying valuable works of literature or scholarship to a community of peers and to the public at large.[17]

Without a doubt, the work of translators has been critical in expanding the field of Japanese literature as a whole, opening up new readerships and revealing hitherto hidden corners of the Japanese literary world even to fellow scholars who are, of course, unable to read everything because of the sheer size of the Japanese book industry. Since 1997, sales of books and magazines in Japan have been falling due to the rise of mobile phones, but even so, the number of new titles published each year in Japan remains extremely high. In 2018, there were 71,661 new book titles in all genres, accounting for a total of approximately 196 new titles every day; meanwhile, there were 2,821 magazines in existence. If instead of looking at new titles, one turns to the number of printed books or magazines and the Japanese market (including both new and older titles still in print), one finds a thriving industry: over the course of the year 2018, there were over 942 million books and 1.835 billion magazines on the Japanese market, which resulted in nearly 700 billion yen of book sales and 593 billion yen of magazine sales.[18]

The Three Percent Problem

Although literary production in Japan is extremely healthy, only the tiniest fraction is ever translated. Readers in the Anglophone world, and the US in particular, are so infamously insular that some publishers even "disguise" translations by removing a translator's name from the cover.[19] It is an often-repeated statistic that only around 3% of all books published in the US each year are translations from other languages; however, as scholar and editor Chad Post has noted, that number also includes non-fiction, including do-it-yourself manuals, self-help books, and all sorts of other genres. If one limits one's purview narrowly to literary fiction, poetry, and drama, he estimates the number of translated texts is closer to 0.7% of all US titles.[20] Open Letter, a publisher specializing in translations of world literature, kept a running database of literary translations published since January 2008. Although the database does not include English translations published outside America, it gives perhaps the best snapshot of any resource regarding the recent state of Japanese literature in translation, especially in comparison to the translation of other literatures.[21] As of January 2020 when this research was conducted, the Three Percent Translation Database contained 4,952 entries, 223 (4.50%) of which are literary translations from Japanese, meaning that there were approximately twenty-five book-length literary texts translated from Japanese published each year in the US during the 2010s. Considering the fact that tens of thousands of literary texts are published annually in Japan, this number is woefully small by any stretch of the imagination.

This does not mean that there were not valiant efforts to bring Japanese literature to Anglophone audiences. Among the publishers who worked especially hard to bring translated Japanese literature to US audiences were Kodansha International, originally founded in 1963 as an imprint of its large Japanese parent company Kodansha, and the independent publisher Vertical, founded in 2001. However, despite their important contributions, both remained relatively small. At its height in the 1980s and 1990s, Kodansha International published as many as twenty-five to thirty titles per year, but the majority of these were non-fiction, non-literary texts, including some related to other Asian countries. However, there were occasionally some spectacular successes; for instance, Kodansha International was the first to put out an international edition of Murakami Haruki, who attracted more attention than any of the other translated authors Kodansha International had published until then.[22] Founded in 2001, Vertical had the ambition of bringing popular Japanese literature—crime fiction, science fiction, and speculative fiction in particular—to Anglophone audiences, but even when it was most involved with the translation of literary texts in the first decade of the twenty-first century, it only produced a handful of titles per year. By later in the same decade, Vertical had shifted emphasis from publishing literature to more lucrative manga, anime, and video game tie-ins. Eventually, in 2011, Kodansha acquired Vertical and reorganized Kodansha International into Kodansha USA, with Vertical becoming an imprint of the larger company. While Vertical and Kodansha USA continue to publish, translated literary fiction occupies a relatively small portion of their catalog, and certain genres like poetry and theater are not represented at all.

According to the Three Percent Database, there are a number of languages that, despite having far fewer speakers than Japanese, produced a remarkable number of literary translations. For instance, during the time that the database covers, translations from Italian accounted for 291 titles (5.88%) Hebrew for 209 titles (4.22%), and Swedish for 207 titles (4.18%). Even though Italy, Israel, and Sweden have far smaller populations than Japan, a major factor elevating the literary position of those languages is the relatively large numbers of English speakers who read them at an advanced level. A second, even more critical factor, however, has to do with institutional support. Many countries and even certain regions, such as Catalonia in Spain, have all created governmentally sponsored organizations that give financial support to translators and publishers to promote their literature abroad.

In 2002, the Japanese Agency for Cultural Affairs *(Bunkachō)* started the Japanese Literature Publishing Project (JLPP) in imitation of those programs, actively matching translators from different languages to Japanese texts and financially supporting the publication of books representing a broad range of literary tastes.[23] Because the number of translated Japanese texts was so small from the start, the JLPP successfully boosted numbers, but the texts selected did not always match readers' tastes abroad, and many went out of print within just a few years. More problematic, however, was the fact that the JLPP texts were, for the most part, not necessarily the kinds of things that Anglophone academics of Japanese literature were talking about—the JLPP titles skewed toward popular literature designed for mainstream audiences. The disconnect between academics and the JLPP selection committee may be one reason that relatively few JLPP titles were picked up for classroom use and that so many quickly went out of print. After the JLPP shifted strategy in 2010, many of the US publishers who worked with the JLPP, such as Dalkey Archive Press, veered away from Japanese literature, ceasing the acquisition of new titles from Japanese. That year, the JLPP lost most of its funding in a series of governmental budget cutbacks, and it changed its goals to incubating new translators through workshops, competitions, and symposia.[24]

The strategy of creating and incubating translators rather than directly supporting the translation of certain titles was also the strategy of the Nippon Foundation, which worked to support Japanese literature during roughly the same years as the JLPP. For several years, David Karashima spearheaded a program at the Nippon Foundation which worked with the British Centre for Literary Translation (BCLT) to host an annual literary translation workshop at the University of East Anglia. The organization selected promising translators from around the world and brought them together to work with an established translator and a well-known author while simultaneously learning about the art and business of literary translation. The project also helped create a successful mentoring system for emerging Japanese translators and hosted readings and workshops in the UK.

Meanwhile, academia, especially in the US, has failed to come to grips with the important role that translation plays in helping to organize and promote the discipline of Japanese literature as a whole. The view of translation as a derivative activity ignores the fact that translations can reshape the entire field by providing readers, students, and budding scholars with new forays into authors, subject matter, and issues. The academic prejudice against translation also ignores the simple fact that translations typically have a far greater reach than scholarly work—the print run of a moderately successful translation may be in the range of 3,000 to 5,000 copies, whereas a moderately successful scholarly tome is more likely to have a print run of 500 to 1,000. Of course, the number of copies sold isn't necessarily the best measure of the influence of a work, yet translations, which can appeal to both scholars, students, and general readers alike, are likely to find their way into more hands than a scholarly book whose audience is limited from the start.

If numbers of citations and reviews are one measure of an academic's success routinely used in tenure and promotion decisions, it is illogical for tenure and promotion committees to disregard translations, which are far more likely than scholarly monographs to be widely read and reviewed. Although not all universities recognize the significance of translation, it is one of the most important things a scholar can do. In 2011, the Modern Language Association (MLA) produced a report advising administrators on how to evaluate translations as scholarship. There, the authors emphasized, "the translation of a work of literature or scholarship—indeed, of any major cultural document—can have a significant impact on the intellectual community, while the absence of translations impedes the circulation of ideas."[25] The final point is an important one: by failing to do the translations that would make their own work understandable to the wider world, Japanese literary scholars are essentially hiding their work from readers who don't read Japanese, tempering the impact and reach of their discoveries. Translator and advocate Esther Allen has noted the irony that it is "a far safer career move for a US academic to write, in English, a monograph on an author whose work has never been translated into English than to translate that author's work into English," although translation would make that author accessible to a wide audience.[26]

The time has come to reconsider this prejudice. After all, how easy is it to take away big lessons from a detailed, deep reading of a text that one has never heard of and has no chance of ever reading? If anything, the failure to translate only reinforces the view of Japanese literary studies as marginal and contributes to the growing crisis of relevancy.

Recent Shifts in the Field

In recent years, there have been signs that the situation is changing. Language and literature programs have been progressively turning to teaching translation as a way of making themselves relevant again. Numerous programs across the US, UK, and Australia have added translation courses—sometimes even an entire component—to their curricula to attract students and to give them a way to connect their literary studies with the larger world. In continental Europe, where so much communication is predicated on translation, the importance of translation has never been in doubt, and so it has been leading the charge, arguing that the traditional ways of learning language, namely focusing on the "four skills"—reading, writing, listening, and speaking—are not enough for our increasingly globalized world where so much communication takes place across languages. The Common European Framework of Reference for Languages (CEFR) has argued that educators should treat translation as an essential "fifth skill."[27] In the US, the MLA has advocated developing courses in translation and interpretation, commenting that there "is a great unmet demand for educated translators and interpreters, and translation is an ideal context for developing translingual and transcultural abilities as an organizing principle of the language curriculum."[28] When universities do develop such courses, they are not necessarily taught by literary scholars; they are just as likely to be taught by specialists in foreign language acquisition and applied linguistics, but the rising stock of translation is welcome, especially since it is a skill that many language learners hope to develop. The status of translation in tenure and promotion decisions is also rising. Even though tenure committees in the US are still unlikely to count translations as fully equivalent to other forms of scholarship, the number of universities actively discriminating against translators is waning, thanks in part to advocacy by the MLA, the American Literary Translators Association (ALTA), and the PEN Club, all of whom have vociferously argued for the value of translation.

Judging from their publications, scholars who came of age in Japanese literary studies during the first decade of the twenty-first century, are increasingly recognizing that despite the skepticism of older generations, translation plays a critical role in making scholarship relevant to broader audiences. Recent years have seen the publication of a significant number of books that have returned to the 1970–1980s "translation-friendly" model of putting translations and original scholarship, such as discussions of a book's historical background or detailed textual exegesis, in the same volume, thus making their books useful to readers who cannot read the original Japanese easily. This pattern is more common in premodern Japanese literary studies because the temporal and physical distance between source culture and target culture makes explanation especially necessary and helpful, but in modern Japanese literary studies too, there have been a rising number of such publications.[29]

At the same time, translations of Japanese literature seem to have been earning more popular attention for Japanese literature than at any time in recent memory. The worldwide success of Murakami Haruki whetted the appetite of publishers for other Japanese writers who could replicate at least a little of Murakami's commercial success. As John Treat has noted in his chapter in this volume, this has led publishers to overemphasize Murakami-style "quirkiness" in their selections, as if novels that explore alternative realities and strange turns-of-events represent the entirety of Japanese literature. Even so, this search for authors who might replicate Murakami's success has opened up a literary space for other writers whose stories veer into the surreal, including, as Rebecca Copeland points out in her contribution to this volume, a wave of prominent women writers, such as Tawada Yōko, Itō Hiromi, Oyamada Hiroko, Ogawa Yōko, and Matsuda Aoko. Among the wave of recent translators who have been particularly successful at putting contemporary Japanese writers on the map of world literature are Tomoko Aoyama, Emily Balistrieri, Polly Barton, Sam Bett, David Boyd, Andrew Campana, Juliet Winters Carpenter, Michael Emmerich, Philip Gabriel, Morgan Giles, Ted Goossen, Kendall Heitzman, David Karashima, Rina Kikuchi, Takako Lento, Sam Malissa, Margaret Mitsutani, Sawako Nakayasu, Allison Markin Powell, Motoyuki Shibata, Stephen Snyder, Ginny Tapley Takemori, Alison Watts, Asa Yoneda, and Hitomi Yoshio. One should note that although a few of the translators just named hold positions within academia, they have strenuously resisted the pressure to abandon translation in favor of other forms of scholarship. If anything, their work has contributed to the visibility of translation, not just through their own publications, but through presentations, conferences, workshops, and mentoring emerging translators.

Translations of Japanese literature have also won significant prizes in recent years, promoting the visibility of the field. In 2018, the National Book Award (NBA) created a category for translations, and when Margaret Mitsutani's translation of Tawada Yōko's novel *The Emissary (Kentōshi)* won, the book quickly attracted international attention.[30] The following year, Stephen Snyder's translation of Ogawa Yōko's *The Memory Police (Hisoyaka na kesshō)* was longlisted for the same prize, and in 2020, Morgan Giles's translation of Yū Miri's *Tokyo Ueno Station (JR Ueno-Eki Kōen-guchi)* won the NBA again, marking the second time in just a few years that a translation from Japanese garnered the prestigious prize.[31] Although no Japanese writer ever won the Man Asian Literary Prize, which was offered from 2007 through 2012, Kanehara Hitomi, Kawakami Hiromi, Igarashi Tsutomu, Ōe Kenzaburō, Ogawa Yōko, Yoshimoto Banana, and Murakami Haruki were all nominees, adding to the worldwide visibility of Japanese writing, especially in the British Commonwealth where the Man Prizes are nearly as important as the Nobel Prize for Literature. Recent years have also seen translations of poets garner new attention in competitions never previously won by Japanese writers; for instance, the Best Translated Book Award went in 2009 to Sawako Nakayasu's translation of Hiraide Takashi, and in 2012 to Kyōko Yoshida and Forrest Gander for their translations of Nomura Kiwao.[32] In 2011, the Harold

Morton Landon Translation Award from the Academy of American Poets went to Jeffrey Angles for his translations of Tada Chimako, and in 2016, the MLA gave Angles the Aldo and Jeanne Scaglione Prize for his translation of *The Book of the Dead (Shisha no sho)*, one of the few novels by poet and ethnologist Orikuchi Shinobu.[33]

Despite certain right-wing US politicians' ardent desire to eliminate the National Endowment for the Arts (NEA), the organization has done valuable work to support translation projects, including several from Japanese, that might otherwise never have seen the light of day. Between 2010 and 2024, the NEA has given six grants to translators working on Japanese authors—namely Sata Ineko, Takamura Kōtarō, Taneda Santōka, Yosano Akiko, Nishi Kanako, and Nakahara Chūya—but even within this time frame, there are many years in which Japanese literature is not represented at all. If anything, this suggests that there are not enough Japanese translators taking advantage of these grants. One hopes it will not be long before the number of books translated from Japanese and published in the United States will rise far higher than the current, sluggish number of two dozen or so volumes per year. There are readers out there, and yes, they are waiting.

Notes

1. For instance, see Anthony P. Carnevale, Ban Cheah, and Andrew R. Hanson, "The Economic Value of College Majors" (Georgetown University Center on Education and the Workforce, McCourt School of Public Policy, 2015), https://cew.georgetown.edu/wp-content/uploads/The-Economic-Value-of-College-Majors-Full-Report-web-FINAL.pdf; Anthony P. Carnevale and Ban Cheah, "From Hard Times to Better Times: College Majors, Unemployment, and Earnings" (Georgetown University Center on Education and the Workforce, McCourt School of Public Policy, 2015), https://cew.georgetown.edu/wp-content/uploads/HardTimes2015-Report.pdf

2. See Paul T. Corrigan, "Jobs Will Save the Humanities," *The Chronicle of Higher Education*, June 28, 2018, https://www.chronicle.com/article/Jobs-Will-Save-the-Humanities/243767; American Academy of Arts and Sciences, "The State of the Humanities 2018: Graduates in the Workforce & Beyond | American Academy of Arts and Sciences," February 7, 2018, https://www.amacad.org/publication/state-humanities-2018-graduates-workforce-beyond

3. Valerie Strauss, "The Surprising Thing Google Learned about Its Employees—and What It Means for Today's Students," *The Washington Post*, December 20, 2017, https://www.washingtonpost.com/news/answer-sheet/wp/2017/12/20/the-surprising-thing-google-learned-about-its-employees-and-what-it-means-for-todays-students/

4. Cited in Martha C. Nussbaum, *Not For Profit: Why Democracy Needs the Humanities*, Revised paperback edition (Princeton University Press, 2016), xviii.

5. Edward Fowler, "Rendering Words, Traversing Cultures: On the Art and Poli-

tics of Translating Modern Japanese Fiction," *Journal of Japanese Studies* 18, no. 1 (1992): 3. Emphasis in original.

6. Marleigh Grayer Ryan and Shimei Futabatei, *Japan's First Modern Novel: Ukigumo of Futabatei Shimei*, UNESCO Collection of Representative Works–Japanese Series (Columbia University Press, 1967).

7. Robert Lyons Danly and Ichiyō Higuchi, *In the Shade of Spring Leaves: The Life and Writings of Higuchi Ichiyō, a Woman of Letters in Meiji Japan* (Yale University Press, 1981).

8. Ishimure Michiko, *Paradise in the Sea of Sorrow: Our Minamata Disease*, trans. Livia Monnet (Yamaguchi Publishing House, 1990), republished as Ishimure Michiko, *Paradise in the Sea of Sorrow: Our Minamata Disease*, trans. Livia Monnet, Rev. ed, Michigan Classics in Japanese Studies 25 (University of Michigan Center for Japanese Studies, 2003).

9. Ishikawa Jun, *The Bodhisattva, or, Samantabhadra*, trans. William Jefferson Tyler, Modern Asian Literature Series (Columbia University Press, 1990).

10. Edouard J. Maunick, "A Library of World Classics," *The UNESCO Courier* 39, no. 1 (1986): 5–6, https://unesdoc.unesco.org/ark:/48223/pf0000068108

11. Maunick, 6.

12. René de Ceccatty, "The Originality of Japanese Literature," *The UNESCO Courier* 39, no. 1 (1986): 12–14.

13. George Steiner, *After Babel: Aspects of Language and Translation* (Oxford University Press, 1975), 291–301.

14. Lawrence Venuti, *The Scandals of Translation: Towards an Ethics of Difference* (Routledge, 1998), 5.

15. Jennifer Howard, "Translators Struggle to Prove Their Academic Bona Fides," *The Chronicle of Higher Education*, January 17, 2010, https://www.chronicle.com/article/translators-struggle-to-prove-their-academic-bona-fides/

16. Michael Henry Heim, quoted in Howard, "Translators Struggle."

17. Catherine Porter, "Translation as Scholarship," *ADFL Bulletin* 41, no. 2 (2009): 12, https://www.maps.mla.org/bulletin/article/adfl.41.2.7/

18. Japan Book Publishers Association, "Statistics of Publishing in Japan" (Japan Book Publishers Association, 2019), 3–4, https://www.jbpa.or.jp/en/pdf/pdf01.pdf

19. Sophia Stewart, "Translators Fight for Credit on Their Own Book Covers," PublishersWeekly.com, October 15, 2021, https://www.publishersweekly.com/pw/by-topic/industry-news/publisher-news/article/87649-translators-fight-for-credit-on-their-own-book-covers.html

20. Chad W. Post, *The Three Percent Problem: Rants and Responses on Publishing, Translation, and the Future of Reading*, Kindle (Open Letter, 2011).

21. As of January 2020, the database contained entries only through April 2018, thus covering nine years, four months' worth of texts. (The database does not include translated manga, which would likely significantly boost the numbers of texts translated from Japanese, but the database does include translations of Japanese light novels.)

22. On the history of the "Murakami phenomenon," see David James Karashima, *Who We're Reading When We're Reading Murakami*, First Soft Skull edition (Soft Skull, 2020).

23. Agency for Cultural Affairs, "JLPP to Wa | About the JLPP," JLPP to wa | About the JLPP, 2010, https://www.jlpp.go.jp/aboutus.html

24. Kōno Shion, "Following Murakami's Path: Japanese Books as World Literature," nippon.com, June 19, 2019, https://www.nippon.com/en/in-depth/d00491/following-murakami's-path-japanese-books-as-world-literature.html

25. Modern Language Association, "Evaluating Translations as Scholarship: Guidelines for Peer Review," Modern Language Association, 2011, https://www.mla.org/Resources/Advocacy/Executive-Council-Actions/2011/Evaluating-Translations-as-Scholarship-Guidelines-for-Peer-Review

26. Esther Allen, "Translation, Globalization, and English," in *To Be Translated or Not to Be: PEN / IRL Report on the International Situation of Literary Translation*, ed. Esther Allen (Institut Ramon Llull Catalan Language and Culture, 2007), 23, https://www.lilec.it/spagnaplurale/wp/wp-content/uploads/2018/03/2007-To-be-translated-or-not-to-be.pdf

27. Directorate-General for Translation, *Translation and Language Learning: The Role of Translation in the Teaching of Languages in the European Union-Summary* (European Union Publications Office, 2013), 6, https://data.europa.eu/doi/10.2782/13232

28. MLA Ad Hoc Committee on Foreign Languages, "Foreign Languages and Higher Education: New Structures for a . . . ," Modern Language Association, 2007, https://www.mla.org/Resources/Guidelines-and-Data/Reports-and-Professional-Guidelines/Foreign-Languages-and-Higher-Education-New-Structures-for-a-Changed-World

29. For instance, a number of books published in the mid-2010s conveniently pair exegesis with translations of key texts within the same volume. In each case, the scholarly apparatus was hefty enough that the scholar-translator could easily have broken it off and published it as a journal article or even an independent book, but that would only mitigate the usefulness of the translations in the classroom where students benefit from having both primary and secondary sources packaged together. See, for instance, Stephen Dodd and Kajii Motojirō, *The Youth of Things: Life and Death in the Age of Kajii Motojiro*, trans. Stephen Dodd (University of Hawai'i Press, 2014); Heather Bowen-Struyk and Norma Field, eds., *For Dignity, Justice, and Revolution: An Anthology of Japanese Proletarian Literature* (University of Chicago Press, 2016); Ineko Sata, *Five Faces of Japanese Feminism: Crimson and Other Works*, trans. Samuel Perry (University of Hawai'i Press, 2016); Orikuchi Shinobu, *The Book of the Dead*, trans. Jeffrey Angles (University of Minnesota Press, 2017).

30. Yoko Tawada, *The Emissary*, trans. Margaret Mitsutani (New Directions, 2018).

31. Yoko Ogawa, *The Memory Police*, trans. Stephen Snyder (Pantheon Books, 2019); Yū Miri, *Tokyo Ueno Station*, trans. Morgan Giles (Riverhead Books, 2020).

32. Takashi Hiraide, *For the Fighting Spirit of the Walnut*, trans. Sawako Nakayasu (New Directions, 2008); Kiwao Nomura, *Spectacle & Pigsty*, trans. Kyoko Yoshida and Forrest Gander (Omnidawn, 2011).

33. Tada Chimako, *Forest of Eyes: Selected Poems of Tada Chimako*, trans. Jeffrey Angles (University of California Press, 2010); Orikuchi Shinobu, *The Book of the Dead.*

Bibliography

Agency for Cultural Affairs. "JLPP to Wa | About the JLPP." JLPP to wa | About the JLPP, 2010. https://www.jlpp.go.jp/aboutus.html

Allen, Esther. "Translation, Globalization, and English." In *To Be Translated or Not to Be: PEN / IRL Report on the International Situation of Literary Translation*, edited by Esther Allen. Institut Ramon Llull Catalan Language and Culture, 2007. https://www.lilec.it/spagnaplurale/wp/wp-content/uploads/2018/03/2007-To-be-translated-or-not-to-be.pdf

American Academy of Arts and Sciences. "The State of the Humanities 2018: Graduates in the Workforce & Beyond | American Academy of Arts and Sciences," February 7, 2018. https://www.amacad.org/publication/state-humanities-2018-graduates-workforce-beyond

Bowen-Struyk, Heather, and Norma Field, eds. *For Dignity, Justice, and Revolution: An Anthology of Japanese Proletarian Literature*. University of Chicago Press, 2016.

Carnevale, Anthony P., and Ban Cheah. "From Hard Times to Better Times: College Majors, Unemployment, and Earnings." Georgetown University Center on Education and the Workforce, McCourt School of Public Policy, 2015. https://cew.georgetown.edu/wp-content/uploads/HardTimes2015-Report.pdf

Carnevale, Anthony P., Ban Cheah, and Andrew R. Hanson. "The Economic Value of College Majors." Georgetown University Center on Education and the Workforce, McCourt School of Public Policy, 2015. https://cew.georgetown.edu/wp-content/uploads/The-Economic-Value-of-College-Majors-Full-Report-web-FINAL.pdf

Corrigan, Paul T. "Jobs Will Save the Humanities." *The Chronicle of Higher Education*, June 28, 2018. https://www.chronicle.com/article/Jobs-Will-Save-the-Humanities/243767

Danly, Robert Lyons, and Ichiyō Higuchi. *In the Shade of Spring Leaves: The Life and Writings of Higuchi Ichiyō, a Woman of Letters in Meiji Japan*. Yale University Press, 1981.

de Ceccatty, René. "The Originality of Japanese Literature." *The UNESCO Courier* 39, no. 1 (1986): 12–14.

Directorate-General for Translation. *Translation and Language Learning: The Role of Translation in the Teaching of Languages in the European Union-Summary*. European Union Publications Office, 2013. https://data.europa.eu/doi/10.2782/13232

Dodd, Stephen, and Kajii Motojirō. *The Youth of Things: Life and Death in the Age of Kajii Motojiro*. Translated by Stephen Dodd. University of Hawai'i Press, 2014.

Fowler, Edward. "Rendering Words, Traversing Cultures: On the Art and Politics of Translating Modern Japanese Fiction." *Journal of Japanese Studies* 18, no. 1 (1992): 1–44.

Hiraide, Takashi. *For the Fighting Spirit of the Walnut*. Translated by Sawako Nakayasu. New Directions, 2008.

Howard, Jennifer. "Translators Struggle to Prove Their Academic Bona Fides." *The Chronicle of Higher Education*, January 17, 2010. https://www.chronicle.com/article/translators-struggle-to-prove-their-academic-bona-fides/

Ishikawa Jun. *The Bodhisattva, or, Samantabhadra*. Translated by William Jefferson Tyler. Modern Asian Literature Series. Columbia University Press, 1990.

Ishimure Michiko. *Paradise in the Sea of Sorrow: Our Minamata Disease.* Translated by Livia Monnet. Yamaguchi Publishing House, 1990.

Ishimure Michiko. *Paradise in the Sea of Sorrow: Our Minamata Disease.* Translated by Livia Monnet. Rev. ed. Michigan Classics in Japanese Studies 25. University of Michigan Center for Japanese Studies, 2003.

Japan Book Publishers Association. "Statistics of Publishing in Japan." Japan Book Publishers Association, 2019. https://www.jbpa.or.jp/en/pdf/pdf01.pdf

Karashima, David James. *Who We're Reading When We're Reading Murakami.* First Soft Skull edition. Soft Skull, 2020.

Kōno Shion. "Following Murakami's Path: Japanese Books as World Literature." nippon.com, June 19, 2019. https://www.nippon.com/en/in-depth/d00491/following-murakami's-path-japanese-books-as-world-literature.html

Maunick, Edouard J. "A Library of World Classics." *The UNESCO Courier* 39, no. 1 (1986). https://unesdoc.unesco.org/ark:/48223/pf0000068108

MLA Ad Hoc Committee on Foreign Languages. "Foreign Languages and Higher Education: New Structures for a . . ." Modern Language Association, 2007. https://www.mla.org/Resources/Guidelines-and-Data/Reports-and-Professional-Guidelines/Foreign-Languages-and-Higher-Education-New-Structures-for-a-Changed-World

Modern Language Association. "Evaluating Translations as Scholarship: Guidelines for Peer Review." Modern Language Association, 2011. https://www.mla.org/Resources/Advocacy/Executive-Council-Actions/2011/Evaluating-Translations-as-Scholarship-Guidelines-for-Peer-Review

Nomura, Kiwao. *Spectacle & Pigsty.* Translated by Kyoko Yoshida and Forrest Gander. Omnidawn, 2011.

Nussbaum, Martha C. *Not For Profit: Why Democracy Needs the Humanities.* Revised paperback edition. Princeton University Press, 2016.

Ogawa, Yoko. *The Memory Police.* Translated by Stephen Snyder. Pantheon Books, 2019.

Orikuchi Shinobu. *The Book of the Dead.* Translated by Jeffrey Angles. University of Minnesota Press, 2017.

Porter, Catherine. "Translation as Scholarship." *ADFL Bulletin* 41, no. 2 (2009). https://www.maps.mla.org/bulletin/article/adfl.41.2.7/

Post, Chad W. *The Three Percent Problem: Rants and Responses on Publishing, Translation, and the Future of Reading.* Kindle. Open Letter, 2011.

Ryan, Marleigh Grayer, and Shimei Futabatei. *Japan's First Modern Novel: Ukigumo of Futabatei Shimei.* UNESCO Collection of Representative Works–Japanese Series. Columbia University Press, 1967.

Sata, Ineko. *Five Faces of Japanese Feminism: Crimson and Other Works.* Translated by Samuel Perry. University of Hawai'i Press, 2016.

Steiner, George. *After Babel: Aspects of Language and Translation.* Oxford University Press, 1975.

Stewart, Sophia. "Translators Fight for Credit on Their Own Book Covers." PublishersWeekly.com, October 15, 2021. https://www.publishersweekly.com/pw/by-topic/industry-news/publisher-news/article/87649-translators-fight-for-credit-on-their-own-book-covers.html

Strauss, Valerie. "The Surprising Thing Google Learned about Its Employees—and What It Means for Today's Students." *The Washington Post*, December 20, 2017. https://www.washingtonpost.com/news/answer-sheet/wp/2017/12/20/the-surprising-thing-google-learned-about-its-employees-and-what-it-means-for-todays-students/

Tada Chimako. *Forest of Eyes: Selected Poems of Tada Chimako*. Translated by Jeffrey Angles. University of California Press, 2010.

Tawada, Yōko. *The Emissary*. Translated by Margaret Mitsutani. New Directions, 2018.

Venuti, Lawrence. *The Scandals of Translation: Towards an Ethics of Difference*. Routledge, 1998.

Yū Miri. *Tokyo Ueno Station*. Translated by Morgan Giles. Riverhead Books, 2020.

PART III

Institutional Responses to the Field

CHAPTER 12

The Many What-ifs of Literary Urbanism

A European Perspective

Gala Maria Follaco

As a university student of Japanese in Italy in the early 2000s, I recall being impressed by the highly pervasive presence of Tokyo in modern literature, as both a space of representation and production. I was under the impression that after the Meiji Restoration, the literary life of the entire country had moved *en masse* to the new capital. I was learning of writers who had come to Tokyo from the provinces to cultivate their literary ambitions and of other writers who, inspired by the new paradigms of urban life, developed novel and sometimes revolutionary motifs and languages. I was in the process of discovering whole neighborhoods where publishing activities were concentrated, to the extent that they became centers of a thriving and increasingly diverse industry.

To some extent, my impression had to do with the multiple processes of periodization, hierarchization, and canonization of literary phenomena that were taking place in Japan during the transition to a modernity that was, in many ways, inspired by European ideals. The many cultural changes that accompanied the country's economic and social evolution after 1868 were a conservative revolution, since many of the questions crucial to the realization of this modernization had already been posed long before the Restoration.

This is perhaps the most defining feature of Meiji literature—and the main reason for the impression I had as a university student. It signals the disruption of the existing balance and the transformation of a relational system at a time when many established categories were being questioned. It marked the start of a process that would give rise to an "imperialist" literature seeking to appropriate a territory of new extension.[1] An appropriation that, apparently, began and ended in the space of the new capital.

The most obvious results of the multiform intrusion of capitalism and Euro-American imperialist policies in the field of writing were the drastic reform of language and a redefinition of the contours of the literary canon. At the heart of the new literature was narrative prose, more precisely the "novel," in a sense closer to its Western European conception than to its Japanese counterparts. This led to a gradual renunciation of Sinitic writing and a devaluation of genres that were difficult to assimilate into Western forms and styles. To be modern, a novel had to tell real stories and had to do so in a language that was as close as possible to the spoken language; one that everyone could understand. A language that had to be "Japanese."

And the space of storytelling was no less important. After the abolition of the status system, society had lost some key identity coordinates.[2] At the same time, Euro-American ideas and techniques were spreading, inspired by massive urban modernization projects. Everything was changing: the city and the lives of its inhabitants, and both the territorial as well as the mental landscapes. On the other hand, as nothing really changes in such a short time, the rhythms and trajectories of everyday life retained the vestiges of the past for longer. Tokyo in the 1870s should be regarded as a space of limbo, a city in transformation, whose status as capital had not yet been established.[3] One of the main characteristics of Meiji literature—being "urban"—did not manifest itself until the end of the century, when novelists inspired by European Realism and Naturalism began to set their stories in urban contexts, most notably Tokyo. They were certainly modern, telling the real story and describing the city as it was at the time, but their representation was not entirely new. Images of European cities from the works of Goethe, Zola, and many others mingled with those of Edo and Tokyo's recent past, just as they appeared in the "useless" *gesaku* prose of fifteen or twenty years earlier; the city's pre-Restoration spatial zoning was still faintly visible, like a watermark, behind the modern scene of the Meiji capital. New problems arose, as the stories of literary characters unfolded in spaces that, very often, were much more than a mere background or setting.

Aside from the debt that any line of research on the modernization of urban space must necessarily owe to Maeda Ai[4] and his effort to read Japanese modernity as part of a worldwide process, it is important to underline the influence of Jinnai Hidenobu's work on Edo,[5] which, especially through the suggestion of a resemblance to Venice, both being "water cities," has shed light on hitherto neglected aspects of urban modernization and its impact on the representation of space. Further, Jinnai has succeeded in convincingly demonstrating that the transition from Edo to Tokyo, far from being a moment of rupture, actually marks a continuity, especially a cultural one, between the two cities.[6] Transformation in waterways as a crucial step in Tokyo's modernization is also at the core of Paul Waley's research on Japanese river culture and its actual, as well as symbolic, connection with spatial zoning.[7]

The importance of looking at urbanism from a historical perspective, not minimizing the elements of continuity but indeed stressing them, is implicitly emphasized by the joint effort by Waley himself and other scholars who, after organizing a session at the conference of the European Association for Japanese Studies in 1997, published a book[8] in which three distinct capitals, Kyoto, Edo, and Tokyo, are studied from multiple points of view and through their numerous representations. This work has the added value of addressing the theme of urban space from an interdisciplinary perspective, also going beyond the Tokyo-centric approach of many studies on Japanese urban modernity, especially in the literary field.

The intersection between space and identity in a context that is not necessarily Tokyo-based is at the center of Stephen Dodd's research in his book on *furusato*,[9] which brings to the forefront the theme of native place within a timeframe (from the mid-Meiji period through to the late 1930s) in which everything that fell outside the (real and ideal) perimeter of the capital tended to be overlooked.

Deserving a mention here is the 2012 volume *Urban Spaces in Japan*, which followed the 2005 conference of the German Association for Social Science Research on Japan and, adopting an interdisciplinary approach based on a set of case studies, offered a critical reflection on the topic of space in Japan. It examines space inside and outside the capital and even beyond strictly national borders, space as the subject of composite and original research, which, through a multiplicity of languages and approaches, brings to light new problems, questions established issues, and imagines future developments.[10] One of the editors, Evelyn Schulz, is a key figure in Europe regarding the relationship between urban and literary studies. Her work on Nagai Kafū (1879–1959) and on *hanjōki* (records of prosperity) relating to Tokyo, not to mention the volume *Tokyo: Memory, Imagination, and the City* that she co-edited in 2018, addresses the topic of collective and individual memory, thus of image-construction and resistance within the space of the city and through the lens of literary writing.[11] The extensive application of urban studies tools in the analysis of literary works signals the overcoming of the many limitations inherent in text-based approaches and the consolidation of a theoretical foundation that greatly enriches the study of a subject with profound rhetorical, if not instrumental, connotations. At the same time, the systematic exchange and continuous engagement with other disciplines in the field of historical and social sciences connected with Japan ensure the accuracy of a broader perspective, which is of fundamental importance when approaching a topic with diverse implications, such as literature (and, more generally, representation), of the modern urban space.

In 2018, a symposium held in Naples sought, through the prism of narrative, to investigate the dynamics of appropriation, representation, and self-representation of urban space in modern Japan. Taking urban centers such as Tokyo, Kobe, and São Paulo as its focus, the symposium explored the ways cultural, political, and economic dynamics interact to shape urbanization models across Japan and along migration routes. It investigated the construction of urban space in the imagination of residents and migrants, as well as according to market dynamics. It also examined discourses and narratives performed by literary writers and historiographers in the rhetorical representation of the "modern Japanese urban space" and the negotiation of identities of urban denizens in literary and historiographical works. Prioritizing the theme of narration and representation, the symposium aimed to stimulate reflection and take a step toward overcoming the fundamental disparity in the exchange between literature and urban studies, namely toward a re-evaluation of modern Japanese literature as a valid tool in itself for interpreting urban phenomena and not just as a reservoir of information and symbolic configurations useful for analysis in other fields of knowledge.

In the current crisis of the humanities, literary studies risk, in Europe as elsewhere, ending up at the bottom of every government's priority list. Emphasis on STEM subjects is sometimes interpreted as excluding other disciplines, and in an academic environment increasingly governed by market forces and strongly encouraged to pursue innovation at all costs, literary studies (especially those related to past eras) are being relegated to an ancillary role in comparison to language instruction. From this point of view, universities that continue to offer—despite enormous sacrifice and amid countless difficulties—area programs that, alongside language learning, include the compulsory study of cultural disciplines related to Japan and/or Asia, sometimes in great depth and with a variety of approaches and content, represent a valuable resource for the survival of literary studies. Compared to two decades ago, students of Japanese have definitely increased, and the motivations behind their choice have diversified. If already in the early 2000s the paths in areal studies related to Asia, and Japan, were no longer perceived as eccentric, in today's Europe there is, on the one hand, a greater solidity of the field, and on the other hand, an audience of students landing at the university with a greater awareness of the most characteristic cultural (but especially popular culture, as also evidenced by Treat in his chapter) elements. One can study Japanese in large cities as well as in smaller university centers, with in-depth study options varying according to the programs offered, with language instruction leading the way for all other disciplines.

This variety and spread, however, is not matched by an equal investment of resources by individual governments, with countries that can count on a more attentive and forward-looking political class, and others that can rely solely on EU funds and Japanese fellowship programs (MEXT, Japan Foundation, Japan Society for the Promotion of Science, and others), or funding from other countries.

Endorsing Richard L. Stein's notion of "the city as a perfect interdisciplinary object,"[12] one might consider the study of the representation of urban spaces in modern Japan as strategic, for it addresses topics that are of global interest today, such as urbanization, gentrification, resilience, migration, and social inequalities, providing interpretative insights drawn from the empirical experience of cities filtered through the sensitivity of writers who grappled with issues of identity, cultural negotiation, and their relationships with authority over a century ago. By, on the one hand, expanding the discourse to the so-called secondary cities to the urban centers of colonial Japan and those where migrant communities settled, and, on the other, to forms of writing which, for reasons of genre, gender, and language, are noncanonical, the relevance of this discourse in the current context emerges even more strongly.

A recent trend in the field of urban studies, specifically on the historical, geographic-cultural, architectural and anthropological fronts, is to read Japanese urban phenomena from a comparative standpoint, looking to other realities in Asia and around the world both in terms of broadening the perspective and deepening our knowledge of colonial and migratory events. Moving beyond the illusion of Tokyo's particularism in order to examine the representation, in various cultural expressions, of other cities, whether they are within or outside the archipelago's borders, is to set as a horizon a much greater awareness of the urban literature of modern Japan. Michael Cronin's recent work[13] on Ōsaka is an example of such a direction,[14] as is Joshua Fogel's longstanding effort to clarify the importance of Chinese territory for modern Japanese literati.[15]

Urban modernization in Tokyo has incurred very high costs. Repeated reconstructions of the capital have drained available resources, often at the expense of secondary cities and more peripheral regions with the intent of giving a tangible dimension to the ideals of prestige and progress pursued by the authorities. But Tokyo was not only a prosperous and bustling city, reflecting unstoppable renewal and an expression of Japanese society on the path to modernity. It was also the destination for internal migrations that highlighted the contradictions of the era. Entire neighborhoods within the city were immersed in degradation and poverty. Some writers immediately captured these realities in their works, intuiting their potential for social criticism. Although they are not canonical forms of writing and are not normally considered to be among the most representative works of Japanese literature of the period, these texts serve as important historical documents and a representation of an alternative image of the city.

The so-called *shakai rupo*, short for *shakai ruporutāju* (social reportage), became particularly widespread between the late 19th and early 20th centuries, when thousands of workers poured into the capital to contribute, directly and indirectly, to its reconstruction, often living below the poverty line. The neighborhoods where these people tended to concentrate were veritable slums. Among them, places like Shitaya and Fukagawa stood out, their cultural significance in the past sharply contrasting with their current state. The reportages were almost always the work of journalists, the most notable of whom were certainly Yokoyama Gen'nosuke (1871–1915), author of *Nihon no kasō shakai* (*Japan's lower-class society*, 1898), and above all Matsubara Iwagorō (1866–1935) with *Saiankoku no Tōkyō* (*Darkest Tokyo*, 1893), a text most likely inspired by *In Darkest England and the Way Out* (1890) by the founder of the Salvation Army, William Booth (1829–1912).

Matsubara's text is considered the main example of *rupo* in Japan.[16] It voices the author's doubts about ongoing modernization, which, from his point of view, had not succeeded in reducing the gap between social classes or eliminating the problem of poverty.[17] On the contrary, it had exacerbated them. What mattered to him was therefore to propose a different image of the new capital, in sharp contrast with the modern and absolutely positive vision promoted by the authorities.[18] On the other hand, Yokoyama's work was motivated on the whole by his determination to give visibility to people who, working anonymously and under often meager conditions, contributed substantially to the modernization of the city.[19]

In his afterword to Matsubara's book, Tsubouchi Yūzō describes it as the "masterpiece of Romanticism,"[20] an anti-canonical definition that sounds almost like an *épater le bourgeois* (middle class scandal) kind of provocation and grasps a fundamental point: in the process of appropriating foreign genres and motifs, and elaborating (and re-elaborating) indigenous tropes, one inevitably proceeds in a partial manner, and this has the effect, in the long run, of canceling altogether—or relegating to secondary or eccentric cultural expressions—representations that might otherwise spark novel insights not only into literary, but also social and political, history.

Looking at the history of cities from the perspective of marginalized groups such as immigrants, the poor, women, and so forth, is certainly a way to enhance the literary representation of otherness in a period of Japanese history characterized by an emphasis on homogenization. Searching for images of cities outside the canonical forms, questioning pillars of modern Japanese literature, such as urban settings (where urban stands mainly for Tokyo-centered), the primacy of the novel, and the Japanese language, is a way of reimagining literature itself and diversifying the picture enough to do justice to its complexity, bringing up themes that resonate with a wide audience today.

In the early Meiji period,[21] Sinitic texts lost their position of authority and were replaced by forms of writing considered more "useful," more "practical," not intended for entertainment, whose language, which was closer to everyday language, as in Western European literature, would facilitate general understanding and therefore convey a greater number of messages. Chinese influence in Japan had a long history, and, until then, Sinitic had been a fundamental component in Japanese literature. In the Meiji era, some books were still being written in Sinitic, and sometimes they sold well. They described and critiqued the real world, and people read them with pleasure; young writers were inspired by them. Topographic texts included the *hanjōki*, chronicles, or narratives, of prosperity, which recounted with biting irony the splendor (and also the decadence) of contemporary urban space.

Robert Campbell defined the representation of society in *hanjōki* as a faithful and facetious "self-portrait," which was successful from 1874 onwards due to its affinity with the work of numerous chroniclers who narrated and criticized the times by focusing on people's lives. All of this took place against the backdrop of the activities of the Freedom and People's Rights Movement.[22]

These texts are organized according to a more or less standardized thematic plan that reveals, through its variations, the most subtle nuances of social change and literary sensitivities. Study of this genre could help us reconstruct the transformations of the Japanese literary polysystem in relation to the West and Asia. *Hanjōki* have to do with "China" while being deeply rooted in a synchronic dimension, inscribed in the temporality of 19th-century Japan. But they are also timeless because they are still part of a tradition, a canon, albeit obviously unofficial.

It is a corpus of prose texts, generally considered documentary and non-fictional, even though they often present narrative insertions that constitute micro-narratives. As a corpus, they pose interesting theoretical problems, especially regarding language, genre, and reception.

If *hanjōki* sold so well,[23] therefore enjoying such wide readership, to the point that several modern writers admitted to being fans of the genre, why has their importance in the literary history of modern Japan almost always been underestimated, and why have they been treated merely as sources of information, at best as satirical texts, in a way that has minimized their literary value in spite of the sophisticated intertextual mechanisms at work in these writings and their potential influence on writers of later generations?

The main explanation is probably their failure to fall into line with the new canon of Meiji literature, which, as noted above, favored the Japanese language, the novel genre, and realistic representation—primarily meaning a depiction of the individual's supposedly true interiority. Influenced by seventeenth-century Chinese pleasure district literature,[24] conventionally thought to be the link between Tokugawa-period anecdotal narratives and the Western-inspired novel,[25] and published at a stage in Japanese cultural history when prose in literary Sinitic was highly devalued,[26] the *hanjōki* seem to defy all the major categories sustaining the discourse of Japanese literary modernity.

Being written in Sinitic, they were read mainly by *shosei*, the college students who would become the writers of the next generation. From 1872 onwards, this language was gradually abandoned in schools and newspapers, as the school system was overhauled to bring it into line with the country's new requirements, that is, to be more open to Western knowledge. The situation was therefore doubly locked: literary Sinitic was no longer the language of scholarship or literature. Certainly, there were still many people who read it—as demonstrated by the great success of some *hanjōki*—but this was leisure reading, in most cases suffused with nostalgia. In the Meiji era, literary Sinitic was not considered the language of modernity. This is the first reason for the exclusion of *hanjōki* from the "serious" canon of literature: they were not written in the dominant language.

A second reason might be that it is quite difficult to attempt a "genre" definition for *hanjōki*. In Japan, as in China, there is a long tradition of writing about space, places, and topographical texts, but the difference between these other texts and *hanjōki* is that the latter often have almost no practical use. They only briefly recount the histories of places but provide no useful information, nor do they include maps or itineraries. As Evelyn Schulz has pointed out, the narrative inserts show that the authors wanted to amuse readers rather than instruct or inform them.[27] But this is not the case for the whole of *hanjōki*, that is, texts that have the word "*hanjō*" (flourishing) in their titles. There were works about the countryside, others focused on particular neighborhoods or life abroad, even works that were structured like *hanjōki* but treated places in the manner of other topographical genres. In short, *hanjōki* were hybrid and varied texts, part fiction and part non-fiction, with illustrations and sometimes verses—texts that, in any case, were impossible to assimilate into genres perceived as "modern" at the time.

As for reception, it was "limited" to students, samurai and other categories of readers who were capable of reading literary Sinitic and understanding the intertextual play within the text, but judging by sales and circulation figures, it may be said that the vast majority of people in these categories actually read them.

To sum up, *hanjōki* were widely read, entertaining, and escapist books, so not taken seriously, but at the same time they were literary texts, which filtered the mentality of the time and literary tradition for the benefit of a very acute and lucid critical spirit toward society. They can be considered one of the "useless" forms of writing par excellence: they are not written in Japanese, they are not novels, they have a nostalgic allure, so they do not seem to carry any progressive contents. In fact, many *hanjōki* authors had an idea of progress that was simply different: they scoffed at the radical positions of advocates of Westernization and did not reject the "new" a priori, but without necessarily being backward-looking.

Texts such as *shakai ruporutāju* and *hanjōki* confront us with contradictions and question the very nature of literary modernity, whose complexity has been known for decades. They are highly effective examples of the limitations of many of the categories that have informed the field's physiognomy and have yet to be rediscussed, if not entirely deconstructed, asking ourselves what the field would be like today if mechanisms of canonization and non-canonization had operated differently. In fact, they may constitute an addition to the discourse of canon-formation described in the second part of this volume. They highlight once again the need for a re-orienting of the scholarly approach to modern Japanese literature through a trajectory that moves away from the solidity of the canon to strengthen the misalignments that emerge from a re-examination of gender, class, language, space, and more. All this urges us to question again the notions of center and periphery in their most immediate, as well as in their symbolic, meanings.

The tools of literary analysis applied to urban thought assuredly appear suitable for reading and decoding problems of such complexity, and what has been done in recent years in Japan, the United States, and Europe is certainly commendable. It is important to continue with work capable of valorizing non-canonical texts, authors, and contexts, clarifying the centrality of literary discourse in the colonial space and urban experience in the context of migrations.

The fact that academic institutions in Europe are predominantly public means that the allocation of research funds is subordinated to political priorities much more than elsewhere. In this context, literary and humanities studies in general are automatically penalized. Thus, the effort described above must not be pursued with the self-serving goal of surviving a crisis in the humanities, which seems difficult to overcome today, but with the intention of contributing to a global debate that wrestles with such issues on a daily basis, and to which modern Japanese literature could provide a number of alternative keys to interpretation. The most important of these is the invitation to temporarily abandon the certainties of canon and to reason along the lines of a continuous and systematic "What if . . . ?"

Notes

1. Munakata Kazushige, "Jānarizumu to akademizumu," *A New History of Japanese "Letterature" Vol. 3: The Path from "Letters" to "Literature": A Comparative History of East Asian Literatures*, edited by Kōno Kimiko, Wiebke Denecke, Shinkawa Tokio, and Jinno Hidenori (Benseisha, 2019), 364–65.

2. David L. Howell, *Geographies of Identity in Nineteenth-Century Japan* (University of California Press, 2005); Yoshida Nobuyuki, *Kinsei toshi shakai no mibun kōzō* (University of Tokyo Press, 1998).

3. Takashi Fujitani, *Splendid Monarchy: Power and Pageantry in Modern Japan* (University of California Press, 1996), 38.

4. Maeda Ai, *Text and the City: Essays on Japanese Modernity*, edited and with an introduction by James Fujii (Duke University Press, 2004).

5. Jinnai Hidenobu, *Tokyo: A Spatial Anthropology*, translated by Kimiko Nishimura (University of California Press, 1995).

6. The Edo-Tokyo transition, and the assessment of Edo's "modernity" is also part of French cultural geographer (and Watsuji Tetsurō's scholar) Augustin Berque's work from the late 1970s. See, in particular, his *Japan: Cities and Social Bonds*, trans. by Christopher Turner (Pilkington Press, 1997).

7. See, for instance, Paul Waley, "Following the flow of Japan's river culture," *Japan Forum* 12, no. 2 (2000): 199–217; Waley, "On the Far Bank of the River: Places of Recreation on the Periphery of the Pre-modern Japanese City," *Ecumene* 3, no. 4 (1996): 384–407.

8. *Japanese Capitals in Historical Perspective: Place, Power and Memory in Kyoto, Edo and Tokyo*, edited by Nicolas Fiévé and Paul Waley (Routledge, 2003).

9. Stephen Dodd, *Writing Home: Representations of the Native Place in Modern Japanese Literature* (Harvard University Asia Center, 2004).

10. *Urban Spaces in Japan: Cultural and Social Perspectives*, edited by Christoph Brumann and Evelyn Schulz (Routledge, 2012).

11. Evelyn Schulz, *Nagai Kafū: "Tagebuch eines Heimgekehrten"—Der Entwurf ästhetischer Gegenwelten als Kritik an der Modernisierung Japans* (LIT, 1997); Schulz, *Stadt-Diskurse in den "Aufzeichnungen über das Prosperieren von Tōkyō" (Tōkyō hanjō ki): Eine Gattung der topografischen Literatur Japans und ihre Bilder von Tōkyō (1832–1958)* (Iudicium, 2004); *Tokyo: Memory, Imagination, and the City*, edited by Barbara E. Thornbury and Evelyn Schulz (Lexington Books, 2018).

12. Richard L. Stein, "Recent Work in Victorian Urban Studies," *Victorian Studies* 45, no. 2 (2003): 320.

13. Michael P. Cronin, *Osaka Modern: The City in the Japanese Imaginary* (Harvard East Asian Monographs, 2017).

14. Although it is not focused on literary representation of urban space, Louise Young's 2013 monograph on Japan's secondary cities in the interwar period is worth mentioning here. Louise Young, *Beyond the Metropolis: Second Cities and Modern Life in Interwar Japan* (University of California Press, 2013).

15. Also in his translation of Liu Jianhui's work on Shanghai, *Demon Capital Shanghai: The "Modern" Experience of Japanese Intellectuals* (Merwin Asia, 2012).

16. Kida Jun'ichirō, *Tōkyō no kasō shakai* (Chikuma shobō, 2015), 11.

17. Maeda, *Text and the City*, 45–48.

18. Tsubouchi Yūzō, "Meijiki romanha bungaku no kessaku." *Saiankoku no Tōkyō*, edited by Matsubara Iwagorō (Kōdansha, 2015), 159.

19. James L. Huffman, *Down and Out in Late Meiji Japan* (University of Hawai'i Press, 2018).

20. Tsubouchi, "Meijiki romanha bungaku no kessaku," 159.

21. See also Fraleigh's chapter on modern Japanese literature and Sinitic in this volume.

22. Robert Campbell, "Ginza bungei no hyakunen (2)," *Bungaku* 16, no. 3 (2015): 217–18; Campbell, "Kaisetsu: shudaika suru toshi kūkan," *Tōkyō hyakunen monogatari: 1. 1868–1909*, edited by Robert Campbell, Toeda Hirokazu, and Munakata Kazushige (Iwanami, 2018), 315–19.

23. It is estimated that the main *hanjōki* of the Meiji era, *Tokyo shin hanjōki* (A new record of flourishing Tokyo, 1874–1876), written by Hattori Bushō (1842–1908), sold between ten and fifteen thousand copies. Miki Aika, *Hattori Bushō den*, in vol. 4 of *Meiji bungaku zenshū* (Chikuma shobō, 1969), 401–2.

24. Emanuel Pastreich, "The Pleasure Quarters of Edo and Nanjing as Metaphor: The Records of Yu Huai and Narushima Ryūhoku," *Monumenta Nipponica* 55, no. 2 (2000): 200.

25. Fukuda Naoto, "Hanjōki," in vol. 4 of *Nihon kindai bungaku daijiten* (Kōdansha, 1978), 431.

26. Okitsu Kaname, *Meiji kaikaki bungaku no kenkyū* (Ōfūsha, 1973), 128.

27. Evelyn Schulz, *Stadt-Diskurse in den "Aufzeichnungen über das Prosperieren von Tōkyō" (Tōkyō hanjō ki)*, 76–77.

Bibliography

Berque, Augustin. *Japan: Cities and Social Bonds*, trans. by Christopher Turner. Pilkington Press, 1997.

Brumann, Christoph, and Evelyn Schulz, eds. *Urban Spaces in Japan: Cultural and Social Perspectives*. Routledge, 2012.

Campbell, Robert. "Ginza bungei no hyakunen (2)," *Bungaku* 16, no. 3 (2015): 217–18.

Campbell, Robert. "Kaisetsu: shudaika suru toshi kūkan." In *Tōkyō hyakunen monogatari: 1. 1868–1909*, edited by Robert Campbell, Toeda Hirokazu, and Munakata Kazushige, 315–19. Iwanami, 2018.

Cronin, Michael P. *Osaka Modern: The City in the Japanese Imaginary.* Harvard East Asian Monographs, 2017.

Dodd, Stephen. *Writing Home: Representations of the Native Place in Modern Japanese Literature.* Harvard University Asia Center, 2004.

Fiévé, Nicolas, and Paul Waley, eds. *Japanese Capitals in Historical Perspective: Place, Power and Memory in Kyoto, Edo and Tokyo.* Routledge, 2003.

Fogel, Joshua, trans. *Demon Capital Shanghai: The "Modern" Experience of Japanese Intellectuals, by Liu Jianhui.* Merwin Asia, 2012.

Fujitani, Takashi. *Splendid Monarchy: Power and Pageantry in Modern Japan.* University of California Press, 1996.

Fukuda, Kiyoto. "Hanjōki," in vol. 4 of *Nihon kindai bungaku daijiten.* Kōdansha, 1978.

Howell, David L. *Geographies of Identity in Nineteenth-Century Japan.* University of California Press, 2005.

Huffman, James L. *Down and Out in Late Meiji Japan.* University of Hawai'i Press, 2018.

Jinnai, Hidenobu. *Tokyo: A Spatial Anthropology*, translated by Kimiko Nishimura. University of California Press, 1995.

Kida, Jun'ichirō. *Tōkyō no kasō shakai.* Chikuma shobō, 2015.

Maeda, Ai. *Text and the City: Essays on Japanese Modernity*, edited and with an introduction by James Fujii. Duke University Press, 2004.

Miki, Aika. *Hattori Bushō den: Meiji bungaku zenshū, vol. 4.* Chikuma shobō, 1969.

Munakata Kazushige, "Jānarizumu to akademizumu." In *A New History of Japanese "Letterature" Vol. 3: The Path from "Letters" to "Literature": A Comparative History of East Asian Literatures*, edited by Kōno Kimiko, Wiebke Denecke, Shinkawa Tokio, and Jinno Hidenori, 364–65. Benseisha, 2019.

Okitsu, Kaname. *Meiji kaikaki bungaku no kenkyū.* Ōfūsha, 1973.

Pastreich, Emanuel. "The Pleasure Quarters of Edo and Nanjing as Metaphor: The Records of Yu Huai and Narushima Ryūhoku." *Monumenta Nipponica* 55, no. 2 (2000): 200.

Schulz, Evelyn. *Nagai Kafū: "Tagebuch eines Heimgekehrten"—Der Entwurf ästhetischer Gegenwelten als Kritik an der Modernisierung Japans.* LIT, 1997.

Schulz, Evelyn. *Stadt-Diskurse in den "Aufzeichnungen über das Prosperieren von Tōkyō" (Tōkyō hanjō ki): Eine Gattung der topografischen Literatur Japans und ihre Bilder von Tōkyō (1832–1958).* Iudicium, 2004.

Stein, Richard L. "Recent Work in Victorian Urban Studies." *Victorian Studies* 45, no. 2 (2003): 320.

Thornbury, Barbara E., and Evelyn Schulz, eds. *Tokyo: Memory, Imagination, and the City*. Lexington Books, 2018.

Tsubouchi, Yūzō. "Meijiki romanha bungaku no kessaku." In *Saiankoku no Tōkyō*, edited by Matsubara Iwagorō. Kōdansha, 2015.

Waley, Paul. "Following the Flow of Japan's River Culture." *Japan Forum* 12, no. 2 (2000): 199–217.

Waley, Paul. "On the Far Bank of the River: Places of Recreation on the Periphery of the Pre-modern Japanese City." *Ecumene* 3, no. 4 (1996): 384–407.

Yoshida Nobuyuki, *Kinsei toshi shakai no mibun kōzō*. University of Tokyo Press, 1998.

CHAPTER 13

The Problem of Scale in Japanese Literary Studies

John Whittier Treat

"Fiction, music, manga, TV, they've all hit some kind of a wall," says a young cosplaying Akihabara habitué plotting "fun revenge" upon a "placid Japan" in Ishida Ira's novel, *Akihabara@DEEP*. "Culture's no different than the economy, really. Things were more robust when people believed tomorrow was going to be better than today." "The future of Japanese culture," adds a fellow co-conspirator, "is pathetic" (260, 306, 331).

This familiar end-times discourse appears in a successful work of fiction, subsequently an even more successful manga and television series. Its profitable trajectory points to the reflexive irony in this lament of decline. That these *otaku* bemoan a cultural crisis they then disprove is a part of the conceit. Or rather: their lament is the routine preface with which much culture in Japan today introduces itself, not so much as an apology as a premise: Japan is dead, long live Japan. This rhetoric of crisis has been our companion for over a century, and it is ahistorical to ascribe it to anything specifically present-day.

So where is Japanese literature now? Statistics from 2015 estimate that Japan's high school girls use their cell phones an average of seven hours a day (Yamada 2015), and those phones receive *keitai shōsetsu* "cell phone novels." The cell phone may have replaced much in Japan, but not reading fiction. Young people are hardly the alliterate (*katsuji-banare*) generation they are decried to be. More internet blogs are written in Japanese than any other language. Everyone can be a *sakka* "published writer" now, if only on a homepage. The author isn't dead; she is everywhere.

But the "end of literature" is still the *cris de coeur* of many in Japan. The end of literature, unlike the end of the world, is never a prediction. It is an assertion. Talk of the demise of literature in Japan typically cites fewer readers and sales; a decline in social prestige; the loss of political engagement; the abandonment of realism; disinterest in moral or ethical questions; and the turn away from subjective interiority. Interestingly, these are lamented subtractions from, rather than unwelcome additions to, literature. They say nothing about what remains behind, or takes its place. Whatever it is, the bookstores are full of it.

Japanese literary studies, like Japanese literature, is also said to be in crisis today. It is and it isn't. There is the crisis of the humanities writ large and then our reduced presence in it. Those of us who translate, teach and research Japanese literature, a subaltern profession not only within the academy but within a social sciences-dominated Asian studies, find ourselves reacting to changes in the intellectual and pedagogic terrain we are not responsible for but which we have to address. If contemporary writing in Japan today strikes readers as lacking, it is not because it is unchallenged by post-post-industrial capitalism, demographics or Fukushima. It may be so because of how it responds to those challenges by depicting alienation. How is the field of Japanese literary studies to make sense of this? We haven't done a bang-up job, and at the end of this essay I suggest how we might do better. But we need to get one thing out of the way right now. Yes, the prestige of the humanities has declined, and within them the value of literary studies has declined as well. During the Great Recession we saw our institutions draw their wagons in an Occidental circle that excluded even a then-fashionable China. Threatened by declining enrollments, we are encouraged to entertain our students rather than edify them. We all feel pressure one way or another: if not from our chairs, than from the fewer receptive journals and book publishers, or the fewer grant dollars to chase after. At the same time, terrified over job and tenure prospects, junior colleagues are risk-adverse in their scholarship. The bewailed state of contemporary Japanese writing risks making us, as Seth Jacobowitz quipped, today's Sovietologists. Younger professors of Japanese literature endeavor to be "relevant," and it is often painful to watch. As Edwin McClellan said decades ago of his graduate students, of whom I was one, if they had aspired to be relevant, they never would have gone into Japanese literature in the first place (82).

First, the field of Japanese literary studies in North America has suffered from a not-always benign neglect by Western national literature and comparative literature departments, and not just there. "You guys just write book reports, right?" said one Japan political scientist to me; and Japan historians, like their discipline, have long been thought more "reliable" than we literary folks. "[T]he conventional wisdom," writes David Wang in his literary history of modern China, "favors history as more reliable than literature" (7). "Reliable" is a curious word. It does not mean "empirical." It means *us*. We defend ourselves, of course. Many Japan political scientists often write simply bad journalism, and more than a few Japan anthropologists have abandoned fieldwork for the rhetorical question whether "Japan" is still a coherent object of study. For those of us in Japanese literature, times can still be good. Just as postwar Britain declined as a world power and grew more renowned for its contemporary culture, post-Bubble Japan is home to remarkable new writers, artists, and composers. In addition, our field is not dominated by any one theory, any one university, or any one set of *genrō* senior scholars. And, as reminded by Steve Ridgely, "The intimacy and intelligence of a literary text is simply unmatched as a research object" (personal communication). But we are asked to do more than that now. As English departments were methodologically flummoxed once the whole world became its purview (what is referred to as Big-Tent English), those of us in Japanese literature were let loose in a big new playground as Cultural Studies encouraged us to talk about everything in Japan. What to say in the face of such liberties became the overriding issue.

In Japan, the 1980s' love affair with postmodernism in hindsight looks like a restaging of the "Overcoming the Modern" debates of the 1940s, and by the 1990s criticism was somewhat tired with itself as a result. Some critics in Japan, such as Karatani Kōjin and his "world history" project, have returned to attempting grand narratives and invite familiar criticisms in doing so. Frankly, as long as we are "post-" anything, I doubt we are talking about the present rather than the past. For these reasons, literary studies in Japan can look cynical. But there's good news, too—many fine critical biographies of canonical writers, a second Nobel Prize and the prospect of a third, the entry of anthropological theory into literary criticism, and useful controversies sparked by historical revisionisms on the left and the right. Outside Japan, younger people have better Japanese than ever, the result of advances in Japanese language pedagogy. Our Japanese colleagues are evermore fluent in English and read and respond to our work. Cheaper airfares and digital technology mean we are in closer contact than ever. Thematically, if "Japanese nation formation remains a perennial issue in scholarship," notes Brian Dowdle, "greater attention is being given to centrifugal alternative communities," which include writings by Okinawans, Resident Koreans and the Japanese diaspora (personal communication). We are free to expand the canon, whereas our forebears in the 1950s and 1960s labored hard just to prove that the Japanese had one. New scholarship pushes the boundaries of what we can talk about and be taken seriously. But the radical gesture of roaming into new pastures means the archive is now potentially infinite.

This is an issue for us. If we are responsible for film, media and popular culture, even literature around the world written by the diaspora, how do we *manage* all this? And older troubles remain. Deans and provosts are always looking for ways to trim budgets, and so our assigned portfolios grow. Our antagonists are not only our overseers in the imperial languages of Europe. "What you guys do, culture," one Japan economist said to me, "will eventually be explained by social science." He had a point unless we have a nuanced and cogent definition of "culture," and often we do not. In its day, Cultural Studies held great promise. I wrote over twenty years ago that "cultural studies is inspired by the common consensus today that popular culture is no longer—if it ever was—limited to the catalogue of baser forms of entertainment or other leisure activities enjoyed by the working classes, but is some convenient shorthand for the myriad ways in which modern people experience what makes them 'modern' or even 'people'" (6). But I did not anticipate that Cultural Studies would collapse into a reified popular culture studies. Little did I know that it would be high culture, and non-commodified mass culture, that needs defending today. Norma Field writes that the release of Japanese literary studies "into cultural studies may be so transformational as to signify its evaporation as object of study" (268).

She was wise to be vague about this transformation. In my view, it has not worked out well. I am asked to referee submissions to journals that routinely do the following: Here is Text A, and it is about social/cultural Trend B, so now let me tell you what I know about Trend B. Sometimes the essay is good, but often it is amateurishly anecdotal in its attempt to uncover sociological or historical insights with little real grasp of the methods needed to do so. The shift of Cultural Studies into "pop cult" amusement classes for undergrad science majors wouldn't be so bad, if it weren't for the fact that "pop culture" is largely configured as only the highly capitalized, highly commodified parts of it. Anime and manga, easily imported to wherever we are, are deployed to stand in for the whole of pedagogic object "Japan." We now spend a lot of time on the internet, and we've been alerted to the consequences. Okuma Eiji warns that "Because of the expansion of the international academic market, it is possible to ignore Japanese studies in Japan, as long as you reference texts recognized in English-speaking countries and write to target the discussions in those regions" (29). If the entry of Rational Choice into social science no longer incites the distress it once did, it is because it is now so omnipresent as to have passed into common sense. One social scientist said to a colleague of mine, "We don't need to know the Japanese language anymore, all the good research is in English." I can guarantee you that at the start of that good research, someone knew Japanese, and knew it well.

In the absence of a Big Idea, such as the recycled critique of Modernization Theory that had little relevance to Japanese literary studies in the first place, we are free of any single imperative to address. This is a boon. But on the other hand, what we have done is move into a "historicist/contextualist paradigm" that Joseph North says has turned literary works into things "chiefly of interest as diagnostic instruments for determining the state of cultures" (1). What North, an Americanist, may not register is that the Orientalist imperative of our discipline has always instrumentalized literary texts to "explain Japan." North usefully points out that approaches to the literary that map out its complicity with imperialism, racism, sexism, functionalism or whatever, is at the same time a "depoliticizing retreat to cultural analysis as a result of neoliberal forces in the economic and political sphere" (18). Neoliberalism, concludes David Harvey in summary, "seeks to bring all human action into the domain of the market" (7), and I will touch upon that later. But first I would like to discuss four trends in North American Japanese literary studies that are already here.

World Literature in a Parochial Academy

Chronically late to the party, we in Japanese have a sadomasochistic relationship with new trends in literary studies. Perhaps we are in an interregnum, which is why so much is "post-" whatever. It is clear the field is looking for something new to do, especially since it's a game of catch-up for us to be, as McClellan diagnosed, "relevant."

Some of the best news for our field has been the advent of many young, talented translators and newer presses and journals to publish their work. Jeffrey Angles's English rendering of Orikuchi Shinobu's *The Book of the Dead* won the MLA's Scaglione Prize for literary translation, a first for any Japanese translator. Still, there is a score to settle. "Translation, like criticism," writes Pascale Casanova in *The World Republic of Letters*, "is a process of establishing value" (23), but only if those translations are into major European languages, above all English; "For a young Korean poet to be translated into Tagalog and acclaimed in Manila is, no doubt, a matter of satisfaction," notes Stephen Owen. "[B]ut it has less cachet than to be translated into English or French and invited to New York or Paris" (533).

Translation has other effects: it is a process of appropriation. When Casanova writes "the importation of literary texts written in 'small' languages or ones belonging to the neglected literatures serves as a means of annexation of diverting peripheral works and adding them to the stock of central resources" (135), we should remember Cecil Rhodes's boast that, his work done in Africa, he would annex the planets if he could. Every Japanese text rendered into English becomes part of the English language's global archive. I do not simply mean that Kawabata and Tanizaki can be taught in the English department; I mean that translated texts are part of the globalized way literary objects are created, not merely circulated. The translator is no adjunct in the literary industry, if she ever was; she is as embedded in the business as the author, the editor, the reader and the critic. The example closest at hand is Murakami Haruki, translator and author rolled into one, and for a good reason. As Stephen Snyder sees it, "Murakami's work begins and ends in translation. He creates fictions that are both translatable and embody translation in their themes and methods" (138). We are not talking about anything new—something similar could be said about Mishima—but more developed. Murakami's ambition, as he translates Raymond Carver and Tim O'Brien, is to be translated into every language himself and move globally like neoliberal capital: mobile, protean, everywhere.

After the twin entry of Cultural Studies and New Historicism into literary studies opened the field of inquiry to anything we nominate as "cultural" or "historical," we faced a hurdle. "The notion of culture as text has a further attraction," writes Stephen Greenblatt and Catherine Gallagher, "it vastly expands the range of objects available to be read and interpreted" (Kopec 330), expanding the field of literary studies synchronically; and Fredric Jameson, when he ordered us to "Always historicize!" expanded it diachronically. Suddenly there was a great deal on our plate, and we saw the downside. How to juggle it all? That, coupled with dwindling enrollments in demoralized English departments on the lookout for new grist for their mill, resuscitated World Literature to solve our woes. It is the monolingual accounting of everything. Once Albanian, Tamil, Quechan, and Japanese works are available in English, they can be added to the syllabus for exotic color—let's see what you *other guys* have done with what we in Europe invented, the modern novel. "All works cease to be the exclusive products of their original culture once they are translated," writes David Damrosch, "all become works that only 'began' in their original language" (527).

Original here has a specific meaning, namely literary works written in what Pascale Casanova called the "small languages" but what Owen nails as "the wrong languages"—including, he adds, the world's most popular, Chinese (524). That World Literature loves to invoke the Sinitic as Exotic, does not mean it receives favorable terms. Franco Moretti is frank when he tells us the European novel is "a perpetual motion machine" "that renews itself each time it enters new geopolitical territory," a comment that is meant for predatory English and comparative literature departments, but suits capitalism as well (Armstrong and Montag 617).

So World Literature turns out to be works written in the wrong languages. How to teach them? Damrosch asks. "[N]on-Western literary works have often been excluded from world literature courses on the grounds that they are too difficult to understand and absorb *in the time available*" (my italics) (523). Too difficult for whom, and in whose time? I do not recall *The Rape of the Lock* excluded from the syllabus of my undergraduate English lit course, because English professors are supposed to know this stuff, and students were expected to devote whatever time and labor was required to acquire that knowledge. But Japan? A bridge too far. "Bad enough that there are many more works of literature than anyone can read; must we really learn about their cultures too?" (Damrosch 514). Well, what if the answer is yes?

World Literature is not short of critics. Jameson once called World Literature "an antiquated and unserviceable notion" that gives rise to such silly questions as "Which is more universal, *I Promessi Sposi*, or *Red Chamber Dream* [sic]?" (North 180). Both in English translation, of course: the practice of World Literature, already skimpy on the discussion of actual literary works, has examples such as Damrosch's attempt to analyze Bei Dao devolved into a comparison of his English translations, because Bei's Chinese is "unavailable" to him. Comparative literature's ACLA 2017 state of the discipline report did little more than put World Literature on trial. Thomas O. Beebee dismissed "the idea of a 'global literary theory' that reflects nothing more than the rest of the world's ability to mimic the language of 'Western' theory" (67). I am less interested in the suspect theoretical underpinnings of World Literature than in its real-world consequences for our field. One recent PhD in our field, Steve Poland, put it this way: "It continues to appear that 'World XYZ' in the Humanities is a strategy for disciplining labor, not any kind of scholarly approach, framework, or method" (personal communication). One can understand the hyperbole here of a young scholar who devoted his twenties to Japanese literature and now finds it on the precipice of being deeded to the English department. "When we read the *Genji* as world literature," says David Damrosch, who frankly has no other choice, "we are fundamentally translating it out of its home culture and into a new broader context" (529). There is no clearer case of making a virtue out of a vice.

Digital Humanities: Counting on One Hand, The Other Tied Behind Your Back

What unites World Literature with interest in Digital Humanities is this problem of scale. Nation-state Japan is too small for some things, too big for others. World Literature and the Digital Humanities are in part responses, once distinct but now overlapping, to the crisis in higher education (systemic defunding, fewer students, and a recession in tenure-track hiring). They share the expanded archive literary studies is now entrusted with: Big Data. The periphery is nowhere in sight: film, media, the postcolonial, the queer, the Anthropocene, animals, monsters. Around the start of the millennium Franco Moretti proposed replacing close reading with "text-mining." What he proposed is a return to the sociology of literature, except that this time, it will be *all* literature. We need a bigger boat.

Cue the computational turn, one of many, but this one generously funded. It is voguish in literary studies because the imperative for evermore "distant reading" finally requires something that can handle more information than any one person can. Computation has come a long way, but the problem remains: a computer can only search what data it is fed it by humans, and its results are subject to amendment by those same humans. Digital Humanities reduce the process of reading from a higher-level functioning position of interpretation and evaluation to a lower-level function of identification and description. It is, as one of my colleagues put it, using a computer to finger-paint. At best, it introduces empty formalization; but it does make us, if you can bear the irony, more "reliable."

At the same time Digital Humanities preserve human intentionality and interpretation via the programming and implementation of its reading algorithms. "Algorithm" has now attained the status of a charmed rhetorical figure in literary studies. There is something magical in its attributed power to not only handle Big Data but to say something objectively true about it, as if the sciences haven't waged war on objectivity for over a century. DH is yet another utopian pursuit, never long absent, to apprehend the universal. And there is no doubt that DH's popularity among many graduate students is a way of hedging their bets—if not a job in a university, then maybe in one of those Valleys. It is also a way for humanities departments to come to the attention of administrations looking to strengthen and extend STEM. But at what cost? We know what advances computational technology brought a field such as molecular biology, but what about the Japanese *shi-shōsetsu*? What does the reduction of reading to collation and differentiation of data have in store for us?

Hoyt Long, a scholar in modern Japanese literature studies, and his colleague Richard Jean So's 2016 essay, "Literary Pattern Recognition: Modernism between Close Reading and Machine Learning," aims to "synthesize familiar humanistic approaches with computational ones" (235). This is another vice made virtue because their effort to enumerate how many English poems in the Modernist archive are *haiku* fails to do so relying exclusively on computational methods, which was perhaps their ambition. Putting aside the question whether "English haiku" is already oxymoronic, like all the forms Stephen Owen wryly calls "modern classical poetry," just why such an accurate accounting would matter, beyond the already known fact that they are "many," is never explained.

Long and So begin by positing three methods, two traditional and one new, for undertaking their task. One is close reading, another New Modernist Studies historicism, and the third computational methods ("machine learning") (237). Haiku, they begin, are short, feature images rather than narrative, and draw these images from nature. "How did we arrive at these criteria?" they ask; "In part by intuition," using a word that will resurface in their essay whenever subjectivity is required (239). Intuition is the basis of their algorithm, which is necessary because checking every Modernist verse for these elements of style "becomes a highly unwieldy method" because there are just too many poems to read (241).

Enter the machine to the rescue, and its potential to undertake simultaneously categorization, representation, learning, and classification. But even so, Long and So are unable to supply their computer with all English verse: they must choose which examples to let the machine loose on. Either self-identified, or so labeled by the poet or critic, they select 400 translations and adaptations. Why 400? Weren't there more? Was the machine's intake limited? No matter, to the 400 they applied the Naïve Bayes algorithm—requiring the purposeful inclusion of "a control case so as to verify that the Naïve Bayes algorithm was identifying textual differences *where we knew them to exist*" (italics mine) (258). Nonetheless, their algorithm still misclassified a nontrivial number of poems, begging the question, who says "misclassified"? Long and So do. "[T] ability to make . . . a clear distinction ultimately depended on the specific features we told Naïve Bayes to account for" (261). Features that Long and So consider inherent to the poem are at the same time the features they decide it must have. The project appears perilously tautological. Finally, this is hermeneutics with fancy gear, and still the human critic's final call to make. Exit the machine.

There is an important place for Digital Humanities, and it lies in pedagogy: modern technologies can deliver our literary, artistic, and musical patrimony to people beyond the classroom. But that aside, digital humanists are too often people who turn on the internet to find out what the temperature is instead of opening the window to discover it is both cold *and* raining outdoors. The presence of a "statistical pattern" seems suspiciously preordained by the intercession of human intention. Long and So's collaboration reproduce such hallmarks of post-industrialism as flexibility, teamwork, efficiency, etc.—and in doing so, dream of contributing to the compressed space and time of the global economy. In such compressed time and space, how can we read *everything*? Maybe we can't. A colleague of mine in Yale's English department has given up and gone into administration.

Queer Theory, Eco-criticism and the Stakes Between Them

Elsewhere, other things once simpler are becoming unmanageable, too. Queer Theory got its papers when Theresa de Lauretis made what she thought was a bad joke at a 1990 conference, but it was already on its way to us. Post-structuralism, second and third-wave feminism, ACT UP, Queer Nation, the longevity of psychoanalytic thinking, and backstage murmurs anticipating the trans movement today meant that the sex-gender system (a lazy hyphenation that needed to be de-coupled) was also exceeding, once more, all previous *scale*, beyond the binary and into the realm of the poly, and we needed new conceptual apparatuses to handle it. Space was cleared for this surplus by positing a radical indeterminacy of both erotic desire and gender that makes "queer" anything not monolithic. English departments again rose to the challenge, where the pejorative "queer" resonated with the long-standing celebration of the recalcitrant modern poet.

LGBT studies was the precursor to this, but it never got far. The cynical thing to say is that "studies" (Black studies, American studies, Woman studies) need office space, administrators, budgets, and I suspect our deans had had enough of this. Theory, on the other hand, is cheap—just a syllabus and the will to weave it into a class. For a theory as notoriously hostile to materialism as Queer Theory was, it seldom queried this part of its institutional welcome. And it looked promising. Queer Theory did important things for us, building on the real-world heavy lifting by groups such as

Lavender Menace and Sex Panic! alongside Queer Nation, all of which carnivalized gender and fought "to remove large stretches of sexual intimate life from [certain kinds of] institutional control" (Seidman 326). A few of its arguments added to the arsenal pioneered by LGBT studies in combatting HIV/AIDS and its stigmas, and at the same time provided a bulwark against gay people being reduced to the product of an "original trauma," the way some Jews have feared their identity as a people has been reduced to that of the Shoah.

But its moment is over. QT's intervention was summary and easily executed, at least in the world of those elite universities where we find what Baldwin scholar Matt Brim—faculty at cash-starved City University Staten Island—calls "rich queer studies." For a movement with roots in both activism and scholasticism, it has remained true to the latter, but with a curious afterlife in popular culture. In the way folks talk today, to announce oneself as "queer," as one might say "goth" or "nerd," is no more than protesting you are not *normal*. If you visit an urban high school, you will notice that what the queer kids perform resembles naive minstrelsy. Who among us wants to think he or she is normal, anyway? "Queerness can never define an identity," Lee Edelman writes in his influential if incoherent *No Future: Queer Theory and the Death Drive*, "it can only ever disturb one" (17). The term is politically useless or worse; it re-installs norms, social and analytical, and I would add, political. Japanese literary studies contributed good work to Queer Theory—no surprise there, given how many of us in the field are out homosexuals. Keith Vincent has made some of the clearest, succinct explanations of the "queer" in Queer Theory as anyone has; and as Jonathan M. Hall says, there is "ample reason to resist the disposing of Queer Theory as yet a further addition to the dust heap of scholarly fashions cycled through Japan studies" (205). At the same time, few tenets of Queer Theory applied to Japanese literature have passed my two smell tests: congruency with my lived experience as a homosexual in Japan and elsewhere, and consistency with my scholarly knowledge of the same.

Queer Theory in our field faces the usual critiques plus a few others. QT's inattention to issues of class have been pointed out by Brim and others, and replicates itself in the application of the theory to Japan in similar measure. The back streets of Harajuku get attention from us, but the back streets of working class Ueno less so. The problem Queer Theory has within Japanese studies is that Japan and its sexual practices have largely been more invented in the West than observed, and the anti-empirical bias of Queer Theory does little to amend the Orientalist take on geisha, kabuki actors, and *new half*. Add to that the failure of psychoanalytical criticism to "suture" well in Japanese literary studies overall. Moreover, Queer Theory's close cleavage with the psychoanalytical has made it ahistorical in its approach. It even boasts of freeing "queer scholarship from the tyranny of historicism." Its "unhistoricism," as Valerie Traub and others have called it out for (21), includes a rejection of the notion of "futurity," which is surely part of rightful historicism as well. Queer Studies by definition demands to be unhistorical, because any move to periodize is to assign an "identity" to a chronological span, and that rubs against the grain of a radically anti-identity movement. Queer Theory's debt to Foucault led it astray from the investigation of the gay subject: in critiquing a more or less stable homosexual identity, Queer Theory jettisoned subjectivity just when we needed it. It is similarly scarce on the ground with what matters most to many, ethical analysis of the social. QT's aforementioned contribution to the HIV/AIDS epidemic could have been much more, had it not dismissed gay *people* precisely when we needed to reach out to people at risk. When ACT UP invaded the New York Stock Exchange—to lower, not protest, drug prices—they weren't looking to *Gender Trouble* or *Epistemology of the Closet* for instructions.

Queer Theory's exploitation of the psychoanalytic, with its insistence that abjection is psychic rather than rooted in any collective social judgment against us, means that in practice Queer Theory had little to say about texts by openly gay writers, be she *Rubyfruit Jungle*'s Rita Mae Brown, *The Sexual Outlaw*'s John Rechy or *Confessions of a Mask*'s Mishima Yukio. Instead, Queer Theory takes its syllabus to the psychiatrist's couch and must "disclose" or "reveal" that the heterosexualist text is, surprise, queer. Keith Vincent is explicit about this, when he writes: "[The] queer reader does not read a text because it has a certain kind of people in it. . . . Indeed, he or she is just as interested in texts populated exclusively by ostensibly 'straight' people" (69–70). His scare quotes about "straight" are there because there are none—we have an *unconscious*, and it must be queer. By re-reading canonical texts in the light of a new critical prism, QT conforms to how the most orthodox literary criticism works nowadays, and is no way radical.

No counter-critique of QT easily makes a dent: as David Halperin has put it, you cannot argue with Queer Theory's "highly developed psychoanalytical wing" because every refutation is dismissed as repression ("Homosexuality's Closet" 38). Gay authors who write gay literature have told me they consider Queer Theory useless to them. The obligatory unconscious must be at work in, say, a Natsume Sōseki novel, for Queer Theory to be interested, and if it is not, psychoanalytical criticism is beside the point and QT is *not* interested. "Is it possible," Halperin asks in a book intended "to put us on guard against a stealth 'return of the normal' within psychoanalytical criticism," "to understand the workings of gay male subjectivity, including its transgressive impulses and our political resistance to them, without recourse to psychoanalysis," currently "the only critical show in homo-town" (*What Do Gay Men Want?* 97, 56, 98)? Yes. One exception Halperin cites is D. A. Miller, whose work "locates psychic life in the social rather than in the personal ("Homosexuality's Closet" 45). I regret that Miller's and Halperin's interest in Japan has come late in their careers, because we need them.

Queer Theory normalizes the world; it does not reform it. I do not believe every critical practice has to have changing the world as its aim, but I do object to Queer Theory's regular insistence that it does when it doesn't. From the point of view of feminist philosopher Martha Nussbaum, Queer Theory has to appear "decadent," as she put it in her well-known takedown of Judith Butler. It is open to charges of an ineffective formalism or an aporetic, ontological reduction that occurs whenever "queer" is abstracted and dehistoricized. "[T]he AIDS pandemic is essentially without origin," wrote Japan historian William Haver years ago, "essentially that being-without-origin that wounding *is*" (40). I disagree—it has an origin, you can see it under a microscope, but Haver's obtuse philosophizing is in keeping with the rhetorical flourishes of Queer Theory. "It is little comfort to persons in the late stages of AIDS to know that sight is a discursive construct," writes disability scholar Michael Davidson, "or that disease is the relatively recent product of a panoptical imperative" (166). Paula Treichler spoke of an "epidemic of discourse," Lee Edelman of "the plague of discourse." They are not wrong but not quite right, either. The real epidemic and the real plague were never discourse, it was and is a virus that Queer Theory, unlike medical research and the efforts of public health, left in place as a fetish when it spoke of it at all. One might, if pressed, blame Foucault: the "political" problem with him is that his analyses of power were "normatively neutral" and the deployment of work after his death served to undermine the potential ground for identification of status that injustice, and justice, require. How, in the end, do queers resist unwelcome domination? And once everything's been "queered" and "queered" again, as QT insists it must, how much has materially changed? ACT UP's direct actions undeniably prolonged lives, but did queer fanzines? "The lasting legacy" of Queer Theory, concludes Yasmin Nair, "is to assume that the mere presence of queer people creates a magical insurgency" (16). Under the very nose of Queer Theory and its colloquia, Nair has pointed out, what has really changed our lives, and not for the better, has been the spread of Homonationalism and its normalizing agenda for sexual minorities—first in the US, and now in Japan, where questions of citizenship and other social enfranchisement are being posed against a neonationalist background.

I return to the problem with which new immensities have confronted literary studies. No scale has been so enormous, and such a challenge to literary studies, as global climate change and species extinction. Philosopher Timothy Morton had to coin a new word, "hyperobject," to "refer to things that are massively distributed in time and space relative to humans," and they "are directly responsible" for what he calls "*the end of the world*" (*Hyperobjects*, 1, 2). Global warming is one of them. Raymond Williams, armed with his critique of "enclosed fictions," might have been the first Eco-critic—how could a materialist be anything else?—but since the early nineteen-nineties others have joined him. "Let us be clear about our situation," says Roy Scranton, "We live in the early stages of a global ecological collapse . . . None of this shit will last" (*Narrative in the Anthropocene is the Enemy*). The twentieth century, which once looked to some as if it would be around for good, has turned out not to be. It is common to hear the opinion that questions of art, and narrative overall, are "marginal to the main task of tracing and identifying environmental issues in texts," which range from pollution, wilderness, apocalypse, dwelling, animals, earth and health. (Zapf 11, 45). But working with all things simultaneously is the greatest juggling act that criticism in and of Japanese literature is auditioning for. Unlike Digital Humanities, World Literature, or Queer Theory, there is no distillable "method," and not because conventional Eco-criticism is heavily thematic and "like patching up the void with duct tape" (Morton, *Ecology Without Nature* 140). Whichever method we devise, it now has to be grounded in the phenomenal world. Japan historian Julia Thomas has shown that we have long thrown up our hands at nature "in consternation at the concept's analytical indeterminacy" (1)—"isms" are disappointing us. Postmodernism, for instance, is on its way out. In the face of what is happening we are interested in the tangible world and less in how it may be a metaphysical or discursive byproduct. Sure, Eco-criticism is pushing us back, willy-nilly, to "grand narratives," but at the same time we now see literature in the late Anthropocene will be quite precise about things, because things will be all that matter.

"Unless we find a way of saying the unsayable," James Bradley observes in a piece called "Unearthed: Last Days of the Anthropocene," "there is no way we can begin to prepare for what lies ahead." Really? Hasn't the "representable" always had its necessary complement of the "unrepresentable," from God to the sublime to the Holocaust to Hiroshima to every sort of trauma and finally to what Amitav Ghosh calls today the "Great Derangement." What's different about *this* now? Many events, as global warming might, have turned out to be "worse than you think" (Wallace-Wells) and yet we've not only gotten used to them but found ways to embed them in our stories. Ghosh and others despair of the novel's ability to depict the "slow violence" of the ecological crisis, against which there stands a representational bias. Ghosh insists that "at exactly the time when it has become clear that global warming is in every sense a collective predicament, humanity finds itself in the thrall of a dominant culture in which the idea of the collective has been exiled from politics, economics, and literature alike" (80).

Timothy Clark says "the basic conception of most novels may at first seem ill-suited to concerns that may involve time frames far exceeding a single human life, which may deal with spatial scales of the very large or small, or with issues that do not fit traditional political polarities of left and right" (4–5). But literature has been pursuing a new real for quite some time, at least since the twentieth century's wars and civilian genocides; one might also say with Queer Theory in mind, that there is a straight line from the actuality of the AIDS virus to the actuality of the world as configured in Eco-criticism. In some ways this world lies beyond our power to intervene. "Planets," Roy Scranton has written, "do not decide to spin" ("Learning How to Die" 113). We cannot stop them and they do not need our help to continue to do so. Hurricanes do not have agency and nuclear power plants do not have subjectivity. As anti-materialist as Queer Theory was, Eco-criticism is incoherent without it.

Contemporary Japan literature is at the forefront of ecological writing. Karen Thornber, Christine Marran, Doug Slaymaker, Rachel DiNitto and others are overseas pioneers of its study. When Jay Parini listed twenty-five writers and critics he deemed central to the environmental studies boom, all were American (Nixon 234); and Amitav Ghosh's list, somewhat more catholic, was still wholly Anglophone (124–25). Here we go again, one is tempted to say, since the one greatest environment threat we face today is still nuclear weapons, a subject upon which the Japanese have had plenty to say. If Bruno Latour says that to be modern is to envision time as irreversible (Ghosh 123), then Takahashi Gen'ichirō, Tawada Yōko, Kawakami Hiromi, Furukawa Hideo and others are not quite modern, since all of them wreak havoc with the parade of history in their environmental writings. Maybe no environmental literature is exactly modern. Replacing the narrative of the modern as continual progress in one of his novels about nuclear power, *Reactors in Love* (*Koi suru genpatsu*, 2011), Takahashi proposes that "order" (*junban*) is replaceable with a casual rather than causal sequence of events: Three Mile Island, Chernobyl and Fukushima (*Koi* 213), and represent a new kind of "history" for us.

Critics such as Christine Marran have stepped back to give us the bigger picture. Her book *Ecology Without Culture* takes us from the strictly literary in its first pages: "When human culture is the primary frame of analysis, as it has been for Enlightenment modernity, it becomes difficult to address the biological, geophysical, and atmospheric aspects of our world" (4). But "our" world? Really? That already sounds anachronistic, because we have surrendered so much of it and are seeing the rest taken away. I don't think Marran really means to say "our" or maybe even "world." I have argued elsewhere that the proliferation of animals in contemporary Japanese literature may be the first step to turning the planet over to other species, and perhaps not merely in our imagination. Marran's intriguing term "obligate storytelling" not only "grants birds and animals the capacity to express" but dismisses the "epistemological question of how we can know whether a stone or an ocean speaks." In her view environmental authors such as Ishimure Michiko are good at letting "things tell stories." If, wondering aloud what literary theory there is to account for "this kind of expressive ontology," Marran timidly suggests the "New Materialism provides a narrow path in," then here's a theory to explore more closely than World Literature, Digital Humanities or Queer Theory, because it may be the last scheme we will ever need (28, 39–41).

Neoliberalist Criticism in Absentia

I conclude with a suggestion. I am not one of those who insist Anthropocene needs to be swapped out with "Capitalocene" in order to place blame where some insist it belongs—humans have been changing the planet since we tamed fire and planted crops—but I do recognize that industrial capitalism (and socialism) have accelerated the process of environmental entropy. It turns out that imperialism is not "the highest stage of capitalism." In the wake of empires' disassemblage after World War I, neoliberalism rapidly filled the void. World Literature, Digital Humanities, Queer Theory, and Eco-criticism are utopian projects in our otherwise dystopian day, four crisis discourses among many. Let me add one to the list: the variously salutary and disastrous impact of neoliberalism in our lives.

The congenialities of Digital Humanities and Queer Theory with neoliberalism are well documented, and making the same critique of the World Literature project is like shooting fish in a barrel. This is not surprising. When Wendy Brown listed the signs of neoliberalism as ranging from the "deregulation of industries and capital flows" to "the conversion of every human need or desire into a profitable enterprise, from college admissions preparation to human organ transplants," from "baby adoptions to pollution rights" to "avoiding lines to securing legroom on an airplane" (28), there is no mention of a novel, a poem, or a play. But they're there. Her things are part of the world we presumably want our contemporary fiction to reflect upon. The neoliberal project is uneven and contingent, and surprises us with unexpected new freedoms from time to time in addition to the forfeiture of others. It is naive to think our work as literary scholars is indifferent to this reshuffling. "As neoliberalism enters into crisis," challenges our Americanist Joseph North, "literary study . . . will once again be re-oriented, and alternatives will have to be found" (4).

Political economists say that Japan, like other developmental states, is late to the game of neoliberal policy-making. Again, this is true and not true. The Japanese state remained a major player in the economy well into the 1990s, but its troubles began in part because of its reluctance to regulate in the first place; and any culture called a *jōhō shakai* "information society," as Japan was by the late 1970s was already neoliberal. More recently Japan has exploited its crises, none more so than Fukushima and the Great East Japan Earthquake, to impose neoliberal policies in inviting private interests to dictate reconstruction.

When talk of neoliberalism became fashionable in the UK and the US, talk of Murakami Haruki did at the same time in Japan. He has been the perfect poster boy for neoliberalism. Breaking the guild rules imposed by the Japanese publishing industry, Murakami was the entrepreneur extraordinaire, flying to New York on his own dime to negotiate directly for space in *The New Yorker*. What Stephen Snyder, who has studied Murakami's business model, calls "the flattening and homogenizing" global literary market has served Murakami well, making his novels the literary equivalent of Cool Japan's exports of "Pokémon and anime and sushi" (134), all of which are now kitsch or sliding inexorably into it—as has Murakami himself. Tim Parks includes Murakami among his global novelists who make sure their work can circulate interlingually with ease—were he writing now, Parks says, even Shakespeare would ease up "on the puns" (28).

At first glance Murakami's novels may not seem so neoliberal. His characters are hardly as entrepreneurial as their author. They are lazy, in fact. One of them, Tsukuru Tazaki in *Colorless Tsukuru Tazaki and His Years of Pilgrimage*, has no real wants or desires; he starts his day with "a simple breakfast," irons his sheets, passes the day sitting in a café, leaving half-finished every beer he orders (244–47, 376). In 1979, when Murakami debuted, Foucault announced his new and timely definition of the neoliberalist *homo œconomicus*, who is "the subject or object of *laissez-faire*" (270): Murakami's slovenly slackers are more accurately *laissez-faire rien*. But take a look elsewhere: Murakami's characters with their psychic maladies express a crisis of freedom, something we are perhaps experiencing because freedom is only an interlude between old and new forms of subjection or coercion. Tazaki's blank life is overdetermined with pathological signs that his freedom (to do nothing) is now migrating over to new forms of compulsion—in his case, to understand his past and that of his friends.

Murakami's characters may live in their own small worlds, but they know they are small: what lies outside is unsurveyable, which returns us to the problem of scale. Things come in multiples for Murakami: the doppelgangers, the two moons, *kochiragawa* and *achiragawa*, the sets of twins, multiple personalities. One of his female characters produces too many eggs; everywhere there is surplus that, like Big Data, must be managed. His characters are nonplussed by what immenseness they stand in front of. This is not neoliberalism but its byproduct. "The neoliberal regime," writes philosopher Byung-Chul Han, "is in the course of inaugurating the age of exhaustion" (133), and this explains to us why, not coincidentally, so much contemporary American writing is concerned with "healing" and so much Japanese with *iyashi* "wellness."

It is a mistake to assert, as do some, that Japanese literature and those of us who write about it fail to confront global issues: we do whenever neoliberalism is mentioned. We use that word in writing about Japan as a fulcrum space within the territorial structure of neoliberal globalization whether we know it or not. "The original dependence of literature on the nation," writes Pascale Casanova, "is at the heart of the inequality that structures the literary world" (39). This remains true because Japan lies so far beyond the West that it barely matters, be it in terms of world politics or World Literature. But when Takahashi Gen'ichirō declares "I am the nation" (*Boku wa kokka da*) (Bungaku 184) he undercuts Casanova, because his declaration only makes sense if the words "I" and "nation" means something different than they once did. The collective entity of the nation needed the atomized "I" as its complement and its constitution. Takahashi collapses and disarms the tension that structured their meaning and usefulness. Writers in Japan from Murakami Ryū to Abe Kazushige to Yokoyama Yuta are doing new things with that "I" and its coordinate concept of nation. The epochal shift in the *raison d'être* of modern Japanese literature, the nation-state, is headed to parts unknown, but my guess is that the minimization of the nation-state in current Japanese writing is linked to the successes and failures of neoliberalism practices. The show is hardly over. As long the Japanese have been human, their tales have been part of the world, a world as varied and limited as human experience. And how we will interpret those tales? I hear the latest thing in literary studies is Thing Theory—what to do with our tools, including computers, when they malfunction and become useless to us. What is Thing Theory's method, you ask? It's not the New Materialism, or indeed anything new. Sit down for this. It's close reading.

Works Cited

Armstrong, Nancy, and Warren Montag. "'The Figure in the Carpet.'" *PMLA* 132, no. 3 (2017): 613–19.

Beebee, Thomas O. "What the World Thinks About Literature." In *Futures of Comparative Literature: ACLA State of the Discipline Report*, edited by Ursula K. Heise et al., 61–70. Routledge, 2017.

Bradley, James. "Unearthed: Last Days of the Anthropocene." *Meanjin*, Spring 2019. https://meanjin.com.au/essays/unearthed/

Brim, Matt. "Poor Queer Studies: Class, Race, and the Field." *Journal of Homosexuality* 1, no. 19 (2018): 1–19.

Brown, Wendy. *Undoing the Demos: Neoliberalism's Stealth Revolution*. Zone Books, 2015.

Casanova, Pascale. *The World Republic of Letters*. Translated by M. B. DeBevoise. Harvard University Press, 2004.

Clark, Timothy. *The Cambridge Introduction to Literature and the Environment*. Cambridge University Press, 2011.

Damrosch, David. "World Literature, National Contexts." *Modern Philology* 100, no. 4 (2003): 512–31.

Davidson, Michael. *Concerto for the Left Hand: Disability and the Defamiliar Body*. University of Michigan Press, 2008.

Dowdle, Brian. Personal communication to the author. 18 May 2017.

Edelman, Lee. *No Future: Queer Theory and the Death Drive*. Duke University Press, 2004.

Foucault, Michel. The *Birth of Biopolitics*. Translated by Graham Burchell. Palgrave Macmillan, 2010.

Ghosh, Amitav. *The Great Derangement: Climate Change and the Unthinkable*. University of Chicago Press, 2016.

Hall, Jonathan M. "Area Studies at the Bedroom Door: Queer Theory, Japan, and the Case of the Missing Fantasy." *Japanese Studies* 23, no. 2 (Sept. 2003): 205–12.

Halperin, David M. "Homosexuality's Closet." *Michigan Quarterly Review* 41, no. 1 (Winter 2002): 21–34.

Halperin, David M. *What Do Gay Men Want? An Essay on Sex, Risk, and Subjectivity*. University of Michigan Press, 2007.

Han, Byung-Chul. *Psychopolitics: Neoliberalism and New Technologies of Power*. Translated by Erik Butler. Verso, 2017.

Harvey, David. *A Brief History of Neoliberalism*. Oxford University Press, 2005.

Haver, William. "Interminable AIDS." *Topologies of Trauma: Essays on the Limit of Knowledge and Memory*. Edited by Linda Belau and Petar Ramadanovic, 33–52. Other Press, 2002.

Ishida, Ira. *Akihabara@DEEP*. Bungei shunjū, 2004.

Kopec, Andrew. "The Digital Humanities, Inc.: Literary Criticism and the Fate of a Profession." *PMLA* 131, no. 2 (2016): 324–39.

Long, Hoyt, and Richard Jean So. "Literary Pattern Recognition: Modernism between Close Reading and Machine Learning." *Critical Inquiry*, no. 42 (2016): 235–67.

Marran, Christine L. *Ecology Without Culture: Aesthetics for a Toxic World*. University of Minnesota Press, 2017.

McClellan, Edwin. "The Study of Japanese Literature in the United States." *Japanese Studies in the United States. Part I, History and the Present Condition*. The Association of Asian Studies (1988): 71–82.

Morton, Timothy. *Ecology Without Nature: Rethinking Environmental Aesthetics*. Harvard University Press, 2007.

Morton, Timothy. *Hyperobjects: Philosophy and Ecology after the End of the World*. University of Minnesota Press, 2013.

Murakami, Haruki. *Colorless Tsukuru Tazaki and His Years of Pilgrimage*. Translated by Philip Gabriel. Knopf, 2014.

Nair, Yasmin. "We Were There, We Are Here, Where Are We? Notes Toward a Study of Queer Theory in the Neoliberal University." *QED: A Journal in GLBTQ Worldmaking* 3, no. 2 (2016): 7–17.

Nixon, Rob. *Slow Violence and the Environmentalism of the Poor*. Harvard University Press, 2011.

North, Joseph. *Literary Criticism: A Concise Political History*. Harvard University Press, 2017.

Okuma, Eiji. "Studying Japan as 'the Other': A Short History of Japanese Studies and Its Future." In *Rethinking Japanese Studies: Eurocentrism and the Asia-Pacific Region*, edited by Kaori Okano and Yoshio Sugimoto, 19–31. Routledge, 2018.

Owen, Stephen. "Stepping Forward and Back: Issues and Possibilities for 'World Poetry.'" *Modern Philology* 100, no. 4 (2003): 532–48.

Parks, Tim. "The Dull New Global Novel." In *Where I'm Reading From: The Changing World of Books, 25–28*. New York Review of Books, 2015.

Poland, Stephen. Personal communication to the author. 20 May 2017. Email.

Ridgely, Steven. Personal communication to the author. 17 May 2017. Email.

Scranton, Roy. "Learning How to Die in the Anthropocene." *New York Times*, 10 Nov. 2013.

Scranton, Roy. "Narrative in the Anthropocene is the Enemy." *Literary Hub*, 18 Sept 2019. https://lithub.com/roy-scranton-narrative-in-the-anthropocene-is-the-enemy/

Seidman, Steven. "From Identity to Queer Politics: Shifts in Normative Heterosexuality and the Meaning of Citizenship." *Citizenship Studies* 5, no. 3 (2001): 321–28.

Snyder, Stephen. "Insistence and Resistance: Murakami and Mizumura in Translation." *New England Review* 37, no. 4 (2016): 133–42.

Takahashi Gen'ichirō. *Bungaku ja nai ka mo shirenai shōkōgun*. Asahi shinbunsha, 1992.

Takahashi Gen'ichirō. *Koi suru genpatsu*. Kawade shobō shinsha, 2011.

Thomas, Julia Adeney. *Reconfiguring Modernity: Concepts of Nature in Japanese Political Ideology*. University of California Press, 2001.

Traub, Valerie. "The New Unhistoricism in Queer Studies." *PMLA* 128, no. 1 (2013): 21–39.

Treat, John Whittier, ed. *Contemporary Japan and Popular Culture*. Curzon Press, 1996.
Vincent, J. Keith. "Queer Reading and Modern Japanese Literature." In *Routledge Handbook of Modern Japanese Literature*, edited by Rachael Hutchinson and Leith Morton, 69–81. Routledge, 2016.
Wallace-Wells, David. "The Uninhabitable Earth." *New York Magazine*, 10 July 2017. http://nymag.com/intelligencer/2017/07/climate-change-earth-too-hot-for-humans-annotated.html
Wang, David Der-wei, ed. *A New Literary History of Modern China*. Belknap Press of Harvard University Press, 2017.
Yamada, Kana. "Survey: High School Girls Use Mobile Phones 7 Hours Daily." *Asahi shinbun*, 10 Feb. 2015.
Zapf, Hubert. *Literature as Cultural Ecology: Sustainable Texts*. Bloomsbury, 2016.

CHAPTER 14

Signposts for the Non-Specialist

Thoughts on a Renewed View of the State of Modern Japanese Literary Studies

Christopher Lupke

Being a Chinese Studies specialist who, like most of us, teaches more broadly (and loves to do so), I have come to realize an unusual and perhaps ironic aspect to my scholarly self: it may be that in certain ways I know the field of Japanese studies better than that of Chinese studies simply because I don't have the confidence or expertise to develop my own, unmediated, grasp of the field of Japanese. For Chinese, I can read the literary works in Chinese myself, watch films, view other cultural materials on my own, and, perhaps most important, draw on my knowledge and training that has deepened with decades of work. For Japanese and Korean, although I am enamored of both places and have read a fair amount from each in English translation, I don't have the confidence to say I grasp the fields broadly or deeply. Thus, I am largely dependent on the English-language scholarship on them. It is with that fact in mind that I provide some comments on this new and exciting volume that represents the best in scholarship on modern Japanese literature and will serve as a critical tool for all scholars in Japanese studies, but perhaps most important also for the rest of us who teach East Asian humanities courses and need all the help we can get keeping up. This volume offers crucial insights to the East Asian Studies instructor in several ways: it helps frame the discussions of modern Japanese literature in terms that are of current relevance to the broader humanities; it helps the instructor contemplate modern Japanese literature in geographical terms that involve a variety of special models, including world literature, the civilizational heritage of Chinese or Sinitic literature, the impact of immigration on Japanese literature, and the impact of translation on the understanding of the literary scene, and others; finally, this volume also helps the non-expert in learning about modern Japanese literature in ways that are practically unimaginable until one delves deeply into it. When we read, far too often we take a *deductive* approach to our subject, which is to say that we often already have an idea of what we are looking for. We then go out and seek it. What many of the essays in the volume teach us is that we should shelve our preconceived notions and stay open to the possibility of new and unexpected insights. Then, we should incorporate those insights into our overall understanding of the region and its literature, sharing these insights with students and inviting them into the discovery process. So, then, how can the instructor whose expertise might primarily be in Chinese, such as me, in Korean, or in comparative or world literatures utilize this volume? This volume contains a plethora of timely interventions into Japanese studies and the study of world literature.

The volume reflects the fact that over the past few decades the intellectual landscape pertaining to East Asia in general and Japan specifically has changed dramatically. For example, as the editors note, the days of subject-object relationships with the exotic other are behind us. This can be viewed in very concrete ways. The editors observe, for example, that the work of such intellectual luminaries as Karatani Kōjin has had considerable impact on major Western theorists such as Fredric Jameson and Franco Moretti, representing a reverse in the information flow back toward the West. Indeed, a hallmark feature of this volume is not just that it signals a major shift in the matrix of area studies but that it directly confronts the area studies paradigms and offers at least six new approaches, or perhaps new topical emphases, to how Japan and Japanese literature is placed in the world, as well as how Japan as a geographical entity is featured in literature and cultural representation.

Rebecca Copeland's essay leads off this section in an admirably provocative way, detailing with courage her early career experiences trying to shift the discourse on early modern Japanese literary studies, especially pertaining to literature written by women. The perilous relationships of power dynamics that she and other women of her and previous generations encountered should be a surprise but sadly are not. In addition to the gender iniquities, her essay also illustrates that not all false ideologies of East Asian essentialism have been concocted out of a Western-centric Cold War worldview, but they have reinforced that mindset. Ultimately, Copeland's rich and detailed essay instructs us on how Japanese literary subject matter, especially written by women, can be organized in other ways than simply "how Japanese (male) writers fit into a universalist conception of human nature" or, the opposite extreme, "how Japanese writers are 'quirky'" (John Treat's term). Modern Japanese literature written by women is sufficient in volume and quality to be taught on its own and on its own terms.

In response to the Truth and Reconciliation Commission's Calls to Action in June 2015, Canada embarked on an ambitious, if horribly belated, attempt to foster respectful relations with the indigenous populations of the country and redress some of the legacy of racism perpetrated against them. Although a similar TRC is still wanting in the United States, the activities in Canada have nevertheless had some knock-on effects down south. Of course, many academics have been working on indigenous, First Nations, Métis, Inuit and Native American cultures and societies for their whole careers. Davinder Bhowmik's career devoted to work on the people of Okinawa is a case in point. We have, until recent times, thought of East Asian countries in unitary ways: *the* Chinese; *the* Japanese; *the* Koreans. But indigeneity is a phenomenon in Japan and elsewhere in East Asia that disaggregates this perceived monolith. Bhowmik's work opens up another avenue through which the study of Japan (and Japan-adjacent, as many Okinawans don't view themselves as part of Japan) can intersect with other humanities disciplines in the North American academy. Bhowmik concludes that studies of Okinawan culture offer a mixed bag with both limitations and strengths. It is difficult to say if the future is an optimistic one, since a major obstacle to further research and teaching is the insufficient number of open positions in Japanese and East Asian Studies in North America.

Bridges's work on blackness in Japanese studies as well as the racist treatment of Japanese Americans, is a further example of the extraordinary work being done in race studies with respect to Japan. In contemplating the question "do Black lives matter to Japanese literary studies," he demonstrates to the reader that for decades prominent Japanese intellectuals such as Kanagaki Rōbun, Nagai Kafū, Natsume Sōseki, Abe Tomoji, Kijima Hajime, and a host of others have been thinking about and interacting with Black intellectuals and literary figures for a long time, sometimes in highly problematic ways. "Black lives have long mattered," Bridges concludes, calling for a more prominent highlighting of Black culture and the interaction between Japanese and Black cultures that is an ongoing activity.

The latter three essays in this section highlight environmental themes and manga in geographical ways. Ecoliterature is an expression of what are fundamentally global issues, although the negative implications are usually very local. Manga and anime enjoy a cult-level fascination among youth in North America, but Adam Kern and Deborah Shamoon show in their respective ways how graphic literature is intimately intertwined with cultures worldwide and that the tendency to brand them as quintessentially or at least originally Japanese is a misconception. All of these essays help us to see that as a geographical phenomenon, Japan is far more than the object of study that an earlier era of instrumentalist national security studies might have predicated for us. The study of Japan through these works and with the interpretive assistance of this cutting-edge research tend to complicate our understanding of Japan in interesting ways rather than clarifying or simplifying that understanding.

The four middle essays in the volume privilege language, but they do so in highly specialized ways. Featuring three essays by Japanese (and Japan-based) scholars along with two from the US, including one who writes Japanese-language poetry, the essays in this section turn the tables on conventional scholarship that sees Japanese literature as sui generis, impossible to understand outside of its own context, and incommensurable with literature from other traditions, especially Western traditions. Japanese literature has never been an entirely national formation, given the fact that, as Matthew Fraleigh amply reminds us, there have been imbrications with Sinitic traditions for centuries. Yoshitaka Hibi's contribution echoes some of the scholarship of recent decades that has focused on Japanophone writing, a colonial tradition that has existed for over 100 years. Considering things from the opposite perspective, YoungRan Kō's essay explores Japanese literature written by immigrants to Japan. Nonetheless, there is indeed a crisis in Japanese studies and the humanities in general that has befallen our profession in the last two decades, a fact that is dissected and lamented very thoroughly in Jeffrey Angles's essay. Recalling a statement written over thirty years ago by Edward Fowler, Angles revives the argument that the translation of literature from languages like Japanese that get very little visibility in the West can help "soften" the image of the other, and specifically the Japanese people, by which I take him to mean that literature in translation helps assign a "face" or individuality to Japanese through the characters and situations depicted in these translated works. I cannot agree more. I did not know of Fowler's essay, but two years ago I wrote an essay on how translation could help "rescue the humanities" by providing the non-expert with direct access to the written work in all of its contradictions and idiosyncrasies. In the old days, many of these translations were funded by various generous granting agencies, some of which were part of the Cold War area studies project. But these days not only has the funding mostly dried up, but enrollments are plummeting, too, mainly because of the public divestment from education, especially the humanities. Should students plunge themselves deeply into debt in order to get a degree or perhaps only take a course or two in a field that has no promise of enhancing one's job prospects directly out of college? Neoliberal education policy has lamentably led to a dumbing down of our understanding of cultures vastly different from our own such as Japanese. I would call this a new kind of Cultural Revolution, a revolution against culture. Like the Chinese Cultural Revolution of 1966–1976, the full damage of this historical moment will not be felt or fully known for decades to come. But it will be catastrophic. The defunding of the humanities will lead to mass ignorance, misunderstanding, and possibly hostility. Despite the rather pessimistic image that Angles draws of literary translation, especially Japanese literary translation, his essay ends on an optimistic note, listing some of the ways in which the most recent era of Japanese literary studies has returned to a sort of "translation friendly" period sustained by new grants and awards that have gone to translators and/or writers and translators. He notes the visibility of Murakami Haruki in particular, a writer well known to most literary-minded people. I would add one thing to this: science fiction. I am not knowledgeable on Japanese science fiction, but Chinese science fiction has captured the attention of thousands of avid readers in the West, readers who otherwise would not be caught dead reading an East Asian novel or poetry collection translated into English. I personally am not very attracted to science fiction, but perhaps one can hope that the popularity of such work in languages other than English and other European languages indicates that there is hope for the rest of us. Perhaps we can hitch a ride on the popularity of science fiction.

When writing an overview of what already is a state-of-the-field book, which is what this afterword tries unsuccessfully to do, we must acknowledge that only a few superficial points can be made and that some of the essays must be overlooked in their entirety while others are given only scant attention. I apologize for that. So let me conclude by returning to my main point from the beginning but also sabotaging it to some extent. This volume represents a fresh, serious, and learned attempt to articulate where the field of modern Japanese literary studies is today. It does so admirably even if incompletely. This book will serve as an essential tool to those in Japanese studies looking for very general assessments of various aspects of the field. For non-experts such as myself, it is an indispensable guide for teaching. But inevitably the book puts the emphasis on the macro-assembly of the field, accentuating the basic affinities that the essays all share and that Japanese literature shares. All, that is, except the last essay by John Treat. Treat takes a meta-level approach to surveying the present circumstances and is not afraid to apply to the current cultural studies trend in the humanities a skeptical critical eye. We are, he states in invoking a quip by Seth Jacobowitz, at risk of becoming today's "Sovietologists." By this he means that we have a compulsion to relevance in a moment in which the humanities are on the ropes, a problem compounded by periodic recessions, tax cuts, and even, I would add, pandemics. But it is precisely the precarious and interwoven nature of the world today, where a major online blunder in the financial sector in Tokyo, Hong Kong, or Singapore could lead to the complete obliteration of a bank in London or New York; where a mysterious virus emerging from god-knows-where in Wuhan could end up killing millions in the US, Russia, and Brazil; and where a conflict among a small number of people in the Middle East, while tragic, has the potential to trigger a full-scale regional war that nobody wants. In such a world, it behooves us to read literature of the world so that we can understand those whom we understand least. Nevertheless, Treat cautions us that reading too broadly could lead to the dangerous conflation of multifarious cultures and languages and result in "the monolingual accounting of everything." He wryly invokes David Damrosch's famous contention that world literature is literature that began in its original language but, in translation, "ceases to be the exclusive products of their original culture. . . ." Well, perhaps in stature, but two features set aside literature from other languages, especially languages that are vastly different from English and other European languages: one is the absolute incommensurability of truly "foreign" cultures; the other is the individual uniqueness of great writers. The main reason we read world literature is to experience firsthand, albeit in translation, an unusual tale rendered in a unique and intriguing way by a master storyteller. I cannot do justice to the thorough-going critique to which Treat subjects various theories of world literature, but I will end on a tone of agreement with him: great literature invites, rewards, and insists upon close reading, for close reading unlocks the entryway into the inimitable storehouse that is great literature. What the essays in this volume do is illustrate that point in numerous ways while also providing an array of paradigms through which we can teach modern Japanese literature.

Contributors

Seth Jacobowitz is an Assistant Professor of Japanese at Texas State University. He is the author of *Writing Technology in Meiji Japan: A Media History of Modern Japanese Literature and Visual Culture* (2016), which won the 2017 International Convention of Asia Scholars Book Prize in the Humanities. His research examines modern Japanese literature, visual culture, and transnational Japanese diaspora. He has translated works such as *The Edogawa Rampo Reader* (2008) and *Dirty Hearts: The History of Shindo Renmei* (2021). He is co-editor of *The Hirabayashi Hatsunosuke Reader: Mass Culture and Intermediality in Imperial Japan* (2025) and currently working on the scholarly monograph *Japanese Brazil: Immigrant Literature and Overseas Expansion, 1908–1945*.

Jonathan E. Abel is a Professor of Japanese and Comparative Literature at Pennsylvania State University. He specializes in Japanese media, film, and literature, with a focus on critical theory, global modernism, translation studies, and new media. Abel's notable works include *Redacted: The Archives of Censorship in Transwar Japan* (2012) and *The New Real: Media and Mimesis in Japan from Stereographs to Emoji* (2023).

Rebecca Copeland is a Professor of Japanese Language and Literature at Washington University in St. Louis. Her research focuses on modern and contemporary Japanese women's writing, material culture, and translation studies. Among her myriad books, Copeland has translated Kirino Natsuo's *The Goddess Chronicle*, edited the collected volume *Woman Critiqued: Translated Essays on Japanese Women's Writing*, researched and written two scholarly monographs, including *Lost Leaves: Women Writers of Meiji Japan*, and authored the novel *The Kimono Tattoo.*

Davinder L. Bhowmik is an Associate Professor of Asian Languages and Literature at the University of Washington and a wonderful human being. She specializes in 20th and 21st-century Japanese literature, with a particular focus on Okinawan fiction. Bhowmik has edited *Double-Exposure: An Anthology of Japanese Fiction and Poetry from Okinawa* (with Steve Rabson) and published the scholarly monograph *Writing Okinawa: Narrative Acts of Identity and Resistance* (2008). Her current research includes a book-length monograph tentatively titled *Off-Base: The Rhetoric of Peace in Contemporary Okinawan Literature.*

William H. Bridges IV is the Arthur Satz Professor of the Humanities and an Associate Professor of Modern Languages and Cultures at the University of Rochester and an energetic interlocutor. His research intersects modern Japanese literature, African American literature, and comparative media studies. Bridges authored *Playing in the Shadows: Fictions of Race and Blackness in Postwar Japanese Literature* and is working on projects related to reparations and the Black Pacific.

Jon L. Pitt is an Associate Professor at the University of California, Irvine. His research explores the intersections of Japanese literature, cinema, sound media, and environmental humanities. Pitt's first book, *Botanical Imagination: Rethinking Plants in Modern Japan*, examines the influence of plant studies on Japanese literature and cinema. He is also the translator of Itō Hiromi's *Tree Spirits Grass Spirits.*

Adam L. Kern is a Professor of Japanese Literature and Visual Culture at the University of Wisconsin–Madison, where he specializes in early modern and modern Japanese popular culture in comparative context. His experiences in Japan, besides research affiliations with the University of Kyoto, the University of Tokyo, and the National Institute of Japanese Literature, include brief stints as an editorial intern with Kōdansha and as a staff reporter for *Kyoto Shimbun.* Kern's recent books include *The Penguin Book of Haiku* (2018), *Manga from the Floating World (Second Edition with a New Preface)* (2019), and the co-edited *A Kamigata Anthology* (2020).

Deborah Shamoon is an Associate Professor of Japanese Studies at the National University of Singapore. Her research interests include modern

Japanese literature, film, manga, anime, and gender studies. Shamoon authored *Passionate Friendship: The Aesthetics of Girls' Culture in Japan* (2012) which traces the history of shōjo manga. She co-edited the volume *Teaching Japanese Popular Culture* (2016) with Chris McMorran. Her next book will be on visual analysis of manga across genres and including comparisons with US and UK comics, tentatively titled *On Text and Image: Making Meaning in Manga.*

Hideto Tsuboi is a Professor at Waseda University, Tokyo, and Professor Emeritus at Nagoya University and also at the International Research Center for Japanese Studies (Nichibunken) in Kyoto. His research focuses on modern Japanese literature, poetry, and cultural history, including a focus on the postwar era and its aftermath. Tsuboi has authored numerous books, including most recently *Sengo hyōgen: Japanese Literature after 1945* (Postwar expression: Japanese literature after 1945; 2023), *Nijūsseiki Nihongo-shi o omoidasu* (Remembering 20th century Japanese-language poetry; 2020), and *Sei ga kataru: nijūseiki Nihon bungaku no sei to shintai* (Sexuality speaks: gender and the body in 20th century Japanese literature; 2012). He is also the editor of *Sengo Nihon no kizuato* (The scars of postwar Japan; 2022), *Sengo Nihon bunka saikō* (Rethinking postwar Japan; 2019), and the six volume series *Sengo Nihon o yomikaeru* (Reinterpreting postwar Japan; 2018–2019).

Yoshitaka Hibi is a Professor at the Graduate School of Humanities, Nagoya University. He specializes in modern Japanese literature, literature of Japanese immigrants, modern Japanese print culture, and computational literary studies. Hibi's research includes the study of representation and privacy in literature and the print culture in Japanese overseas territories. He is author of *Purabashī no tanjō: moderu shōsetsu no bungaku-shi* (The birth of privacy: the troubled history of romans-à-clef in Japan; 2020), *Bungaku no rekishi o dō kakinaosu no ka: nijūseiki Nihon no shōsetsu, kūkan, media* (How to rewrite literary history: the novel, space, and media in 20th century Japan; 2016) and *Japanīzu Amerika: imin bungaku, shuppan bunka, shūyōjo* (Japanese America: immigrant Literature, print culture, and internment camps; 2014).

Matthew Fraleigh is an Associate Professor of East Asian Literature and Culture at Brandeis University. His research interests include classical and modern Japanese literature, cultural and literary exchange between China and Japan, and Sinitic poetry and prose in East Asia. Fraleigh has authored *Plucking Chrysanthemums: Narushima Ryūhoku and Sinitic Literary Traditions* *in Modern Japan* and translated *New Chronicles of Yanagibashi and Diary of a Journey to the West*, which won the Japan–U.S. Friendship Prize for the translation of Japanese literature. Recently he collaborated with scholar and translator of Chinese classical poetry Jonathan Chaves to publish *The Same Moon Shines on All: The Lives and Selected Poems of Yanagawa Seigan and Kōran* (Columbia University Press, 2024).

YoungRan Kō is a Professor at Nihon University. Her research focuses on modern Japanese literature, antiwar movements, and representations of pacifism. Her recent book, *Shuppan teikoku no sensō: futeina monotachi no bunka-shi* (The publishing empire at war: a cultural history of defiance; 2024) examines the cultural history of resistance in Imperial Japan. She is also the author of *Sengo to iu ideorigī: rekishi, kioku, bunka* (The ideology of the postwar: history, memory, and culture; 2010) and co-editor of *Ken'etsu no teikoku* (The empire of censorship; 2014), both of which have been translated into Korean.

Jeffrey Angles is a poet, translator, and professor of Japanese literature at Western Michigan University. His collection of original poetry written in Japanese, *Watashi no hizukehenkōsen*, won the Yomiuri Prize for Literature. He believes in the role of translators as activists and has focused on translating socially engaged, feminist, and queer writers. Recent translations include Orikuchi Shinobu's modernist classic, *The Book of the Dead* (2017) which won two awards for translation, the Miyoshi Prize and the MLA's Scaglione Prize; the feminist writer Itō Hiromi's long novel *The Thorn Puller* (2022); and the queer poet Takahashi Mutsuo's poetry collection *Only Yesterday* (2023). His translation of the collected poems of the 1930s Japanese modernist Nakahara Chūya is forthcoming from Penguin Classics in 2026.

Gala Maria Follaco is an Associate Professor of Japanese Language and Literature at the Università Degli Studi di Napoli "L'Orientale" in Italy. Her research focuses on urban representation in modern and contemporary Japanese literature. Follaco has translated works by several modern and contemporary Japanese authors, and is the author of *A Sense of the City: Modes of Urban Representation in the Works of Nagai Kafū* (2017). She is the editor of the two-volume *Cultura Letteraria Giapponese. Le mille forme della scrittura dal VII al XXI secolo* (Japanese literary culture: The myriad forms of writing from the 7th to the 21st century; 2023).

John Whittier Treat is a Professor Emeritus of East Asian Languages and Literature at Yale University. His research includes modern Japanese literature, Korean studies, and LGBT studies. Treat has written several scholarly monographs including *Writing Ground Zero: Japanese Literature and the Atomic Bomb* (1995) and *The Rise and Fall of Modern Japanese Literature* (2018). He is also the author of several novels, including *First Consonants* and the forthcoming *Seventh City of Refuge.*

Christopher Lupke is a Professor of Chinese Cultural Studies in the Department of East Asian Studies at the University of Alberta. His research focuses on modern Chinese, Taiwanese, and Sinophone literature and cinema. In addition to co-editing four volumes on Chinese literature and poetry, Lupke has authored *The Sinophone Cinema of Hou Hsiao-hsien: Culture, Style, Voice, and Motion* (2016), and translated *A History of Taiwan Literature* by Ye Shitao (2020). The latter received the MLA's Scaglione Prize (2022).

Index